D0243904

Praise for Paul Tomkins and The Tomkins Times

"Phenomenal ... Absolutely quintessential reading for Liverpool fans."
The Redmen TV

"The Tomkins Times is an indispensable website whose diagnosis of all
things Liverpool is beyond compare."
LFCHistory.net

"Perhaps the most intelligent guide to LFC available on the internet."
The Independent on Sunday

"Gold-dust analysis"
John Sinnott, BBC

"[Football analysis] is best left to the professionals, like the admirable
Mr Tomkins."
The Daily Telegraph

"An ingenious and intelligent look beneath the surface to reveal what
the headlines too often don't tell us. Fascinating."
Jonathan Wilson

"Another triumph of impeccable research, Pay As You Play brings
much-needed factual insight to a discussion previously dominated by
half-truths."
Oliver Kay, The Times

"Liverpool do happen to be blessed with supporters whose statistical
analysis provides a lucid interpretation of where the club's strengths and
weaknesses lie, accessible through the Tomkins Times website."
The Independent

For Joyce Tomkins.

And for Alex Tate.

Paul Tomkins is the author of over a dozen football books, an academic paper on the role football finances play in success, and the novel *The Girl on the Pier*. In addition, he was a columnist on the official Liverpool website between 2005 and 2012. In 2009 he set up the website *The Tomkins Times*.

www.TomkinsTimes.com

© 2019 Paul Tomkins and The Tomkins Times.

All rights reserved. No part of this publication may be reproduced, distributed, or transmitted in any form or by any means, including photocopying, recording, or other electronic or mechanical methods, without the prior written permission of the publisher, except in the case of brief quotations embodied in critical reviews and certain other noncommercial uses permitted by copyright law.

Mentality Monsters: How Jürgen Klopp Took Liverpool FC From Also-Rans To Champions of Europe

Paul Tomkins

Contents

Foreword

Fireworks fizzed and popped and sprayed as the phalanx of scarlet coaches inched along the streets. Flares and smoke bombs spread a red mist across Merseyside, explosions of sparkling confetti shot again and again from an air cannon into the blue skies, as the best part of a million Liverpool fans thronged the route, sitting astride traffic lights and hanging out of windows, risking life and limb to get a glimpse of the returning heroes. Jürgen Klopp, lager bottle in hand, one leg slung over the back of the open-top bus – also apparently risking life and limb – beamed a grin that would send the Cheshire Cat to the dentist in shame, as his players – all wearing shirts with the number six on the back (as if it was some kind of bizarre Dejan Lovren convention) – took turns to lift the European Cup, or film the hundreds of thousands of fans gathered along the pavements and roads, who were of course filming them. The Liverpool manager looked at his clenched fists, then extended one finger, then two – until, one by one, he had counted to *six*. Another huge grin in the pyro glow, before, half-cut, he almost fell off the back of the bus.

Boom!

Liverpool Football Club, Champions of Europe.

For a sixth time.

In the build-up, Klopp faced the unthinkable hell of a seventh successive defeat in a cup final; Liverpool themselves facing their fifth, dating back to 2012, and a second in this very competition in 12 months. To lose would – paradoxically – be made all the worse after racking up the third-best points haul in English football league history and *still* only being runners-up; the agony due to being so brilliant and yet so unrewarded, in terms of silverware (if not love and respect, and of course, healthy renumeration). The pressure during the three-week lead-up to the game was intense, and so, a day after despatching Spurs 2-0 in a sweltering Madrid, the entire playing, coaching, fitness and analytics staff, as well as the owners, were on a bus weaving its way through a sea of onlookers and well-wishers, finally able to relax and, in Klopp's case, drink a crate of beer.

(As hundreds of thousands of Liverpool fans from all over the world poured into the city one could only imagine all the Everton fans *streaming out*. They must have some kind of evacuation procedure in place for these occasions over the past five decades.)

It was only the third time a club had won a game against a team from each of Europe's big-five leagues in a single season in the competition, after Bayern Munich in 2012/13 and Rafa Benítez's Liverpool in 2004/05. Victory took Liverpool clear of Bayern and Barcelona – two teams the Reds happened to beat en route to Madrid – and, with six, ended the season behind only AC Milan and Real Madrid in the all-time standings. It also put the Reds one clear of Manchester United – 24 to 23 – when adding together the two really meaningful trophies: the league and the European Cup.

But this is not a story of one-upmanship; this is not about bragging rights, but about *a great journey*, with the most satisfying of endings. (And if it shuts up a few snarky trolls and bitter rival fans, as well as those eager to label Klopp a failure and a fraud, then all well and good.)

The Long Journey

A late, late Divock Origi goal, hit from the inside-left position, the ball flying into the far corner of the net. Cometh the hour, cometh the Origi. The players in red – as one on the final whistle – saluted the Liverpool fans who had come to watch them play.

But this was not the Wanda Metropolitano stadium in Madrid in 2019.

This was Anfield, the 13th of December, 2015 – when *all this* essentially all began. That day perhaps marked Ground Zero. Jürgen Klopp had been in charge for a couple of months, having inherited a mixed squad assembled with muddled thinking by factions within the club who were never going to see eye to eye. Going into the 96th minute, Liverpool were losing 2-1 at Anfield in the Premier League to lowly West Brom. But up stepped that man – Origi – to rescue a point. To general bewilderment, Klopp took the team, hand in hand, to the Kop to salute those who remained for their support; plenty of fans having filed out around the 80-minute mark (an issue Klopp would also address in his press conferences, in terms of making the football so good that they would not dare leave). Supporters of other clubs laughed and mocked; trolled and snarked. Some Liverpool fans cringed. "Is this what we've become? Celebrating a home draw against rubbish like West

Brom?" But if you had even an ounce of imagination, you could see what the German was trying to do.

And – to use his own parlance – fucking hell, *did he do it.*

"Mentality monsters" is how he described his team three and a half years later, with the addition of the requisite Kloppian F-bomb. That was not the case in 2015, with a team and – let's face it, a fanbase (myself very much included) – that had become punch-drunk on mediocrity. Losing no longer hurt that much, because – well, it was just another defeat.

His reign started two months earlier – against Spurs, of course. A lot has been made of the bench that day at White Hart Lane, but there were quite a few injuries, which meant some fringe squad players had to be called upon to fill in as subs. Even so, the team was Simon Mignolet, Nathaniel Clyne, Mamadou Sakho, Alberto Moreno, Martin Škrtel, Philippe Coutinho, James Milner, Adam Lallana, Lucas Leiva, Emre Can and Divock Origi; none of whom started in the 2019 Champions League final, with most sold or offloaded by the time this season rolled round. The subs were Ádám Bogdán, Kolo Touré, Connor Randall, Joe Allen, Jordon Ibe, João Carlos Teixeira and Jerome Sinclair – not one of whom were at the club the following season (they were loaned, sold or released). By stark contrast, the Spurs team that day included Hugo Lloris, Toby Alderweireld, Jan Vertonghen, Danny Rose, Christian Eriksen, Dele Alli and Harry Kane, who all began the match in Madrid less than four years later, while Erik Lamela, an eighth starter from that day, was on the bench in 2019; plus, Kieran Trippier and Harry Winks were on the bench for Spurs in Klopp's first game, and then starters in Madrid. Spurs, as a project, were already largely together in 2015; Liverpool at that point were merely ripe for ripping apart.

Players like Origi, skipper Jordan Henderson, and utility man James Milner, had emerged through years of criticism to come within a whisker of landing the league title for Liverpool ... before – having to all intents and purposes been "knocked out" in the first leg of the semi-final in Catalonia – securing a sixth European Cup. They were amongst the few survivors. Perhaps the greatest moment from the whole weekend was Henderson, in tears, embracing his father, whom he nearly lost to cancer a few years earlier, as if neither dare let go. Anyone who didn't join them in crying must have had their tear ducts surgically sealed.

Klopp, on the back of six consecutive final defeats, including two in the Champions League – and fresh from yet another runners-up medal in the league, to add to a couple from Germany – was not about to become football's nearly man; seven years on from the second of his sensational *Bundesliga* successes with Borussia Dortmund, he had his third *major* honour, albeit his achievements with lowly Mainz prior to that perhaps the ones achieved against the steepest of odds. He probably deserved to have winners' medals from half those unhappy finals, but it was to prove lucky seven; and indeed, in terms of European finals with Liverpool (or Champions League finals with his two main clubs), *third time lucky*. Here is a manager who, three full European campaigns into his career with the Reds, possesses a record that reads: finalists, finalists, winners. He has still to lose a two-legged tie with the club, despite facing Manchester United, Dortmund, Manchester City, Bayern Munich, Roma, Barcelona and a whole host of others.

The point against Spurs that day in the dim, distant past – a 0-0 draw in which Origi went close, hitting the bar – took Liverpool up to the heady heights of 9th. That's how far off they were when he took over, for the ninth game of the league campaign.

This book will chart the rise from the chaos of the final 15 months of Brendan Rodgers' tenure, and how a club divided became a club united. (Incidentally, while *United* became a club divided. How these things turn, and Liverpool are back on their European perch.) I will seek to explain, as best I can, how the club has transformed from, frankly, a bit of a shambles, to the most envied operation in the world game.

And it certainly wasn't smooth sailing in Klopp's first two years; reaching two finals in his first season, but losing the Europa League, after leading 1-0 at half-time, to Sevilla; and before that, edged out by Man City in the League Cup final on penalties. But the league form was inconsistent: some big wins, and some heavy defeats. Two years in, Klopp's record was identical to that of Brendan Rodgers, although Rodgers' record in his final 50 league games was deteriorating rapidly, after a sensational run in the second half of 2013/14 had given him a fairly impressive win-percentage midway through his tenure. And yet by 2019, Klopp was absolutely streets ahead of Rodgers' overall record, having created a team on a whole different level.

In May, after landing the title, Pep Guardiola said: "You give credit for the titles and how huge our rival is. In my career as a manager, I played against incredible sides and there are two that were 'wow'. One is the Barcelona of Luis Enrique with Neymar, [Lionel] Messi and [Luis] Suárez in front. The other is this Liverpool. I think they're the best two sides I've faced as a manager."

By the time the Reds had lifted their sixth European Cup, the Elo Club rankings system had them listed – with beautiful symmetry – as the 6th-best team in European football history, based on the cumulative achievements of reaching the final in 2017/18, and racking up 97 points in what had, by the reckoning of the model, become the strongest league on the continent. So while it seemed that Guardiola was perhaps being a little disingenuous, it seems that he was utterly *right*.

Ironically, the revival under Klopp seriously kicked in after a humbling 4-1 defeat to Spurs in October 2017; and since the start of 2018 Liverpool's form, domestically and in Europe, has largely been sensational: two Champions League finals – one won – and a 97-point league season. There could be no denying that Liverpool were now one of the best teams in Europe and, with a better record in the two biggest competitions than Man City (who edged Liverpool out by a point in the league but crashed out of Europe two rounds earlier), arguably *the best*.

A Quick Note About This Book

In many seasons – dating back to 2004/05 – I commenced writing a book at the midway point about Liverpool's unfolding campaign, never quite knowing where it would end. As with that first book a decade and a half ago, I didn't expect things to turn out *quite* this well for the Reds; although at least this time there was a serious sense of something special by the turn of the year, whereas the miracle of Istanbul was too insane to even dream about. In some seasons, these books ended up documenting nothing better than near misses, which led to hundreds of Manchester United and Everton fans leaving trolling reviews on book websites, as if I had purposefully set out to write a book about finishing 2nd, or losing a Champions League final. No, the story takes me where it takes me, and if that's with the team as an unlucky runner-up, as in 2018, 2014, 2009 and 2007, so be it. For a while it looked like this book would be about winning the title after 29 years; and then it felt like it would be a book about yet more agonisingly close finishes, with no cigars and no silverware. Still, it would hopefully have been an interesting and enjoyable read all the same, with part of the emphasis on the process of *improvement*.

But of course, you can't beat a glorious ending. And so, I have to thank everyone at Liverpool FC, from the players to the manager, the owners and all the backroom staff, for (indirectly) helping me to write a book that documents something better than finishing 2nd or being beaten finalists. (I look forward to seeing how many Manchester United and Everton fans review *this* book.)

Of course, this book doesn't cover *everything*. And this may not be the *definitive* book on Liverpool's rise to a sixth European title – with others sure to be published, some by writers with far better contacts – and proximity to the action – than me; but hopefully there won't be any others quite like it (capturing the joy, detailing the process and analysing the context.)

Briefly – as this isn't always the most interesting part for the reader – I'd also like to thank, in particular, Daniel Rhodes and Andrew Beasley, for their help with this book, which has shape-shifted as the season unfolded; and to Chris Rowland, for keeping his editorial eye on *The Tomkins Times* whilst we knocked this tome into shape (apart from when he went swanning off to Madrid in a camper van). I'd also like to thank Daniel Marshall for all the excellent design work, and Mick Thomas for being an additional pair of eyes in the proofing process.

And a big thank-you to all our subscribers, who have kept us in business for a full decade now – paying to read our paywalled material and be part of a wonderfully welcoming, intelligent and troll-free community – and whose preorders of this book helped fund the project.

Finally, I'd like to thank Sergio Ramos, for making *all this* feel so much better. The dastardly villain ruined the ending to the first film, but in the sequel he gets a right royal comeuppance, and the heroes – in their bright red shirts, with the heartbreak still fresh in their minds – are pushed all the way to greater glory.

The Greatest of the Great European Anfield Nights

Nothing was won; at least, nothing silver and tangible. But a team can only be in with a shout when the trophies are handed out, and at 8pm on May 7th, 2019, Liverpool had next to no chance of progressing to the Champions League final in Madrid, just days before they still had a chance of winning the Premier League crown, albeit with Man City simply needing to match whatever the Reds achieved to retain their crown.

Across the media, journalists admitted that they were turning up to write the story of Lionel Messi, arguably the world's greatest ever player – and certainly the best since Diego Maradona (whose career, unlike Messi's, faded badly upon substance abuse) – and how Messi was heading to yet another Champions League final.

According to the data-crunching websites *FiveThirtyEight* and *Gracenote* the probability of Jürgen Klopp's side progressing was between 4-6%; but no one had ever turned around a 3-0 first-leg deficit in the semi-finals of the Champions League/European Cup, with the only time such margins were overturned involving an away goal. To have to do so against a Barcelona side that had just wrapped up the *La Liga* title a week earlier and rested its *entire XI* in the league game six days between the two legs when Liverpool had a tough away game – and when that game at Newcastle, along with others, left the Reds without so many key players – kept the odds lengthening. As such, it was a 50-1 shot at best at kick-off. Jürgen Klopp was still yet to lose a two-legged European tie as he took his team into the final two-legged game of his third European season, but this time it looked beyond even his powers of motivation.

And yet …

Barça strolled into town, 3-0 up from the first leg, looking confident in their luminous yellow kit; again fielding two ex-Liverpool players who fought to leave the club for the glory of Spanish football and a more suitable "cultural" fit. Going into the game, neither of them were being missed by the Reds, but there they were in the opposition lineup, ready to do damage. By contrast, the Reds were almost decimated by injuries. Watching from the stands, or at home undergoing treatment, were Mo Salah, Roberto Firmino, Naby Keïta, Alex Oxlade-Chamberlain, Adam Lallana, and by the second half, the injured Robertson, who had been cynically kicked by Luis Suárez. The five missing from the start had scored 40% of the Reds' goals in 2018/19 (while Oxlade-Chamberlain, capable of goals, had barely played 20 minutes), and, after inflation, their transfer fees represented around one-third of the squad's overall cost.

And yet Liverpool still didn't need Philippe Coutinho or Luis Suárez. Barcelona, meanwhile, when they desperately needed them, *couldn't find them.*

This was only half a Liverpool team, against a whole, fully rested and buoyantly confident Barcelona.

And yet…

After the impossible was made possible, Liverpool's players and manager were almost speechless, and in tears, in explaining how *this* happened. The emotion of football can be overplayed, and sometimes we see players as mercenaries, only in it for the money. But *BT Sports*, on their live broadcast, had to interview several Liverpool players before anything even remotely coherent was uttered. The TV station knew better than to live broadcast an interview with Jürgen Klopp; but, noting it was past 10pm, the German duly obliged. "You mean – and you'll have to bleep this, my fucking mentality monsters". Gary Lineker, back in the studio, said he had been asked to apologise – but refused, on the grounds that it was late at night, and who *wouldn't* want to swear right now? Liverpool had been desperately unlucky to lose the first leg, let alone lose it 3-0; but it just laid the foundations for an even better story.

It all made for the greatest Champions League/European Cup semi-final comeback ever, to place right alongside the greatest final comeback, back in 2005, in some place that just happens to be hosting *next year's* final. Each time a three-goal deficit had to be overturned against a more expensive and experienced team.

Just seven minutes into the game the odds were back down to around 12-1, as Sadio Mané seized on a loose Jordi Alba header to dart towards the box; the final-third regain again as effective as any playmaker. The ball broke to Jordan Henderson, who – in an advanced role – smartly evaded a tackle and just about had enough time to get away a prodded shot, with no back-lift possible; Marc-André ter Stegen got down sharply but could only parry the ball into the path of the onrushing Divock Origi, the hero just a dozen minutes earlier (in playing time) on Tyneside, who followed up his logic-defying winning header with a tap-in against Barcelona.

So often in these games the chasing team – pumped up, with nothing left to lose – gets the early goal; the crowd goes wild, hopes rise, and then the opposition gets one back – and with the away goals rule – the tie is dead. A great atmosphere suddenly dissipates to pin-drop silence, and you're just glad your team gave it go; where they maybe grab a late second, to take the consolation of winning the game 2-1, but losing the tie.

Or, if the deficit is somehow cancelled out – and it goes to 3-3 – the fearlessness evaporates, and the team that had everything to lose, staring down humiliation, suddenly is the one with nothing left to lose. It happened in Istanbul; AC Milan were utterly shellshocked by the Reds' comeback until it went 3-3, then suddenly they came back to life, as Liverpool grew nervy. It happened again here, only to a much smaller degree; Barcelona came out fighting at 3-3, but without ever creating anything gilt-edged. They still only needed one goal to make Liverpool need two more to progress, but it was a night when they drew a blank at Anfield, the remarkable Alisson Becker dealing with anything Barça could throw his way.

Unlike Jerzy Dudek 14 years earlier, Alisson didn't really have to pull off any wonder-saves, but as Klopp explained after the game, the Brazilian is not a maker of eye-catching saves – *but he's always just there.* Just as Virgil van Dijk rarely makes a tackle – he's too good at reading the play to need to – then Alisson's game is all about judgement and positioning and anticipation, rather than being forced into the theatrical arched-back saves that the cameras love so fondly. Often he just thumps the ball away with two hands, either with his fists or as an open-handed barrier. In this game Barcelona had two clear-cut chances; Alisson dealt with both. At the other end, Liverpool had five, and came away with four goals. The Catalans must be sick of the sight of him; the goalkeeper playing when Roma overturned a three-goal quarter-final deficit a year earlier, which set up Alisson's own first experience of Anfield on a frenzied European night (and when it was Liverpool's turn, in the away leg, to stare down the possibility of throwing away a big advantage). At least this time he was on the right end of the drubbing; but he had helped sow the seeds of doubt in this superstar opposition.

There were Liverpool heroes everywhere. In particular, Fabinho – booked early, but still able to win tackle after tackle, and even lead a crazy-legs counterattacking charge late in the game, like a rugby player just trying to gain distance until someone takes him out, no other goal in sight. Joël Matip looked every inch as good as Virgil van Dijk, just as he is every inch as tall as him. Sadio Mané, sans Salah and Firmino, channelled his inner Diego Maradona (the good side, not the coke-snorting lunatic side) to dribble past players and retain his balance, and not even let anyone get a sniff of the ball.

Man City, ahead of the final weekend's Premier League fixtures, will have watched their old friend James Milner, moved from midfield to once more become a makeshift left-back, making a headed tackle whilst on the floor. That's what this Liverpool team would give. It's almost beyond description, without resorting to expletives. It has pace, power, goals, aerial dominance and agility – but it also has a player who will tackle someone *with his face.*

The villain on the night was clear: not so much Philippe Coutinho, who had left more recently under a cloud of acrimony (simply from him twice going on strike to get the move), but the man who played the first leg like he was trying to get every Liverpool player sent off, and celebrated his goal as if it was against just any other club (a less serious crime, perhaps). Luis Suárez returned to Anfield suggesting the fans would give him a good reception, but as he stood on the centre-circle to take the kick-off – which was delayed for what felt like a minute until the television broadcasters were ready – he was mercilessly booed and whistled and jeered. Before long there would be chants of "Fuck off, Suárez!" The fact that his children were there as Liverpool supporters must have made it an unbearable evening, given the enmity pouring towards their father; but once he crosses the line Suárez frequently *crosses the line*. He has never helped himself. In time he will be remembered fondly again, when the wounds from the Nou Camp heal, but for now he was the enemy.

In the first half he missed a good chance, scuffing his shot across goal for an easy Alisson save. Half of the passes Suárez completed in the second half were kick-offs, and his most effective kick in the first half was into Andy Robertson's shin, forcing the Scot off at half-time. Similarly, Jordan Henderson was in agony just before the break after an opponent's studs slid into his knee. "Just give me everything. A jab, tablets. Both. Everything," he was reported to have said at half-time. He managed to solider on – indeed, he was heroic in is endeavours – but Suárez had put paid to Robertson's night. Almost all of Liverpool's key wide creative forces were now absent.

And yet even getting rid of Robertson rebounded on the returning Uruguayan. On came Gini Wijnaldum and, with goals scored in the 54th and 56th minutes – exactly echoing the times of the first two scored in Istanbul – he turned the tie Liverpool's way; even more reminiscent of 2005 was Wijnaldum's header, to make it 3-3 on aggregate, which bore a lot of similarities to Steven Gerrard's towering leap at the Atatürk. The Dutchman's second goal came just 31 seconds of playing time after his first, albeit with a 90-second interim for the wild celebrations and a VAR investigation into a "possible red card event", which was presumably when Wijnaldum pushed ter Stegen in an attempt to get the ball back – in the usual antics that ensue when a further goal is required and the opposition team decides to try and hide the ball. The Liverpool no.5's eagerness to grab that ball was rewarded when, just half a minute later, he rose like the proverbial salmon – if that salmon was the bastard child of Duncan Ferguson – to thump a header into the top corner, as the whole place shook on its foundations. Any louder, and Anfield would have needed rebuilding. There's nothing quite like a quick-fire second goal to take an atmosphere into *frenzied*, with the crowd yet to calm down from the previous strike, but what followed 23 minutes later – while all the more remarkable – was also perhaps slightly *unbelievable*.

Running down the wing, but unable to work room for a cross, Trent Alexander-Arnold realised that he was getting closer to the byline. A quick movement later – dummying to cross – he was able to play the ball onto Alba's leg to win the corner, which was the best he could hope for in the situation. The ball bounced back off the advertising hoarding and onto the pitch, while the ballboy helped get another ball onto the corner spot. As Origi kicked the first ball back off the pitch, Liverpool's no.66 turned away, as if to let Xherdan Shaqiri take it, for an inswinging left-footer, having just assisted the previous goal. But then Alexander-Arnold turned back and, in almost one movement, whipped in the cross to the unmarked Origi, loitering on the edge of the six-yard box. Origi was only *half* paying attention, with quick glances; but that was more than any other player on the pitch. Quite how the young Liverpool right-back spotted the opportunity is hard to know; the vision was of a world-class playmaker (something that his crosses were already starting to resemble on a regular basis). In an almost surreal moment, Origi swept the ball, with a powerful shot from his instep, into the top corner. Because no Barcelona players were even remotely ready it seemed as if the referee *had* to disallow the goal – as if it was taken too quickly; but unlike a free-kick, you cannot take a corner too quickly – once the whistle has gone and the ball has been placed, it's fair game; unless, of course, the referee has already blown his whistle a second time, to halt proceedings due to some scuffling in the box. Even Klopp and his staff missed the goal. It needed young substitute Ben Woodburn to tell the manager what had happened.

Was this another feather in the cap of Liverpool's analysts? In the first leg Barcelona, as they so often do, had spent so much time surrounding the referee after every single decision – to good effect, from their point of view, in terms of intimidation (Messi seemed to spend both games trying to *be* the referee) – but as such they would often not be paying attention to the opponents. In the era of marginal gains, here was one: be alive when the opposition has switched off. It's the kind of detail that is easy to overlook.

You also cannot overestimate how difficult the chance was for Origi. Week after week I write about someone somewhere in football missing a "sitter" from a ball coming in from wide; any time there's even just a little pace on the ball it becomes difficult to judge which foot to use (and sometimes, the additional confusion is whether or not to go with the head or the chest, or even the knee or thigh). If there isn't time to let the ball come across the body, the striker is often swinging with a certain lack of control. Add that this was a bouncing ball, that skipped off the turf on the half-volley, and the Belgian could easily have just got it a fraction wrong, from which point it's in the Kop rather than the back of the net. Indeed, it wasn't a million miles away from the breakthrough corner Wijnaldum lashed in at Cardiff, after the Dutchman had pointed out to Alexander-Arnold at half-time that there was a space in front of the six yard box the Welsh team were leaving unguarded.

It perhaps also felt unreal as Origi isn't the most demonstrably ecstatic of scorers; just days earlier he'd looked confused and maybe embarrassed at scoring the winner at St James' Park. Was this *really* a goal? The aforementioned Wijnaldum goal in Cardiff and the Jordan Henderson strike at Southampton led to scenes of delirium from the scorers; here, Origi merely looked *fairly chuffed*. And of course, there was the added spectre of VAR, ready to rule out a goal after it has been celebrated; as happened so famously, and painfully, for Manchester City in the dying seconds of their victory over Spurs in the quarter-final second-leg, with unbridled joy turned to tears by the subsequent offside decision, picked up by the video referee.

It was such a surreal night that even Jose Mourinho appeared humble on beIN Sports, using the Spanish word for comeback. "For me, this *remontada* has one name: Jürgen. I think this is not about tactics, nor philosophy, this is about heart and soul, and fantastic empathy that he created for this group of players.

"Jürgen deserves this result. This is about him, a reflection of him and his personality, to never give up, fighting spirit, every player giving everything, and not crying about the quantity of matches that they have to play, and not crying about not having a certain player. Today is about Jürgen's mentality.

"They had the risk of finishing a fantastic season without anything to celebrate, and now they are one step from being European champions. I think Jürgen deserves, you know, the work they are doing in Liverpool is fantastic."

Perhaps it helped that Barcelona, like Liverpool, are perhaps Mourinho's biggest enemies in football, aside from all the Real Madrid, Chelsea and Man United players he has fallen out with; and praising Liverpool could be seen as a dig at those at United who refused to back him. But just like Pep Guardiola, he found it hard to disguise his admiration for what's going on under Klopp's guidance, even if there was surely some self-serving motive wrapped within.

Writing in *The Guardian*, Jonathan Wilson said, "…in the cauldron of Anfield, when crosses – at last – found their man and deflections fell Liverpool's way, it was not enough. Barcelona's front three between them didn't make a single tackle – an extraordinary statistic for a team under such pressure with a lead to defend. They made only two interceptions, both by Philippe Coutinho. Suárez had only 31 touches (of the ball, that is: there were probably at least that many on the legs of Andy Robertson). Messi's brilliance transformed the first leg and his level of genius can probably be afforded a certain latitude, perhaps even requires it, but defending a man down – two men down given Suárez's no-show – against a side as good as Liverpool leaves a team horribly susceptible."

Guillem Balague, Spanish football journalist and ex-Merseyside resident, gave his views on *BBC Radio 5 Live* after the final whistle: "Jürgen Klopp understood what happened in the first leg better than Ernesto Valverde. In that game Liverpool had a lot of chances and played a high tempo that Barcelona struggled with. Klopp said they didn't do much wrong in the first leg and they did not have to change much so they did the same again tonight.

"Over the two games, for three quarters of them Barcelona were inferior, scared and unable to find answers. For me, Messi was saying 'how do I influence the game?' For the last hour where was he? Not many teams have ever done that to him.

"After the first leg, Messi warned the Barcelona players that the game was played at the pace Liverpool wanted, and he said they [Barcelona] were all exhausted and couldn't play at that pace again, but that's what has happened again … Barcelona have not played a team like this in a long, long time."

The Guardian's resident Spanish expert, Sid Lowe, wrote: "At the end Leo Messi collapsed to the floor and for a time he just lay face down on the grass, until a teammate eventually came and lifted him to his feet. Exhausted, he was barely able to breathe. Barely able to believe it, either. When at last he walked, the noise deafening as he headed towards the touchline, he was still wondering how it could have slipped through their fingers like that.

"This is not Anfield, this is the Camp Nou six days earlier.

"When Ousmane Dembélé scuffed the last kick of the first leg, producing a shot unforgivably bad, Barcelona led 3-0 but it felt like it mattered, which was telling in itself – and because it felt like it mattered, it did matter. Barcelona still did not feel safe; they had seen Liverpool up close and knew how good they were, Messi admitting to feeling 'asphyxiated'. Deep down, they also knew of their own vulnerability."

After that first game, Cesc Fàbregas told the *BBC*: "Hats off to Liverpool, what an amazing performance. You can only lose a game like that if against you there is a good team but especially a player that is well above the rest."

If Messi was *asphyxiated* in the first leg, then the second leg must have felt worse. He'd been here before, 12 years earlier, but he was not a *phenomenon* back then – merely an amazing kid; and they were not necessarily expected to qualify for the next round, after losing the first leg 2-1 to Rafa Benítez's men on home soil. But there can be no doubt that his good friends, Suárez and Coutinho, knew the power of Anfield; how it makes strange things happen. If you've been on the beneficial end of such noise and passion then you will be nervous stepping into the arena as an opponent; especially if you didn't necessarily leave on the warmest of terms (both players essentially went on strike to leave, but then again, players have done that to join Liverpool.)

And in the end, all this night did was further fire the folklore; yet another legendary night, to add to the oeuvre. The more frequently nights like this happen, the more they can get into the heads of the opposition, before the whistle has even been blown; a virtuous circle. A year earlier the Reds went 5-0 up against Roma in the semi-final, having gone 3-0 up against Man City in the quarters; and in May 2019, Liverpool found themselves 4-0 up against a Barcelona side absolutely blown away.

Klopp reflected after the match: "I said to the boys before the game, 'I don't think it's possible but because *it's you* we have a chance'".

Fucking *mentality monsters*, every last one of them.

PART ONE

Analysing Liverpool FC – A Quick Explanation of Some of the Data, Context and Terminology Used Within This Book

As you will discover, this is not a statistical book; however, it is a book that *uses some statistics*. (Lest we be burned at the stake for such crimes.) While at *The Tomkins Times* we don't want our application of stats – or analytics – to be impenetrable to anyone who hasn't got a PhD in quantum mechanics (not least as we certainly *haven't*), it's impossible to do any credible football analysis in 2019 and not to use the wealth of data that is shaping the game.

(Disclaimer: if you're a fan of Andy Gray, and the type of guff he and his ilk peddle, then please slowly step away from this book.)

This book is also about the *joy* of football; the *beauty* of football. Hopefully it captures the spirit of Liverpool becoming the Champions of Europe, and the brilliance of racking up the third-highest points tally in the history of English football; and it will share some of the stories of the rise from also-rans in 2015 to being back on the European perch. But it's a book of *analysis*; about understanding what creates success, and how success is to be fairly and objectively measured; and as such, different ways of measuring – and weighing – the value of all *relative* success is required. Establishing some of those methods at the outset seems the most logical way to proceed. Liverpool ended the season with the Champions League trophy, but how can you accurately assess just how far the team has come? As both Jürgen Klopp and Mauricio Pochettino hinted at before the final in Madrid, their *bodies of work* would be the same, win or lose. But perceptions are altered by trophies.

Regular readers of *The Tomkins Times* will know a lot of what I'm about to outline here, but for anyone new to our work, it's worth taking a little time to explain the methodology. And some of what I will set out here is largely in the public arena anyway; if you don't know what Expected Goals is by now, where have you been?

Expected Goals

For the past few years the metric Expected Goals (xG) has become so widespread that even *Match of the Day* shares its data at the end of games, even if Alan Shearer and co. would never lower themselves to actually *discuss* it. The media is, of course, heavily populated by 'Proper Football Men' (as *Football365* like to call them), who think that any stat other than the scoreline is meaningless; and hark back to a golden age of stats-free ignorance.

And yet, if all that matters is the scoreline, why even bother analysing *anything* about the match? Surely the aim is to get beneath the surface and tell us what went on *beyond* the moments when the ball crossed the goalline? Expected goals essentially works on the probability of a goal being scored from each shot taken in a match, from the 1% chance of a shot 35 yards from goal to the 99% chance when faced with an open goal from point-blank range (with the probability based on years of data, and thousands of shots); and with everything in between. These are then added up to make an xG scoreline for each encounter. The better models take into account further variables such as goalkeeping position and the number of defenders – or lack thereof – in the way of a shot. But even basic models have their uses.

As such, xG is perhaps the best judge of how good a football team actually is, and provides the wider context for each individual match, even if not all good attacks end with a shot (although some models, like the one used by *FiveThirtyEight*, calculate "non-shot xG" – and as such, give value to attacks with no final attempt, such as a dangerous ball across the goalline that no one can quite get a toe to, or when a striker is in on goal but is forced wide by the goalkeeper and the ball runs out of play; both of which would be termed "a chance" by anyone watching the match without any shot actually fired at goal).

Sometimes a team will deliberately stop looking to create chances – such as when finding themselves 1-0 up and choosing to "shut up shop" – and so *game state* plays a role, too. (See: final, Champions League, 2019.) But look at a team's xG performance over 10 or 20 games and you get a much better idea of what that team is all about. While the very best players will outperform xG – Lionel Messi will usually score more goals than expected from the shots he takes (although in one season he did not) and David de Gea will usually save more than expected (albeit not this season) – all efforts will be judged against the average outcome from such situations. (As an aside, for goalkeepers there are two forms of "expected saves": one based on the same method as expected goals, which looks at the location at where the shot was taken, and a second, based on where within the goal-frame the ball is placed; with top-corner obviously being the hardest to save, and straight at him generally easier to stop.)

Expected goals is essentially like the vital signs of a match: pulse rate, blood pressure, respiration rate, temperature, and so on. The scoreline is the outward appearance – you may *look* totally fine, but that won't tell you if you have early stage cancer, or are about to enter cardiac arrest.

And in many ways, xG is actually changing the way the game is played, not least in partially killing off the long-shot. As such, xG has surely been a part of Liverpool's in-game planning, so whether or not you like the stat, *it has a clear role in modern football*. According to stats collated by Andrew Beasley for an article on *The Tomkins Times*, Liverpool took 48% of their shots from outside the box in Brendan Rodgers' final season; then 46% across the season when Rodgers departed in October and Jürgen Klopp arrived; then 40% in 2016/17 – with the emerging pattern clear, as fewer and fewer potshots were taken. By 2017/18 it was down to 39%, and yet the biggest drop was to come in 2018/19 – the total percentage of long-range efforts taken by Klopp's team had fallen to 34%, or roughly a third of all shots, down from a half just a few years earlier. Is this accidental? Surely not.

At times Liverpool seem to play one too many passes, but the same is often said of Man City, who at times *literally* do seem to want to walk the ball into the net. Given that Liverpool have got better as a team in every season since 2014/15 – from a starting point when long-range shots were almost 50% of all efforts at goal – it's clear that shooting from closer to goal is a *tactic*; unless becoming a better team simply means you naturally create better chances, and we all know that better chances, on average, will be much closer to goal (even Proper Football Men know that).

Which isn't to say that the blast from distance is dead; Klopp himself is on record as saying that against low-block teams (those encamped with every man in their own area) it's worth taking aim from further out now and again, with the obvious potential benefit of a deflection or an unsighted goalkeeper. This could be seen against the ultimate low-block side, Burnley, who were leading the Reds 1-0 at Turf Moor in the second half in December 2018 when James Milner squeezed a low drive from 20 yards through a defender's legs in a crowded area and into the corner of the net, with Joe Hart hardly moving (although that may just be symptomatic of Joe Hart these days).

But what you don't want is shot after shot after shot being wellied from 25 yards into the backsides of the hoary defenders putting their arses on the line for their team. While Steven Gerrard famously saved Liverpool against Olympiakos in 2004, and in the last-minute of extra-time in the 2006 FA Cup final, with shots from "don't shoot from *there!*" range, it was essentially his eight low-value second-half shots against Chelsea in 2013/14 – and not his slip – that proved costly, as he desperately sought redemption for his error. (That said, how can you *blame* a player that good for a rare off-day?)

In January 2019 – in an article for *TTT* about Liverpool's loaned-out long-range expert Harry Wilson – Daniel Rhodes shared the data for all Liverpool's current players across their full careers (albeit with data from the top divisions of major leagues only); and only one had a success rate from shots outside the box that was better than 10%: Divock Origi, who had seven goals from 49 longer-distance efforts, a conversation rate of 14%, from an average xG per shot of 0.04 – or, on average, a 4% chance of scoring; therefore, when he gets the ball 30-yards out, it is appropriate to scream "*Shoooooot!*". (He's quite good from a yard out when playing against Everton, too.) Since the article appeared Origi has scored six more goals – one from outside the box against Wolves in the FA Cup, and five from inside.

(Indeed, as a totally bizarre example of his ruthlessness – this season, at least – he had just nine shots in total when excluding that game against Wolves, and scored *six* goals. In the Champions League he had just three shots, and each hit the back of the net – to send Liverpool to the final, and then to seal the victory once there.)

In January 2018 Liverpool sold a long-range shot specialist in Philippe Coutinho. According to all the available league data, he had attempted 280 long-range shots in his career up to January 2019, with an average of 0.03 xG per effort. In total those 280 shots would usually be worth – via the xG models – a total of 8.7 goals; yet he had scored 21. Even when outscoring the xG model by over double, that's still only a 7.5% conversion rate, half Origi's, albeit on a much larger sample. Could Liverpool's improvement after the Brazilian's departure be in part due to removing the hundreds of "wasted" longer-range shots? (Or would Liverpool be *even better* had he stayed? Coutinho wasn't exactly noted for his work-rate and pressing, so that could be another area where the team now performs better, even if the Brazilian's qualities would be a nice *option* to call upon.)

Earlier in the season, Wilson – one of Coutinho's heirs apparent – was making a name for himself at Derby County with some stunning long-range goals, often from free-kicks. His career total as of January 2019 (which included his previous loan spell with Hull City) was 89 shots – at a rate of 2.9 per 90 minutes, with, according to Daniel:

"... 57 from outside the box – or 64% of his total, which is incredibly high (and usually not in a good way). His overall conversion rate from *all* shots, having scored 17 goals, stood at an elite-level 19% (for example, Roberto Firmino's is 12.3%, and Mo Salah's is 20.3%). Having scored with nine of his shots from outside the box, that also gives him a sharp-shooter conversion rate of a whopping 15.8%".

Of course, this figure puts him only a little ahead of Origi, but well ahead of the rest of the Reds. Can he maintain such red-hot form?

There are definitely some players who just should simply never shoot, certainly from distance. Between them, as of January 2019, Joël Matip, Nathaniel Clyne, Dejan Lovren, Virgil van Dijk, Joe Gomez, Andy Robertson and Fabinho had taken 161 long-range shots in their senior top-level careers *without scoring a single goal from outside the box*, albeit not all of these when wearing a Liverpool shirt; Clyne with *forty-four* of them in his time in the top-flight. Aside from van Dijk and Fabinho – who are capable of hitting special shots (van Dijk scored some stunning free-kicks with Celtic) – then unless they led to corners or deflections to other players that led to goals, these were all *utter wastes of possession.*

Not only does it give away possession and allow the opposition time to compose themselves – as the goalkeeper wastes time with the resultant goalkick (or easy catch) – but it's one less attack Liverpool can create. Even Daniel Sturridge, with his world-class last-gasp goal against Chelsea that kept the Reds in the early-season title-chasing pack, had failed to score with his previous 70-or-so league shots from distance. They look great when they go in, and in this case it proved vital, but what's harder to measure are all the better chances that keeping possession and looking for a smarter pass could have created. In Madrid, Spurs resorted to several long-range shots and reduced their own chances of scoring.

Naby Keïta, with five goals from 55 shots from distance, is the only Liverpool player, Origi (and Wilson) aside, to have a conversion rate from long-distance over 9%, although all of the Guinean's long-range goals to date remain with RB Leipzig. (But it shows his *potential*.) Xherdan Shaqiri ranked just behind Keïta, at just under 9% (11 goals from 128 shots), but then came Mo Salah, with eight goals from 101 shots outside the box up to January 2019; a conversion rate of 7.9%. Of course, the Egyptian king had one more sensational long-range effort in his locker for later in the season: an absolute *Exocet* that almost broke the Kop-end net against his old club, Chelsea.

Given that the average value of those 101 Salah shots meant they would *usually* be "worth" four goals, to score eight is still doing twice as well as could be expected (although of course, all the shots by players like Clyne go into the calculations); and so, like Coutinho, what Salah does is often wasteful *in a way*, but worth taking on every now and then. (And after all, a team that *never* shoots from distance would in many ways become more predictable; defenders wouldn't have to worry about getting their bodies into blocking positions and could just focus on marking the strikers; it's often the *threat* of the long-range shot that will see a defender sprawling to block, from which point the shot can be used as a decoy. And, of course, the planned reinterpretation of the handball laws, as of June 2019, means that more accidental handballs will be punished if the arms are not clearly at the player's side – which may prompt an increase in powerful shots looking to draw the instinctive movement of a hand or an arm.)

However, players like Clyne, with 44 shots and no goals, are those who – to paraphrase Jon Bon Jovi – give shooting from distance a bad name.

£XI

Another X we find important at *The Tomkins Times* is the "£XI" – the term Graeme Riley and I coined for our inflation-adjusted model which details how much any given team cost, on average, across a full Premier League season. We first used the term in our 2010 book *Pay As You Play*, and it was also included in an academic paper, *Financial Doping in the English Premier League*, from August 2017 (with Hywel Iorwerth from Cardiff Metropolitan University), as well as an earlier European Union report looking at spending in football.

So, in order to appreciate the arguments raised in this book, a little understanding of how inflation works in football spending is required, not least because, by 2018, the average price of a Premier League player was more than *27 times higher* than it had been in 1992; whereas standard UK inflation had merely doubled in that same time. Indeed, the average price for a Premier League player more than doubled *between 2016 and 2018 alone*; and so, someone bought in the 2016 market, when adjusted to 2018 prices, would have their fee retrospectively doubled – almost directly as a result in the massive hike in TV money; a good example being Raheem Sterling, who left Liverpool for Manchester City in 2015 (admittedly a year earlier than 2016) for £50m, but where, in 2018 money, that equated to £106.8m.

(Note: for now, all figures are 2018 money; our update to 2019 money will only be concluded after the release of this book.)

This is important, not least because Liverpool spent a lot of money in 2018 (albeit also when recouping a lot), and yet even someone like Virgil van Dijk – at £75m – does not cost as much, after inflation, as Man City outcast Eliaquim Mangala (like Sterling, also £106m when adjusted to 2018 money, albeit from the starting point of a £42m fee in 2014). That said, Mangala doesn't alter Man City's *£XI*, as he never plays. But Sterling certainly does; as do Kevin de Bruyne (£120m), David Silva (£87m) and Sergio Agüero (£159.5m).

Because Man City locked down a lot of these expensive players *before* inflation hiked prices, these deals can start to feel cheaper than they actually were. It's easy to forget the shock of City paying £42m for Mangala in 2014, as £42m doesn't seem such an outrageous figure now, with our sense of "cost" always primed towards the current market (we don't think of how much a car or house cost in 1967 as having any relevance whatsoever to what a car or house costs now, do we? Yet football inflation moves even faster than the housing market). Without doubt, £42m was still an *enormous* sum in 2014. This is all-important, as without inflation, Liverpool would rank as the 3rd most expensive team in England in 2018/19; but with inflation they rank 4th, still £100m behind Chelsea, whose fee for Eden Hazard – alone – is now equal to £127.9m.

In the past season, Liverpool's £XI was only c.50% that of Manchester City's; their massive financial advantage gaining them just one extra point (but a point that made all the difference.)

In 2018 money, the most expensive Premier League transfers since 1992 are the trio of Andriy Shevchenko, Wayne Rooney and, with his move to Man United (having earlier cost a fortune when Leeds bought him), Rio Ferdinand – all at around the £200m mark; and the player ranked 10th in the list – Ángel Di María – equates to £149.3m. While no club in England – *sans* inflation – has yet paid £200m for a player (or even £100m), £100m-£200m is now the going European rate for an elite striker; as seen with Neymar's move to PSG in 2017. And of course, Liverpool sold Philippe Coutinho – a similar kind of player (South American playmaker) at a similar age (26) to Di María in 2014 – to Barcelona for much the same Man United paid, *after* inflation, for the Argentine. In fact, to really highlight the importance of factoring in *football* inflation, the £15m Newcastle paid in 1996 for Alan Shearer wouldn't now buy the left boot of a Lebanese left-back; but that £15m works out at £162m in 2018 money. And if you still don't trust our inflation model, ask yourself, what would an elite English striker (such as Harry Kane) cost now – £15m or £162m? This concept is vital to establish before getting onto the bones of the book.

Because he's still playing, Sergio Agüero's £38m fee from 2011 somehow – illogically – still gets treated as £38m; yet it was *eight years ago*. Just 14 years before that, the £15m for Shearer now equates to £162m; and from 2011, the £38m for Agüero equates to an almost identical amount (£159.5m).

Given that we've proven over the years that there's a strong correlation between the £XI and final league position – even if a model cannot predict the randomness that also crops up in football – we therefore think it's a kind of gold standard for such analysis, even if no financial ranking system will see all teams perform exactly to par.

We have used the system for almost a decade now, and apply it the same way, no matter where and when Liverpool spent their money.

Tomkins' Law

One more thing to come out of our Transfer Price Index work was my study into what percentage – from what at the time was 3,000 Premier League transfers – could be labelled clear successes; something regular *TTT* contributor, *Anfield Index* podcaster and professional data analyst Dan Kennett dubbed Tomkins' Law (although it doesn't appear to have wheedled its way into the public consciousness, despite my shameless and desperate attempts). In 2011 I created a coefficient to take the fee paid and any possible transfer fee recouped (both adjusted for inflation), and, based on the other data we had on file, factored in the number of games each player started in the Premier League. Each game played was worth several points (to reward the fact that the player was *getting onto the pitch*, which suggests a degree of success), whilst any profit (after inflation) was rewarded in the coefficient in two ways: first, the sum of the profit (say, £20m), and second, the scale of the profit in relation to the original fee paid (so that anyone who cost £1m and was sold for £10m could be fully appreciated – which is particularly relevant for smaller clubs – when the profit of £10m on its own might not mark that player out as an outstanding buy). The ideal situation would be a cheapish buy, who then played 500 league games for the club, and was sold for a profit just before his legs were about to give out.

What I found was that just under half of the players had negative or neutral scores – where virtually no impact was made, and financial losses were often incurred. There were myriad players across all clubs who came for a fee, played a few games (or maybe none) and then vanished. What was surprising was that, the greater the fee paid, the chances of that player being successful only increased marginally: from the overall total of about 40% to the 60% of the most expensive 100 players. For example, the top 20 most expensive players in the Premier League, after inflation, include Andriy Shevchenko (Chelsea), Sean Wright-Phillips (Chelsea), Angel di Maria (Man Utd), Juan Sebastian Veron (Man Utd), Jose Antonio Reyes (Arsenal), Hernan Crespo (Chelsea) and Adrian Mutu (Chelsea), whilst Michael Owen to Newcastle ranks 21st, with Andy Carroll to Liverpool 22nd. Some of these players had bright moments, but none was a clear success; and most were flops. The last time I updated the coefficient, in 2017, the top 15 most successful buys were, in order: Cristiano Ronaldo (Man Utd), Gareth Bale (Spurs), Nicolas Anelka (Arsenal), Jussi Jääskeläinen (Bolton), Shay Given (Newcastle), Kolo Touré (Arsenal), Frank Lampard (Chelsea), Tim Howard (Everton), Patrick Vieira (Arsenal), Cesc Fàbregas (Arsenal), Mark Schwarzer (Middlesbrough), Kevin Davies (Bolton), Luis Suárez (Liverpool), Sami Hyypiä (Liverpool) and Petr Čech (Chelsea). As you can see, it's not *necessarily* the very best players, but those who provided greatest value.

It's harder to apply this analysis to players who are still at their current club; it only really works – fairly at least – when they've been sold on, or when they've retired. Because every player has the chance to turn around their career at a club and, like Moussa Sissoko at Spurs, go from a costly flop for a couple of seasons to a key midfielder in his third (albeit one who helped Spurs lose the Champions League final). Equally, a player can have an amazing first season and then vanish without trace, perhaps due to injuries, or other issues. Plus, no matter how good some signings are, they can't *all* play a ton of games; some will keep others out of the team.

So it's therefore difficult to apply Tomkins' Law to Liverpool's recent transfer work – certainly since Jürgen Klopp arrived – as pretty much everyone bought has been such a success that they haven't been sold; which is in itself a sign of success, just not one easily measured by the coefficient. But it's clear that if you had to apply Tomkins' Law to Liverpool since 2015 – without data, but just on *impact made* – then the trend has been thoroughly bucked in the past four years.

Additional Context For the Start of 2018/19

There were two other issues where some type of analytics helps to explain the context of the summer of 2018, and how Liverpool hoped to improve. Indeed, the first of these – just like the xG analysis from across the whole of 2017/18 – suggested that Liverpool were *already* much closer to Manchester City than the 25-point difference portrayed. As such, they are worth quickly explaining.

University of Bath Study 2017/18 – The Luck Index

It's long been obvious that there is no way for luck to "even itself out" over the course of a season; there is no omnipotent hand to make the alterations necessary to achieve balance, such as giving a team the 15 penalties they are "owed" in the final game of the season. Some seasons you will have more luck than others; but in 2017/18, Liverpool's luck *stank*. And with that being the case, it stood to reason that any kind of better fortune in 2018/19 would likely lead to an increase in league points, if even just the same level of performance was maintained.

I wrote about it throughout that maddening league campaign – with the issue of a lack of penalties, in particular, a big issue in the league; and an even bigger issue at Anfield; and the biggest issue of all *at the Kop end*. As this pattern has been going on for years now, I stopped assuming that it was down to bad luck and have concluded that, while referees are almost certainly not corrupt, their *thinking* about Liverpool and penalties at the Kop end certainly is. They are bending over backwards – ignoring what they see – so as to not *appear* biased. Anyone who has seen a referee try to even up the mistakes after making a gaffe, or giving a decision to whomever happens to make the first or loudest call, knows that decisions aren't cold, hard, rational conclusions; they are totally *influenced*. Indeed, it's very hard to judge almost any situation in a fast-moving game.

A quick glance at social media or football discussion pages any time Liverpool get a favourable decision at Anfield will find the outpouring of utter outrage, with talk of this kind of outrageous fortune happening *all the time*. Except, it almost never does; not anymore. In the 1970s the Kop was a fearsome terrace, and Liverpool, when attacking it – as the best team in Europe at the time – would indeed win a lot of penalties; mostly due to being *good*, one presumes (without the benefit of being able to go back and study evidence of television footage for a lot of those games), but perhaps due to referees being intimidated, back in the age when the home fans were *all* the referees had to answer to. Now, with almost every game televised, streamed live and live-blogged and live-tweeted, the referees instead have to answer to the "neutrals", who tend to make the loudest noise. (And who, of course, *are not neutral*; they support rival clubs. As the Stranglers almost once sang: no more neutrals anymore…).

Whenever Liverpool *do* get a penalty at Anfield – and unlike in European games, it's very rare – the old stereotype of the Kop influencing the officials gets dragged out by rival fans steeped in the myth; and if the manager of the team that concedes a penalty is an ex-player from these shores, you can bet your bottom dollar that he will say something like "Liverpool always get the decisions" and "the ref caved in to pressure from the Kop".

But the data shows that actually, *they don't.*

And nor do a lot of the other big clubs get "all the decisions" – because in terms of penalties won in recent seasons, inoffensive mid-ranking Premier League teams lead the way. Which is utterly illogical.

That said, Liverpool still get an unusually low proportion of their league penalties at Anfield (a long-term trend), and a *really bizarrely* low proportion at the Kop end. (More on this later in the book, as it's definitely not a case of bad luck when you see the strange patterns. This includes Liverpool being about four times as likely to win a penalty in the Champions League than in the Premier League; and of course, that run continued in Madrid.)

But at least some writers and academics with a genuine non-Liverpool FC bias backed up my red-tinted assertions, made throughout the 2017/18 campaign; even if the academic study didn't look into the psychological reasons why referees are terrified of giving decisions to Liverpool at Anfield, and at the Kop end *in particular.*

In August 2018, Gabriele Marcotti, the noted journalist and senior writer at *ESPN FC*, discussed the University of Bath study, which the *ESPN* team, along with Intel, helped create. It was certainly no surprise to see who ranked as the unluckiest team by the measures they set out in the season the Reds finished 25 points behind Manchester City.

"… you can forget that silly cliché that decisions even themselves out over the course of a season," Marcotti wrote on *ESPN.* "We know that's not the case. In fact, you can work it out for yourself by simply flipping a coin: the more times you flip, the less likely it is that you will get an equal number of heads and tails.

"Likewise, on the pitch, every time there is an error it can be in your favour or against you. (Of course, football supporters usually only see the bad luck that goes against them – sort of the opposite of rose-tinted glasses. Goes for the managers, too.)

"But how much does luck – good and bad – really play a part? To find out, we devised and created a study, along with our friends at the University of Bath, to find out the degree to which luck and refereeing decisions impacted the 2017-18 Premier League season. After the numbers were crunched … the Luck Index was born, along with an alternative Premier League table.

"The headline result? Manchester United were the most fortunate side, gaining six additional points, while Liverpool were the unluckiest: strip out the effects of luck and Jürgen Klopp's crew would have had an extra 12 points, enough to finish second [with 87 points] ... and above arch-rival United."

And on top of bad luck through officials' decisions, Liverpool were unlucky based on the xG results that season – just as, in Pep Guardiola's first season in England, the underlying stats said Manchester City were better than their 3rd-placed finish suggested.

Just as the scoreline is rarely a full, *detailed* reflection of a game, then the league table is never fully truthful, either; particularly earlier on in a season, when different teams can have vastly varying difficulty levels to their games. And luck would probably take half a century to even itself out in any truly meaningful way.

Indeed, if Liverpool left some of the terrible Premier League luck of 2017/18 behind in the new season – even, in December 2018, *winning some penalties* (before a stop was put to that, post-haste) – a new threat had emerged: the unkindest of all fixture lists imaginable. To truly appreciate how good a job Klopp has done, you really need to see just how each recent season has started with his team thrown into the deep end.

The Start From Hell

In October 2018, some ten games into the new season – with Man City arriving at Anfield for the 11th – *LFCHistory.net* and regular TTT contributor Terry Dolan confirmed what many of us at the site suspected: that this really had been an *awful* fixture list for the Reds; and this was following on from the season before, where the fixture list had also been historically unkind. This time, by contrast, the European draw was at the heart of the difficulty, although the Reds were still presented with an intimidating set of league games, in no small part due to the Big Six fixtures often packed around those extra-tough European encounters.

"Last season I analysed Liverpool's very difficult start," Terry noted, "with an unusual group of six away games in seven consecutive fixtures, and showed that it was the 3rd-toughest for the Reds in Premier League history after 15 games ... I decided it was time to look again and see how this season's challenging start compares to others. Is it really the most difficult this decade? Spoiler alert – yes it is!"

Terry used the Elo rankings: a method, named after its creator Arpad Elo, for calculating the relative skill levels of players in zero-sum games; initially for chess, but later used for football. (Zero-sum games are where the total gains of the participants are added up and the total losses are subtracted – so, if a team wins three points and the other team loses three points, the sum is zero. As such, Elo is not to be confused with a 1970s' orchestral pop band.)

Terry continued: "By my calculation, 2018/19 represents Liverpool's most difficult 10 games in all competitions in the Premier League era. That is, this is the most difficult start *in over 25 years*. For the seasons in the Premier League era, I selected all of Liverpool's games in all competitions up to game 10, added up the Elo rating (as of 1st August in that season) for each opposition team and then divided the total by the number of games played to give a measure of the quality of the opposition for that season – the average opposition Elo score. Here are the top five seasons, sorted by the average opposition Elo rating after 10 games:

      1st 2018/19 – 1,763
      2nd 2017/18 – 1,735
      3rd 2006/07 – 1,712
      4th 2007/08 – 1,701
      5th 2016/17 – 1,683"

At first, upon reading Terry's words, I assumed that these were all Champions League seasons, with the highness of the scores due, in part, to playing elite European teams. But of course, 2016/17 saw Liverpool face no European football at all; but they did start with a run that included games against Arsenal, Chelsea, Spurs and Manchester United. Which means that, under Jürgen Klopp, Liverpool have *consistently* had tough Premier League starts.

Indeed, when I filtered out the figures for the two Champions League games from the figures Terry provided on the 2018/19 start – against high-level opposition in PSG and Napoli – and also removed the League Cup game against Chelsea, the average Elo score of the opposition fell, as expected, but only to 1,724 – which would make it even harder, in terms of league games, than 2016/17.

(Although this increase is in some small part because of the *overall* increase in Premier League ratings in the past few years – with, as of early April 2019, the average at 1,733; but before that, going back a season at a time, it was: 1,719; 1,701; 1,694; and 1,687, after a fairly big drop from 2014, where it was 1,713. However, while 1,733 was the Premier League's average score in April 2019, this was with four of the quarter-finalists of the Champions League, and two of the quarter-finalists of the Europa League, being from England. As of September-October 2018, the Premier League's average score was just 1,706; so, on average, Liverpool still played Premier League teams with a higher Elo score.)

And, somewhat challengingly, Liverpool's 11th game of the season – and eighth in the league – was against Man City, just days after an away trip to Napoli, and within a week of an away trip to Chelsea. That all made for three Big Six clashes in the first eight league fixtures, with two ultra-tough Champions League games thrown in, plus Chelsea in the League Cup. No fewer than *six* of Liverpool's first 11 games were against opposition from the top-15 ranked clubs in Europe – Spurs, Chelsea (twice), PSG and Napoli.

Which is interesting, particularly when you consider the outpouring of jubilation when England reached the World Cup semi-finals on the back of a particularly easy draw; doing well, clearly, but failing to beat a single nation of note. This is worth mentioning because, halfway through 2018/19, one journalist, speaking on *Sky's Sunday Supplement* ranted – and it *was* a rant – about Jürgen Klopp having won nothing with Liverpool (incidentally, stated as part of a defence of Jose Mourinho's tenure at Man United), claiming to be baffled as to why there was all this praise for the job the German is doing, only to then, much later in the same show, praise Gareth Southgate for lifting England's spirits and doing his country proud in Russia during the summer.

Somehow, Liverpool getting to a Champions League final (beating the higher-ranked Manchester City 5-1 on aggregate *en route*) and, months later, being top of the Premier League, was not worthy of any praise, but beating Tunisia (ranked 14th going into the World Cup), Panama (55th), Colombia (16th, beaten only on penalties) and Sweden (23rd) – all below the 13th place that England occupied – was this *miraculous* achievement. England lost twice to higher-ranked Belgium, and also lost to lower-ranked Croatia in the semi-final. Which isn't to say that Southgate did anything other than a good job; but the double-standards from some quarters with regards to his and Klopp's work simply astounded. (But hey, that's some tabloid journalists for you. And hey, Klopp has just had the last laugh.)

As of June 2019, Liverpool had moved clear at the very top of the European Elo rankings, with the best ranking points total in their history, at 2,043.

Not only that, but it ranks them the 6th-best team *in European football history*.

(Uefa's own coefficient has Liverpool at only 11th, up from 48th when Klopp took over; but it is based on a rolling five-year period, and ranks Europa League progress more highly than it really should.)

While Terry Dolan's method looked at the Elo rankings at the time of the fixtures, another method – the ratings performance index (RPI – a method used mostly in the vast, unmanageable landscapes of American sports, to fairly differentiate between teams who will never face each other) – was first applied to the Premier League on *TTT* by Tim O'Brien, before both Terry and Graeme Riley created their own versions, with subtle tweaks, designed to remove the flaw of the system when the teams *do* all play each other.

These RPI tables looked at the form and league position of all opponents (weighting any points won accordingly), and when running the model partway through the season – and then running it for past seasons – Liverpool ranked top in the autumn, even when not top of the league table. Standard RPI models tend to become less revealing once everyone has played each other, as the formulas end up including the same data – just in a different order (everyone has played everyone, so it co-mingles) – but a tweak of this glitch (which doesn't have to be ironed out in American college sports) allowed the creation of a non-repeating picture.

Graeme's conclusion, running the new formula in all 23 of the 20-team Premier League seasons (as the three seasons with more games confuses the formula), was that Liverpool had *by far* the best score after 23 games of any other team in that two-decade sample; greater even than the Chelsea team of 2005/06 and the Man City team of 2017/18, who were the only two teams to have had a better points record after 23 games of a season in the history of English football, aside from Spurs in 1960/61.

While the form of any club can sometimes just fall off a cliff for no discernible reason, the RPI – just like the xG scoreline – suggested (before a lot of people took them as seriously as they should) that Liverpool were the real deal.

That this was achieved with a much lower £XI than the best Chelsea or Man City sides just underlined the job Jürgen Klopp was doing. What it couldn't necessarily foresee was Man City going on an insanely long winning streak having been vulnerable over the winter, but that's football – you can never predict it all.

And if you could it would be no fun at all.

The Summer of 2018 – From Despair To … Where?

The men in red slumped to the ground on the Ukranian turf that, under the floodlights, glowed an almost unnatural, phosphorescent shade of green; the men in white ran around, eyes wide in jubilation (or perhaps, if a repeat of the 2017 final as reported through the Football Leaks revelations, due to *dexamethasone).*

They say that cheats don't prosper, but that wasn't true on May 26th 2018; *Der Spiegel* having alleged in the autumn of 2018, based on those Football Leaks documents, that Sergio Ramos had failed a test for that particular drug (which can enhance performance, and aggression) after the *previous* Champions League final, and that Real Madrid had a history of disrupting drugs tests on their players; and also that on another occasion, Ramos disappeared for a "shower" when he should have been peeing into a jar. And this before the unpalatable underhand tactics of the wide-eyed, but dead-eyed, Madrid centre-back on the night.

It wasn't so much the fact that Liverpool lost the Champions League final in Kiev to Real Madrid – there's certainly no shame in that, with the Spanish giant's gargantuan spending over the years and their back-to-back European titles heading into the final – but the *manner* of it was sickening. Loris Karius 'chose' this game to make his first costly mistakes of the season (you will often see the word 'chose' in situations like this, even though no one makes that *choice*), but only after Ramos – with a sociopathic gaze – had used what Olympic experts called an *illegal* martial arts move to dislocate Mo Salah's shoulder to the point where the Egyptian left the pitch in agony, thus considerably reducing the Reds' chances of winning (having been the better team up to that point), and grinning as his victim left the game in tears; and, unseen by only the most distant of television cameras, plant an elbow into Karius' head.

There followed a debate about head injuries, with Liverpool, Jürgen Klopp and Karius mocked for suggesting – after the goalkeeper saw a world-renowned specialist in concussion in Boston (where a lot of work has been done on the shocking brain injuries caused to NFL players) – that he was probably concussed as a result. Unlike a bruise, a compound fracture or a bloody gash, concussion cannot be seen by the naked eye, and therefore – to those who don't understand such things –

probably doesn't exist; especially if the player wasn't knocked unconscious at the time. With accusations that Ramos was a serial doper – or at the very least, dope-test *avoider* – emerging several months later (along with myriad accusations against Manchester City for *financially* doping), it added a further sourness to the memory. In all truth Real Madrid were likely to be the better team – they certainly had the stronger bench – and substitute Gareth Bale's overhead kick was undeniably sensational. But it hardly felt like a fair fight.

Whatever the cause of Karius' mistakes – concussion or big-game jitters – rescuing the goalkeeper's mental state presented, without doubt, Klopp's toughest job in football. Even the team that worked on Steve Austin – back in the 1970s, with *Six Million Dollars* – would have struggled to rebuild Karius' confidence. Klopp wanted to try, clearly. But in preseason the goalkeeper made a couple of small errors, and they were magnified into "calamities"; back-page headlines and social media memes from utterly meaningless games against minor opposition. Karius became a global joke figure, in this most vicious of ages; social media taking society back to the days of public humiliations, which were outlawed in England and America the 1800s *for being too cruel*. Before long Karius looked like a nervous wreck; understandably so, given that he is, after all, merely human. There was nothing else for it: for the sake of the team, and maybe the player himself, Liverpool needed a new goalkeeper.

In late July, two full months after the final, Klopp opened up about the events in Kiev, after a series of tit-for-tat media messages involving himself, his players and a certain pumped-up Spanish central defender.

"We are opening *that* bottle again?" said Klopp, speaking before the International Champions Cup game against Manchester United. "It is action-reaction-action-reaction and I don't like that but – if you watch it back and you are not with Real Madrid – then you think it is ruthless and brutal.

"I saw the ref taking charge of big games at the World Cup and nobody really thinks about that later. But in a situation like that somebody needs to judge it better. If VAR is coming then it is a situation where you have to look again. Not to give a red card but to look again and say: 'What is that?' It was ruthless.

"I'm not sure it is an experience we will have again – go there and put an elbow to the goalkeeper, put their goalscorer down like a wrestler in midfield and then you win the game. That was the story of the game. Ramos said a lot of things afterwards that I didn't like. As a person I didn't like the reactions of him. He was like: 'Whatever, what do they want? It's normal.' No, it is *not* normal. If you put all of the situations of Ramos together then you will see a lot of situations with Ramos. The year before against Juve he was responsible for the red card for Juan Cuadrado. Nobody talks about that afterwards. It is like we, the world out there, accepts that you use each weapon to win the game. People probably expect that I am the same. I am not."

At the time Klopp spoke about the Cuadrado incident it was still not known that Ramos had failed a drug test for that match, for a substance that boosts both energy and aggression. Real Madrid denied the accusation, but according to *Der Spiegel*, "Uefa deemed a positive doping test by Ramos to be an 'administrative mistake', after the Real Madrid team doctor failed to disclose a pre-match injection of a banned substance."

Of course, who would take the fall? As the story said, "After Uefa investigated the incident and asked the club and player for expectations, it was the doctor who would take the blame – claiming 'human error'."

As reported by *The Independent*, based on those *Der Spiegel* articles, "The German publication also reports that the club [Real Madrid] interfered with a random doping test of 10 players in February 2017. Clubs are committed to ensuring that doping control officers are able to do their jobs independently and without interference but Uefa reported internally that Madrid's medical staff took the samples for some of the tests. Those same doping officers say they accepted this only 'due to the situation of tension' created when Cristiano Ronaldo had kicked up a fuss about being tested."

By then it had started to sound like something from the murky world of professional cycling, or the BALCO scandal that rocked baseball and athletics at the turn of the millennium, but nothing appears to have been done about the actions of Real Madrid and their biggest stars. Perhaps it really was all just a series of innocent mixups, and Sergio Ramos is as honest as the day is long. (Some might add: as long as a day *in an Arctic winter….*)

How To Get Over It
Earlier in the summer of 2018, as the Reds tried to shake off the disappointment, the club had been pursuing an elite creative, goalscoring midfielder, in the shape of Nabil Fekir, the Lyon attacker who had made a few appearances on the way to France winning the World Cup in Russia; an ideal replacement for Philippe Coutinho, who left six months earlier, given that Fekir was a bit more combative – to press aggressively, as well as to create with skill. Liverpool fans were

salivating at the arrival of this powerful, gifted player who could form part of a devastating front four. But then, during the medical, the full extent of Fekir's past injuries, and the toll they had taken, were revealed.

There can be no doubt that the club pulled out of the deal after the full details of the player's past knee surgeries were revealed in the medical; which, after all, is why clubs spend all that time and effort to vet a potential new signing. Fekir had been largely able to stay fit since returning from missing most of 2015/16, albeit with a modified training regime and without playing as many minutes as other players; but one awkward challenge or slip could see the Reds lose their new £50m asset for the season – or perhaps for good – and presumably the insurance, with the preexisting serious condition, would not cover such an eventuality. With Alex Oxlade-Chamberlain already due to be out for the whole of 2018/19 with his own complicated knee ligament injury – he would end up returning two days after the anniversary of being stretchered off against Roma in the Champions League semi-final, just in time to be ready for Barcelona at the same stage of the 2018/19 season – it would have been reckless to buy a player in a similar position who had a similar injury. In the end the Reds plumped for the £13m alternative of Xherdan Shaqiri, who certainly made an impression in the autumn, with six vital goals in the league before the turn of the year, albeit then largely disappearing from the picture.

Whether or not Brazilian goalkeeper Alisson Becker would have been pursued had Fekir not failed his medical is something else to ponder; because, by the time the Fekir deal faded, it became clear that Karius was now beyond hope – unless he could rebuild his career away from the spotlight. Instead of £50m or more on Fekir, it became a combined £79m on Allison and Shaqiri, and Karius went to Beşiktaş on a two-year loan. While the Alisson deal was touted as a world record at £66m, it's worth noting that he would not be the Premier League's costliest goalkeeper when inflation was taken into account (that was David de Gea, at £79.3m), and that, applying English football inflation to Serie A, Gianluigi Buffon cost the equivalent of over £200m when joining Juventus in 2001.

Liverpool were already committed to the £52m transfer fee for Naby Keïta, the 23-year-old Guinean midfield sensation from the *Bundesliga*; up from the proposed £48m when RB Leipzig qualified for the Champions League. And just a couple of days after the Reds' bitter disappointment in the Ukraine, Brazilian midfielder Fabinho was toasting his move to Liverpool from Monaco on an Instagram post, as he and his wife shared a glass of champagne.

That immediate response to Kiev was evidence that Liverpool were going to hit back, and hit back hard, for the new season. "We have signed a fantastic player," the manager said, as Fabinho was unveiled, "but someone who is an equally fantastic person I think. His reputation as a character in the dressing room and his attitude in training has come through from everyone we speak to. He has a lovely family also – adding a person like this to our dressing room only makes us even stronger. What we have – in terms of our environment at Melwood and in the team – means anyone coming in must be of that build. They must be the highest quality person and player.

"He has ability and mentality to play at the highest level in a number of positions. He can play [as a] 6, 8 and 2. This is cool. He is tactically very strong and football smart. I think he improves our squad and there aren't that many players you can say that about in this moment, because the quality we have already is so high."

Liverpool, it was widely agreed across the media, had "won" the summer transfer window, although the previous summer that tag went to Everton, who ended up in a relegation battle. Liverpool's contrast with Fulham's buying – where the Cottagers, like Everton in 2017/18, bought a whole raft of highly-rated players, with a high net-spend – could be seen when the west London club were relegated at the start of April. You can have too much of a good thing, and buying what amounts to a whole new team in one summer is not the smartest way forward.

Indeed, Liverpool were now arguably regarded as the smartest club in world football. After quite a few years of – at times – rank stupidity, this was a big step forward. Liverpool spent money wisely; doing their due diligence on signings and then helping them to acclimatise. They got more bang for their buck than Man City, but Man City, for the past decade, had banged a hell of a lot more bucks on transfers, wages, coaching staff and a glittering academy replete with its own stadium.

But even with all that spending, and all their brilliance, Guardiola was yet again unable to guide City as far as Klopp guided Liverpool in the Champions League: City, one 'round of 16' and two quarter-finals; Liverpool and Klopp, two finals, one of which was won.

Go back to the start of 2018/19, however, and the two clubs were set to lock horns in possibly the greatest title race British football had ever seen; at least in terms of the overall points garnered. And while Guardiola just about edged it, 98 points to 97, Klopp once again took Liverpool to Champions League football in May; this time, with a far happier ending.

Raring To Go – Football Returns

Football was back; 76 days after the painfully deflating Champions League final in Kiev, the next competitive fixture arrived: West Ham at home – a rare Anfield start to a league campaign. The visitors had bought almost a dozen new players during the transfer window, and several were picked to start at a ground where they found victories rare. Liverpool fielded two of their own new buys, Alisson Becker and Naby Keïta, while the other pair of new signings – Xherdan Shaqiri and Fabinho – had to be content with a place on the bench.

Having been at what was then all eleven of Liverpool's European finals over the years – and, in May, seen the Reds lose their third in a row since Istanbul – *The Tomkins Times'* editor Chris Rowland was back at Anfield, and raring to go.

"I'm in my seat ten minutes before kick-off," he noted on the site. "A friend makes an interesting point about the contrast between post-2013/14, when it felt broken, and now, when it definitely doesn't. There's undeniably a good vibe about the place. And we're very easy on the eye just now. The bloke to my left greets the West Ham fans' anthem with the pithy retort 'You can stick your fuckin' bubbles up yer arse, sideways', an impressive feat of physics I feel. A sideways bubble – how can you tell?"

The Reds opened the scoring in the 19th minute when new signing Keïta picked the ball up in the midfield and burst forward, with four West Ham defenders ahead of him, and only Sadio Mané and Mo Salah in amongst them. Keïta dribbled at pace, turning to his left before stroking a lovely inside-left pass with the outside of his right boot – to the onrushing Andy Robertson. In no time at all, the Reds now had four men on the edge of the box, plus Roberto Firmino and James Milner rushing to join them. When Robertson hit the first-time cross it was now five Liverpool players against six defenders in the box, but Keïta, Mané and Firmino – almost lining up just outside the six-yard box – were not needed, as the ball fizzed across the Salah, whose right-foot touch, three yards out, flashed into the back of the net. It was fitting that the Egyptian grabbed the first goal of the campaign, right in front of the Kop, after the way the previous season ended in hospital. And from the first moments of the season it was clear that Robertson would again be a vital outlet on the left. It was a poacher's goal by Salah, gambling on the cross beating the goalkeeper, to leave a close-range finish that any kind of true contact would turn into a goal (but where a slightly more open angle of the foot could send such a fizzing ball wide).

Trent Alexander-Arnold went close with a free-kick, before Keïta then part-danced, part-fumbled his way past four players in the box, Gini Wijnaldum steering the shot wide when the ball broke his way. Marko Arnautović had a half-chance on the break, which he screwed wide; and then another, with the same end result.

The first-half was also notable for the Reds' new £66m keeper dinking the ball over the leg of the onrushing West Ham striker, in an act that seems part inspired, part lunacy.

Chris: "We agree we may have to accept Alisson will give us kittens on a regular basis and that there may be a couple of instances during the season where he costs us a goal, hopefully when we're 3-0 up rather than the deciding goal against a Manchester club."

Another Robertson cross created the second goal, just on the stroke of half-time, as his deep ball was brilliantly recovered by Milner on the lunge, and for the second time in the game one of Liverpool's fabled front three was a few yards out with an open goal at his mercy – albeit this time the ball was a fraction behind Mané, and the finish a tad more difficult than he made it look.

In the second half, Michail Antonio – scourge of Liverpool in the past (albeit with consolation goals) and scourge of Liverpool in the future (in a more costly manner) – missed a header from point-blank range. Soon after, Firmino looked set to play in Mané, but took another two touches before releasing the pass; Mané was then offside, the ball was smashed into the back of the net on the swivel, and the linesman – perfectly in line – somehow missed it. Not only were Liverpool playing a rare home game on the first day of the season, but now the officials were helping their cause, in stark contrast to the nightmares of 2017/18. There was just time for Daniel Sturridge, on as a sub in the 88th minute, to prod home an 88th-minute goal from a corner – after he'd essentially run into the box straight from the bench – to mean that the Reds had now scored four times against the Hammers four times in a row; a new top-flight record for the club against any single opponent. But West Ham, it turned out, would be back to haunt the Reds in early 2019.

It was a great start. Jürgen Klopp was pleased, especially as Liverpool fielded a fairly diminutive midfield trio of James Milner, Naby Keïta and Gini Wijnaldum, with the more physical Jordan Henderson being eased back after the World Cup, and the one midfield giant – Fabinho – not used as he adapted to the physical and tactical demands the manager places on his charges. "They were obviously taller than us today," Klopp noted after the match, "so that was always a bit tricky, with the wind also." (Indeed, the wind almost became a theme of the season.)

"Then we scored in the perfect moment before half-time, absolutely perfect, then we scored the third one and the fourth one when Daniel was kind of eight seconds on the pitch – that was really cool. So result good, performance good, let's carry on."

If Liverpool were handed something of a home-banker on the first weekend, the Monday night trip to Crystal Palace eight days later was a much trickier tie on paper.

The highlight of the game was Naby Keïta's sublime turn and lofted through-ball to Mo Salah, who took the difficult pass coming over his shoulder down with aplomb, but the ball flicked up onto his midriff, leaving no time to steady himself – after the ball fell down again – before getting too much on a lobbed finish over the onrushing goalkeeper.

Andros Townsend came close to scoring the first goal of the season against Alisson, but his curling shot from 20 yards thumped off the crossbar. The game then swung firmly in Liverpool's favour when the first of several controversial penalties during the season was awarded to Salah; a controversy which, aside from the one at home to Newcastle on Boxing Day, was hard to fathom. Here, ex-Red Mamadou Sakho was all over him like a rash, grabbing the striker and also aiming kicks that, if meant for the ball, only got Salah's shins. James Milner duly converted the spot-kick.

Palace applied some second-half pressure, but the win was essentially secured when Salah, clean through on goal, was taken out by Obi Wan-Bissaka (whose real first name may be Aaron). After what happened the season before – when an identical situation at Anfield saw no punishment for Jamaal Lascelles of Newcastle – it was something of a surprise to see the referee send him off; but the official was the Premier League's best – Michael Oliver – who would also award Liverpool rare penalties at Anfield later in the season.

With the game heading towards a 1-0 win, as Palace sought an elusive equaliser, Virgil van Dijk rose majestically to head away two corners; on the second, Salah, as the Reds broke, played the ball from his own half through to Mané, who, as he ran at speed towards the area, was fouled by Patrick van Aanholt in an almost identical manner to Wan-Bissaka on Salah. Somehow Mané stayed on his feet, despite being off-balance, and jinked around the keeper, to slot in from a fairly tight angle.

While not happy with the Reds' attacking play, Jürgen Klopp was more than satisfied with the defending. "We expected Palace to be that strong and clear in their approach against us, playing a big number of long balls. [Wayne] Hennessey – when I saw it before the game warming up, I thought 'wow, that's really difficult!' In the game they were not that long, but they were long enough. I don't know a lot of defenders in the world that can defend Christian Benteke in nearly 100 per cent of the situations, clear without a foul. It was very important that Virgil was there and that kind of presence, but still the ball drops and then it's a second ball. That was their plan as well, so it is difficult to be 100 per cent clear in these situations."

On the imperious van Dijk, Klopp added: "It was really, really good. It's obvious. Quality costs a specific price, it's with cars like that, with a lot of things like that and with players as well, that's why we paid it [the £75m fee]. Nobody thinks about it anymore and that's good because he's a player in this market, in the moment, he's at least worth it. We don't know what will happen in the future [with transfer fees], but it's not important to us. He loves playing with these boys and that's the most important thing for me."

Liverpool's next game was at home to Brighton – a tepid, disappointing encounter, with few highlights, as the Reds never quite hit top gear – but still deserved the victory.

Three games in, the Reds moved top on goal difference from Chelsea and Spurs, after Manchester City surprisingly drew at Wolves; while Man United, trying to build on their second place finish from the season before, had played three and already lost two.

The Reds' trip to Leicester was a lot more eventful than the narrow, uninspired victory over Brighton. As he would later in the season in the reverse fixture at Anfield, Sadio Mané opened the scoring against the Foxes, taking Andy Robertson's pass – after the full-back bustled forward – inside the box and smashing the ball past the helpless Kasper Schmeichel. Alisson then made a smart save from Demarai Gray, down to his right, but soon the Reds were two-up. James Milner, on his 100th Liverpool appearance, swung in a dangerous corner which, thanks to Roberto Firmino's powerful downward header, turned into the 80th Premier League assist of the vice-captain's 16-year top-level career.

However, with Liverpool looking rampant, Gini Wijnaldum gave away the ball in midfield and the entire momentum of the game seemed to switch. In the second-half Joe Gomez made a sensational block as James Maddison's shot looked destined for the back of the net, but it was only delaying what had started to feel a little inevitable.

If Alisson – on the back of three clean sheets – thought that this goalkeeping lark in England was a doddle, the visit to the King Power stadium proved a rude awakening. As often happens in England, any kind of mistake by a goalkeeper using his feet is deemed a case of trying to be "too clever"; with *cleverness* mistrusted by the game's dinosaurs. Alisson, close to the intersection of the edge of the box and the touchline, Cruyff-turned his way into trouble when none of his team-mates offered themselves for the pass; Kelechi Iheanacho tackled him – albeit with the use of a shove – and squared to Rachid Ghezzal to smash the ball home. The more you look at the tackle on Alisson the clearer the additional shove in his back, effectively to push him both off the ball and off the pitch, but if the officials were only looking at the two mens' feet, and the ball in between them, it looked perfectly legal. Plus, there's the sense given off by English referees that any *fanciness* from a goalkeeper is worthy of punishment.

It was something Alisson clearly learned from – it would be months before another Cruyff turn (which worked fine) – although he hadn't been bought just to whack every ball into touch.

Jürgen Klopp was obviously grilled about Alisson's gaffe after the game. "It was last week when he did what he did [a piece of skill against Brighton] and the way everybody spoke about it, it was clear that it would happen one day that we conceded a goal because of that. But we still want to use it. I have to watch it back but I thought Joe Gomez could have cleared the situation, then Virgil for sure could have cleared it. In the end, if Alisson with the first touch puts the ball away, everything is fine. For some reason, he didn't do that, he dribbled and they scored the goal. That's it. I said to him, it's the best game to do it because we still won the game and we ticked that box.

"… It's only positive that he is that good a footballer. But we all have to learn to use it in the right way still. That means, pass the ball in the right moment, then immediately make another offer for him, open some passing options. That's the job for the team, play the pass in the right moment, not on a dry pitch, not hard enough. Don't do it in these moments."

Liverpool were still top on goal difference, ahead of Chelsea and Watford. Now Spurs – Liverpool's next opponents, at Wembley – had joined City in dropping points; losing 2-1 at surprise package Watford.

'Spursy'

On September 15th Liverpool returned to the scene of a horror-show from less than twelve months earlier. That day, the Reds simply never got going; conceding two early goals and Dejan Lovren, looking all at sea, hauled off well before half-time.

This time the Reds were the early harassers, with James Milner's cross flicked in at the near post by Roberto Firmino, but the goal was disallowed as Sadio Mané was in an offside position, in front of the goalkeeper, attempting to play the ball (but missing). While this was a correct decision *if the law is applied logically*, Liverpool would later concede goals in a similar manner that were allowed to stand, not least at Burnley (and also at home to Chelsea in the League Cup); so while the Reds got some luck across the season with offside decisions, there were still instances where the rule was applied in a hugely inconsistent and baffling manner. Indeed, in the home game against Spurs in 2017/18, Harry Kane was standing *two yards* offside when the ball was played to him, and was in an offside position when the ball deflected off Lovren. While standing offside when the ball comes off a defender does not count as offside, he's still offside *from the original pass* if that pass is aimed in his direction (as it was).

Anyway, this time the offside decision didn't derail the Reds, as another tight call went in their favour – with yet another goal from a James Milner corner. Michel Vorm flapped haplessly at the delivery, and with the ball cleared to Gini Wijnaldum ten yards out, the Liverpool midfielder sent a looping header goalwards, towards the top corner. Obviously, being away from home in the Premier League, the Dutch midfielder was unlikely to score against his compatriot; Wijnaldum having scored all his league goals in English football at Anfield or, when a Newcastle player, St James' Park. Vorm, partly obstructed by his own defender, parried the ball out, but goalline technology showed that the ball was over the line. If this time it came to the Reds' rescue, the goalline cameras were not so helpful in a later Big Six away game, when the ball was mere millimetres from being fully over the Man City line.

Incredibly, Wijnaldum finally had an away goal in the league.

Soon after half-time Lucas Moura hit the post for Spurs after a rare Joe Gomez error, but then Vorm – arguably the Reds' most creative player on the day – was on hand to present the Reds with a second: Andy Robertson playing in Mané in the inside-left position, and his cross deflecting off the post before the Spurs' keeper somehow let it slip through his grasp. From about an inch out, Firmino produced his trademark no-look finish as he rammed the ball home. Minutes later the Brazilian was literally unable to look *anywhere* as Jan Vertonghen's fingernail scraped away at his cornea; indeed, in some gruesome still photos it looked like the Belgian's middle finger could almost have exited through the back of Firmino's skull.

Spurs grabbed a late retaliation, when Érik Lamela smashed home from a tight angle following a Spurs corner, to make the score 2-1; and in fairness, the home side were unlucky not to be awarded a penalty when Mané appeared to clip Son Heung-min. Perhaps this was a bit of the luck Liverpool had lost when Spurs won not one but two penalties at Anfield in the space of a few minutes the season before. (And of course, Liverpool had more luck in Madrid on 1st June.)

Klopp didn't want reminding of what happened in October 2017, as he rightly pointed out all that had changed in the interim. "You all remind me of our performance last year, I wouldn't think about it for a second if you wouldn't ask constantly. It was not part of the preparation; different game, different team, different situation, everything is different, so why should I use it? The only thing we used more was the home game we played against Tottenham, to be honest. Not because the result was better, only because it was not that long ago. The performance today, for me, was better than the result. The result is the most important thing and the result is perfect. Winning here is so difficult, unbelievably difficult, so I never expect that. Because we came here and tried to do it, you need a really outstanding performance – and that was what the boys delivered today. We could have scored more, we controlled the game.

"Let me say, it was the best game of the season for us for sure. We had in all the games really good moments. Today, we had 85 brilliant minutes and then unfortunately we didn't finish the game off. That means Tottenham have the quality to strike back, that's what they did after a corner."

However, despite not finishing the game off, as Klopp put it, the Reds left Wembley with all three points.

Klopp was certainly not going to get carried away with the 100% start. "I am not the personality to wait for problems, but I am old enough to know they will come. I was not really often surprised in my life when I've had some. We all have the same situation in the football team. I am long enough now in this business to know no-one plays a perfect season – not even City last year played a perfect season. It's no problem, it's still early, five games. It's fantastic we won all of them, it's fantastic we improved and this today was by far our best performance of the season, so I like that development. Now we have to prove it and do it again, again and again. We will see if we can do so."

After match-week five, Liverpool's unbeaten start was now only rivalled by Chelsea, with Watford finally falling away. But the Reds were no longer top of the league; Maurizio Sarri's men sitting above them by virtue of an extra goal in their favour on goal difference.

Enter PSG

The next game for the Reds was against petrostate glory-team Paris Saint-Germain, fresh from them winning every trophy in France for what felt like the past 20 years. Liverpool were looking to put the nightmare of Kiev behind them, and perhaps even return to the final – although at the time that felt a long way away.

The Reds began the game without Roberto Firmino, whose eye probably still contained remnants of Jan Vertonghen's fingernail. The visitors lined up with the stellar trio of Kylian Mbappé, Neymar and Edinson Cavani, while Liverpool turned to Daniel Sturridge in the absence of Firmino. And it was Sturridge who opened the scoring from what became a half-intentional trademark move for the Reds: Trent Alexander-Arnold whipping in a cross that just evaded everyone and ran through to Andy Robertson, to repeat the attempt from the other side. This time it landed right on Sturridge's head, a few yards out, and yet again the Reds' hitherto go-to man for goals – six years after he last started in the Champions League – was having a good start to the season.

Later in the first half, Juan Bernat scythed down Gini Wijnaldum when the Dutchman turned sharply and James Milner calmly converted the spot-kick.

However, yet again Liverpool were undone by the weird application of the offside rule, where Cavani's failed attempt to volley at goal when in an offside position was ignored, and Thomas Meunier swept home a fine shot. After half-time, Mo Salah thought he'd restored the two-goal advantage but the close-range strike was disallowed for a clear foul by Sturridge on the visitors' keeper, Alphonse Areola. Sturridge then failed to get enough contact on a similar chance to the one he scored from, before Mbappé – after Neymar had seized on a mistake by Salah – smashed home from 12 yards with just seven minutes left.

But with 91 minutes on the clock Firmino, on as a sub, took a pass from Virgil van Dijk – who was now playing as a no.10 – and, despite having only one functioning eye, turned the full-back inside out before drilling a low shot into the far corner.

Liverpool's Champions League season was up and running, with three points in the bag, but where qualification from the group stages would later be thrown into doubt after losing all three away fixtures. In hindsight, Firmino's late, late winner was the vital moment, just as Spurs – themselves facing elimination at the group stages, and in later rounds – found some vital late goals to make it to the final.

But at that stage there was a long way for Liverpool to go to get to Madrid. Understandably, Klopp was pleased with the start. "It was good, really good in all departments pretty much. It is so difficult to defend them, but we did. Good organisation and a big heart is always a good combination for defending. All 11 players were involved in that. A good performance against an outstandingly strong opponent; it was necessary we played good. The atmosphere was fantastic, so special to do these things in this stadium."

Liverpool's subsequent 3-0 victory over Southampton was most notable for another new player making his first start. The unleashing of Xherdan Shaqiri was something of a mixed affair for the player; having a big hand in the way the Reds ran up a 3-0 half-time lead, before he was surprisingly substituted at the break due to some failures in his off-the-ball work. The opening goal came when he received a fine pass from Sadio Mané down the inside-left channel and cut inside on his *right* foot. The shot wasn't too bad, considering he takes what feels like 90% of his efforts with his left, but it needed not one but two deflections off flailing Southampton defenders to squirm over the line.

Salah almost made it 2-0 when receiving a sharp low pass from Robertson with his back to goal, holding off the giant Jannik Vestergaard, whose arms – as so many central defenders seem to do – were up around the Egyptian's shoulders. Salah turned, played a deft one-two with Roberto Firmino, and just as he was about to stroke home, Cedric Soares slid in to knock the ball behind. This time it was Trent Alexander-Arnold who provided the pinpoint corner and Joël Matip rose to head home – in a game where the giant German-Cameroonian completed almost 100 passes, made three interceptions, one block, eleven ball recoveries and won five aerial duels.

Salah then came close to scoring one of the goals of the season. Robertson slipped on his own six-yard line when trying to make a block but, as Alisson came to claim the ball, the defender somehow scooped a pass to Firmino. Salah ran across the lumbering Vestergaard as Firmino lofted a lovely long-range pass into the channel. The ball drifted a little wide, and so Salah had to cut across the Southampton defender for a second time; in the act of doing so, he left the ball behind, but improvised with an audacious backheel that drifted inches wide.

On the stroke of half-time the Reds won a free-kick, which Shaqiri absolutely thundered against the underside of the bar, perhaps with a tiny touch from the keeper, Alex McCarthy. As players from both sides sprinted in to the loose ball, Salah was the quickest, prodding home from virtually on the goalline, to score his 30th Anfield goal in his 31st game. Southampton switched to a five-man defence at half-time, and Liverpool conserved their energy for two games against Chelsea.

It's perhaps easy to forget – given how "Sarriball" subsequently lost its lustre – that when Liverpool went to Chelsea, the Blues were level on points with Manchester City, each with five wins and a draw from their first six games. Liverpool were top, by two points, and this was a game that almost – despite the Reds playing well – ended in defeat.

Chelsea took the lead when Eden Hazard was played though on goal after a wonderful midfield interchange, with the Belgian winger's third-man run seeing him face up to Alisson and smash the ball in the far corner. But Liverpool had chances to equalise.

Mo Salah then rounded Kepa Arrizabalaga – the man who usurped Alisson as the world's most costly keeper (obviously without inflation taken into account) – only for Antonio Rüdiger to stab his shot off the line. In the second half, Sadio Mané wriggled his way into the area and forced a fine low save from the Chelsea keeper. As the game ebbed and flowed, Hazard was in once again down the inside-left channel; Alisson stood his ground and then, when Hazard looked down at the ball to take the shot, the Liverpool keeper charged towards him, blocking the ball. Later in the game, Xherdan Shaqiri, on as a sub, side-footed Andy Robertson's low cross wide; one of those examples where the foot has to be "opened up" to a perfect degree, or it either hits the goalkeeper or drifts wide – with a first-time effort from a low or bouncing cross often the most difficult "easy" chance. That miss looked like ending Liverpool's unbeaten start to the season; and another chance went begging, with Roberto Firmino's downward header blocked on the line by David Luiz, who was having one of those days where you can see what all the original hype was about, all those years ago.

But then, enter Daniel Sturridge.

Sturridge had hit more than 70 unsuccessful shots from outside the area in the Premier League since his previous goal from distance. This time he picked the ball up from Shaqiri and, 20-25 yards from goal at a slight angle, lifted his head with the ball firmly under the control of his bright yellow left boot. He then swung that phosphorescing foot and hit a powerful curing shot over the dive of Arrizabalaga, arcing beautifully into the top corner; something he'd tried days earlier in the League Cup tie (which Liverpool narrowly lost), only to see his effort cannon off the bar. This was one of those shots where time seems to stand still – although it wasn't a slow curling shot, it still wasn't exactly a net-buster. It simply had *enough* speed, with the accuracy taking it right into the metaphorical postage stamp. It moved him up to 2nd in the Reds' all-time substitute scoring list, after the famous 'supersub' David Fairclough.

It was telling that Liverpool made over 150 sprints during this match, when a high number for the Reds would be 120, and where plenty of clubs don't even manage 100 in a game. At the end, both managers smiled and embraced, full of joy at one of the most intense – but skilful – games of football you will ever *see*.

Klopp was understandably ebullient after the match. "Of course we deserved a point – we would have deserved to win, but it's all good with the result. Both teams deserved a point, but we only had more chances. We had more chances on Wednesday. Chelsea are a super team and it is quite difficult to play them, but I thought we did it in a really impressive way, to be honest."

Having taken off Mo Salah to some criticism as the Reds chased the game, Klopp was eager to praise the goalscorer, Daniel Sturridge. "Three days ago he had a similar situation and hit the crossbar. He is a fantastic footballer and had a full pre-season. He is the best shape since I have known him. It's as simple as that and really cool, I am really happy for him. He works hard, he is just a good lad, when he came in the dressing room after 20 minutes or so, it was pretty loud because the boys are all happy for him. He really is in a good moment."

Liverpool then travelled to Napoli and, just days on from the record-breaking sprints against Chelsea, looked absolutely exhausted in a 1-0 defeat, with the Italians scoring in the last minute.

In just a few weeks Liverpool had played Spurs, PSG, Chelsea twice and Napoli. Days later they were at home to Man City, with the Reds – as would happen at the end of 2018 and into early 2019 – facing their title rivals on the back of a gruelling fixture list. (In early January Liverpool had just played Arsenal days earlier.) The tougher Champions League draw was partly expected, given that Liverpool were seeded to be in the third pot, which meant two big names were potentially there to be drawn; although it was still cruel to face two teams that had racked up over 90 points in their league the season before. And now came City in the league, fresh from their 100 points; albeit now only top on goal difference, as both teams started the game on 19 points.

It was interesting to see this cagey, tactical affair from my vantage point in the Lower Kenny Dalglish stand (in what was my old season ticket seat before I transferred it to a friend), as both teams largely cancelled each other out. It was something of a surprise to see City's full-backs rarely advance past the halfway line, as Pep Guardiola set up his team not to allow any space for Liverpool to tear through them in the way they had in the previous three meetings, which had seen Liverpool bag eight goals. The added spectre of Ederson wasting lots of time with his goal-kicks and also Guardiola's men delaying throw-ins (and the slowest of slow-walk substitutions), you could see how much a point meant to them.

Liverpool lost something by not having the (admittedly tired-looking) Trent Alexander-Arnold as the out-ball on the right, with Joe Gomez ploughing upfield (and back) brilliantly, but never able to look like a winger in disguise. He was there to muffle and muscle Raheem Sterling, and he pretty much did just that, while also swinging in a couple of decent crosses. Gomez's presence was missed at centre-back, however, where his dribbling is more in the elite bracket when compared with Dejan Lovren, who came in; whereas out wide as a full-back Gomez can only really go on the outside and try to cross, rather than bamboozle with skill or a cut infield. Lovren had an excellent game, but more as an old-school stopper, whereas Gomez appears more creative at centre-back.

There was one clear chance, right at the end, when Virgil van Dijk, with a rare error, clipped Leroy Sané as the German speedster looked to get past him in the box. Riyad Mahrez – who had missed four of his previous seven Premier League penalties – stepped up, and, with unerring ferocity and accuracy, sent the ball into the Goodison Park car park. With no goals to cheer at the other end, this felt as good as scoring, and Anfield bounced with glee at the let-off.

After the game, Klopp chose to focus in some depth on the team around him, and why he prefers football to another sport from his youth.

"I'm a team player 100 per cent. I prefer football to tennis because I want to have my friends around me, I want to be a member of something bigger.

"I think everybody at Melwood at the moment has the right feeling when they come to work. They are all really important to us – really, really important.

"In the end, there's always that one person that makes the decisions and that's very often me, but we've created a situation where I can have all the best information from the best people before I reach it.

"I would say one of my biggest strengths is common sense to be honest, because I'm not too smart, but I understand life in a specific way to realise I don't have to know everything.

"There are people who know much more in specific parts so we brought them in. And I'm naturally confident, because I know that I'm not perfect, so I don't think that anybody else should think I'm perfect – I have no problem asking questions.

"I brought a few fantastic people together for the benefit of the club and the project, because, as I said when I came in I didn't want to change things immediately.

"I wanted to understand why English football teams, especially Liverpool, do things the way they did. And so we changed it little by little and we brought quality in for sure. That is something I'm very proud of.

"One of the things that I love most about my job is that I've met some really good, good people, which has made my life much more enjoyable."

The Smartest Men in the League – How Liverpool Went From Also-Rans To Serious Contenders

In football, very few managers, directors of football or clubs in general have a transfer record that remains unblemished for too long. While mistakes can, and do, happen to every manager and director of football, their 'winning streaks' in the market seem to come crashing down before too long, for one reason or another; and often their skills are simply not transferable to other clubs, because it is the organisational fit, and the coaching and man-management – and the relationships therein – that helps players to thrive.

Sometimes there's some serious selection bias in the assessments made by outsiders, as people list only the flops or the successes, and make their entire cases around one or the other. Sometimes mistakes just don't get noted, or tallied up. For 15 years I've been pointing out that Arsène Wenger's initial transfer record at Arsenal was very mixed indeed, with a whole host of flops, but at the same time he absolutely nailed a series of era-defining transfers, and that was what helped them win three league titles. Some chose to just ignore Alberto Méndez, Christopher Wreh, Luís Boa Morte, Kaba Diawara, Igors Stepanovs, *et al*, and some may not even have noticed their arrivals and swift departures – and treat it like everything Wenger touched turned to gold. But either way, it was a handful of absolutely inspired signings that transformed Arsenal into double-double winners, and 'Invincibles', between 1998 and 2004. To focus on the duds would be to obsessively state that the Beatles weren't very good because of songs like *Rocky Raccoon, Blue Jay Way* and *Wild Honey Pie*. However, as the money grew tighter upon the building of the new Emirates Stadium, and then, as Wenger appeared more and more reluctant to spend the money that was there (along with the diminishing fitness work compared to other teams), the Frenchman's ability to make outstanding signings dwindled. In the 2000s he still bought some brilliant players; but by 2010-2018 they were few and far between.

Ramón Rodríguez Verdejo – AKA Monchi – who helped Sevilla discover Diego Capel, Alberto Moreno, Jesús Navas, Antonio Puerta, Sergio Ramos and José Antonio Reyes (who sadly died in a car crash just before this book went to print) – and who bought bargains Adriano, Dani Alves, Júlio Baptista, Federico Fazio, Seydou Keita and Ivan Rakitić – found himself out of a job after less than two years with Roma as he failed to replicate that success, having swapped his homeland for Italy in April 2017; and was soon back at Sevilla once more. Prior to the deserved exaltation of Michael Edwards as the head of Liverpool's football strategy, Monchi was *The Man*.

In 2015/16, the hitherto canny transfer business of Steve Walsh at Leicester City – including insane bargains like Riyad Mahrez, Jamie Vardy and N'Golo Kanté – had underpinned the most unlikely title triumph in English football history. A year later Walsh went to Everton and, despite helping them to spend a small fortune, he was sacked in May 2018, as the team lacked identity and quality. Even the fortunes of Michael Zorc, at Borussia Dortmund, were transformed by the arrival of Jürgen Klopp; and while Dortmund have continued to buy some excellent players, and had some good seasons, they haven't been as effective as the ones signed during Klopp's tenure. Meanwhile, a key, respected scout at the club, Sven Mislintat, moved from Dortmund to Arsenal to take charge of transfers, but that didn't work out and within almost no time he had departed.

Even Damien Comolli was seen as a transfer guru, before his time at Liverpool put paid to that impression. As I've often noted in the past, for all his flops, Comolli was the person in charge of transfers when Spurs signed Gareth Bale, Dimitar Berbatov and Luka Modrić, and when Liverpool signed Luis Suárez, three of whom have gone on to win numerous Champions League and *La Liga* trophies, and are still starring in Spain, after huge transfer fees took them to *La Liga;* while Berbatov also won league titles after moving to Man United. (And of course, Comolli signed another Champions League winner – a certain Jordan Henderson.) After inflation, the sales fees for those players are: Bale £241.3m (2nd, in terms of inflated sales fee rankings, behind only Cristiano Ronaldo); Berbatov £99.5m (38th); Modrić £131.9m (14th); and Suárez £190m (7th). And so, despite a fair few flops, Comolli – friend of Moneyball pioneer Billy Beane – had a hand in some of the most impressive signings in the Premier League era.

And of course, it was Comolli who brought Edwards to Liverpool. What was seen as a mistake by FSG – bringing in the Frenchman as Director of Football – was in fact underpinned by logic; it just took time for the analytics-based influence to spread. Perhaps Comolli wasn't the right man to take the club forward, but he set in place the principles that thrive today.

The excellent (and fellow bald Leicester-based football writer) Jonathan Northcroft of *The Sunday Times* spent time at Melwood in December 2018, and described the scene at the club's HQ: "Across from Klopp's office at Melwood is that of Edwards. Both doors stay open, each dropping in on the other when they are not chatting on WhatsApp. Edwards apprises Gordon daily by phone. Gordon, a cerebral voice down the line from Massachusetts, loves an aphorism and one is 'speaking your mind at Liverpool isn't allowed – it's mandatory'.

"Edwards is sparky, confident, his office bright. He is nothing like the geek in a green visor, goggling at a laptop in a darkened room, that Gordon jokes is the image of a Liverpool recruitment guy, thanks to FSG's associations with 'Moneyball'. Edwards, in fact, was a player, once in Peterborough's reserves. He became an analyst and flourished at Harry Redknapp's Portsmouth after striking a connection with Joe Jordan. He worked with players but never talked to them about stats, believing — having worked for Prozone — that much traditional football data is fatuous. He was then head of performance analysis at Tottenham.

"Gordon, a Boston asset-manager drawn into FSG, took over the daily running of Liverpool in summer 2012. His outside-the-box appointment was Ian Graham, a Cambridge physics graduate whose football research firm was producing revolutionary data for Spurs that inspired several Daniel Levy transfer coups. Graham was a Liverpool fan and frustrated that Levy would not fund him to perfect his model. Edwards knew he could get him. They had worked closely and Edwards was a convert — provided the data would be used alongside traditional tools. Gordon looks back on the signings in January 2013 of Daniel Sturridge for £12m from Chelsea, and Philippe Coutinho for £8.5m from Inter Milan, as the point when he knew a corner had been turned. Despite the brilliant 2013-14 season, however, an obstacle was Brendan Rodgers – because the then manager did not believe in the model."

(My own brief interactions with most of the people mentioned tally with those of Northcroft. Indeed, I even bumped into Northcroft in a stationery shop the morning after he got back from Liverpool's Champions League semi-final in Rome – and which started to look like a bald-football-writers' convention, as we theorised about the departure of Željko Buvač.)

In May 2019, Comolli told Jack Pitt-Brooke of *The Independent* how he ended up bringing Edwards to Liverpool: "I made a few enquiries around the Premier League and people who worked around the Premier League, data providers, that kind of company. I just said 'tell me who is the best in the Premier League and I want to go and get him.' The name that was coming back was Michael Edwards, Michael Edwards, and I got in touch with him and got him.

"He is just someone who … you are struck with how intelligent he is. That type of guy. I like the fact that he challenges the conventional wisdom, like Billy Beane. Because he's got an analytical hat on. 'Why should we do that? Because it's been done the same for the last 60 years? But what if it's wrong? Why should we look at it in that way, when the data tells us that we should look at it the other way?' And that's exactly why I appointed him at the time."

Clubs like Lyon, Swansea and Southampton were held up as paragons of buying and selling players, and of shrewd managerial appointments, but the magic inevitably runs dry at some point; the luck changes, and often, panic sets in at a club and sackings are made before the situation can be reversed. Virtuous circles quickly turn to vicious cycles. And yet, that's life; nothing lasts forever.

So Liverpool's transfer record in the coming years *could* take a hit, just based on the law of averages (AKA Tomkins' Law); indeed, by the spring of 2019 many were already labelling Naby Keïta as the first costly flop of the Klopp/Edwards era, but it was surely too early to draw a line under a player with so much talent; indeed, Klopp rushed to his midfielder's defence, with talk of how the Guinean was still adapting: "Sometimes it takes longer, that's how it is. People lose patience, that's normal – but we don't. For a young boy, he made a big move from Leipzig to Liverpool; he wants to do it right."

(No sooner had I drafted this paragraph, in early April, than Keïta came in and scored a vital equalising goal against Southampton, hit the post and should have won a penalty; and scored again, in a man-of-the-match performance at home to Porto – with his change of luck clear in the deflected goal. He had struck a much better shot away at Burnley, but it hit the post. He grabbed a third goal at home to Huddersfield, after some truly sensational pressing, before a groin strain curtailed his season. In the 25 league games he played for Liverpool in 2018/19 they did not lose once; while fellow midfield newcomer Fabinho is another yet to taste defeat in the Premier League in games which he started.)

However, Liverpool are clearly doing things the right way. It's just that, as with a team that plays a good game of football, that doesn't always mean success immediately follows. Had Liverpool failed to beat Spurs in the Champions League final it wouldn't have changed the excellent work undertaken; just the perceptions of that work.

Having only the very best people is only half of the solution; in the same way that bringing together a lot of talented footballers does not mean they will play as a team. One of the greatest differences to the results Edwards' and the scouts' work in recent seasons is the collegiate relationship engendered by Klopp. Without that, the Reds would still have disparate departments doing their own thing, with any creative thinking hitting the road block of a stubborn manager. For someone like Michael Edwards it was a sea-change from the previous situation, with Klopp an absolute dream to work with; with Dave Fallows, as head of recruitment, and chief scout Barry Hunter, all given the licence *to do what they do best.*

The club's most successful transfer in recent seasons – arguably even more so than Luis Suárez (in that he was relatively cheaper, and has scored even more goals) – was a case in point. "We were sure he can help us," Klopp said in late 2017 after Mo Salah hit the ground running, with 12 goals in his first 17 games. "Michael Edwards, Dave Fallows and Barry [Hunter], they were really in my ear and were on it: 'Come on, come on, Mo Salah, he's the solution!'," Klopp told the official Liverpool website.

"When you have 20 players on the table, different players, it's difficult to make an early decision, but we all were convinced about it so could make the early decision so we could really get him. He's a fantastic person, a nice lad and a really good football player."

In the next 87 games Salah, in addition to many assists, scored a scarcely believable 59 goals – only six of which were penalties; meaning that in just two seasons he had almost matched Suárez' output from *three and a half* seasons (71 goals in 104 games versus 82 goals in 133 games). As such, Salah was named the 2017 African Footballer of the Year, 2018 African Footballer of the Year, 2018 PFA Player of the Year, 2018 Football Writers' Footballer of the Year, 2018 Premier League Player of the Year, and was the winner of both the 2018 and 2019 Premier League Golden Boot – before, most importantly, adding a Champions League medal to his collection of honours.

It's not just that Klopp listened to Edwards and co., but – in stark contrast to how Brendan Rodgers handled the Joe Gomez deal in 2015 – *publicly gave credit to the transfer experts*, as opposed to purposefully misdirecting it away from them. Klopp had the chance to try and show how clever he was – a triumphant "Salah was all my idea" – but instead he highlighted the qualities of those around him, and how he had to be talked around to the idea (initially, at least).

Klopp, who worked alongside a sporting director at both Borussia Dortmund and Mainz, expressed his support for Edwards' promotion to Sporting Director in November 2016, saying: "This decision is hugely positive for us. It will make us better and stronger in managing the process of building and retaining playing talent at all age groups. Development is so important and it makes sense to have a position, within the football structure specifically, that focuses on where we can improve.

"It's no secret I like the concept of a sporting director and having worked under this model previously I have found it to be nothing but positive and forward-thinking. Michael is absolutely the right person for this. He has the knowledge, expertise and personality to flourish in the role and I was delighted when he told me he would be accepting the position. Importantly, he also has a fantastic team of people around him, who have all played a significant role in putting together the talent we currently have in the first team, development squad and at even younger age levels."

Klopp made the point of saying that signings would be "his", but did not stress this fact in order to take credit – instead, to shoulder the blame should any not work out.

"If somebody is not happy with whatever and you ask: 'Is that your player or his player?' It's always my player. I can't blame anyone for anything. I can take the pressure. In this business, the manager is not allowed to be a one-man show. I'm a specialist in football things, I know a lot, but not everything like finances. I like to have the best people around me and Michael is for sure one of the best I have met."

Outsmarting the Richer Clubs

Liverpool did not reach the Champions League final in 2018 by spending a lot of money; nor did they compete with Man City for the 2019 Premier League title and win the 2019 Champions League final by doing the same, other than to wisely reinvest a *big* pot of money received on player sales, and the proceeds from the aforementioned European final; losing the not inconsiderable talents of Philippe Coutinho to fund a change in approach that turned Liverpool from a defensive laughing stock into arguably the world's best; conceding far fewer goals in the league in 2018/19 than Barcelona, Bayern Munich, PSG and Juventus. Whilst still not paupers, Liverpool achieved these serious attempts at the major silverware with the 4th biggest budget in England (based on £XI), some way behind Chelsea in 3rd place, and miles behind the two Manchester clubs. Including this season, 14 of the past 15 champions have had a top-three ranked £XI.

Having written more than a dozen of them, I'm only too aware that football books can date quickly, especially where predictions are concerned; whomever seems clever now can quickly be labelled stupid if results turn. But right now a lot of smart people are saying that Liverpool are the smartest club in the world.

Whether or not the Fenway Sports Group are pure of heart and intent – and let's remember, even if we *lean left* in life, like Jürgen Klopp, there are not many socialist benefactors in sport – or just fattening the calf for a sale somewhere down the line – you cannot argue when the custodians, after an admittedly shaky start and a few mistakes along the way, *run the club extremely well*. If a 1933 rickety and rusting Rolls-Royce Phantom is purchased after being discovered in an old barn and, in time, restored to an elite condition with the best possible care and attention, then it's hard to be indignant if the result is something that is not only befitting of the brand, but also, worth what it *should* be worth – whether or not it is kept, or sold at the new market value. This is the opposite of running something into the ground and seeking to make a profit simply because the value in antique cars has risen anyway (arguably, the Mike Ashley approach at Newcastle United, as well as the Glazers at Manchester United). And unlike their predecessors, FSG did not perform a risky and unpalatable leveraged buyout, where a club is bought with borrowed money, and then the club itself repays the debt and all the steep interest it accrues. Equally, FSG were never going to be sugar daddy owners, who just pump billions of their own oil-gotten gains into a vanity project. They are not oligarchs, nor petrostates.

It's not hard to forget that when FSG arrived – with the acronym NESV (New England Sports Ventures) – they were hailed as "the smartest men in the room". (Given that, at the time, the company was comprised solely of men, and as the old saying relates specifically to men – rather than *people* – I will stick to referencing that specific term; whilst acknowledging that women are of course no less smart than men. And of course, Henry's wife, Linda Pizzuti Henry, is now listed as a partner in FSG. Also, as far as I know she is possibly the only member of FSG to score a goal at the Kop end, albeit after the season ended; and *definitely* the only member to do so in a pink dress and stilettos.)

That said, the smartest men in the room will always seek to learn from those around them, and never assume that *they are the smartest men in the room*. An intelligent leader will know that he or she cannot know everything, and that assistance is required. Often, a leader has to have a grasp of myriad basics, but needs to take soundings from those with specialist knowledge.

Jürgen Klopp is perhaps the paragon of this phenomenon within the field of football management. A very intelligent man (intellectually and *emotionally*), he will always speak about learning more, and bringing in people who can teach him things. This is what psychologists call a 'growth mindset', rather than the more limiting 'fixed mindset'. A fixed mindset will show no adaptation, no progression, with time and experience. A fixed mindset is also connected to the belief in *natural talent*, rather than hard work and pooling knowledge. If God *gave* you these gifts, why do you need to work at them?

But this is not just me – as an obvious Liverpool fan – extolling the virtues of the owners, management, coaches and human infrastructure (such as the "backroom" data teams, fitness staff and dietary experts). It seems inarguable, based on what everyone at the club has achieved throughout their careers relative to historical pressure and financial might. Liverpool have not been financially doped back to the top table of European football. The Reds have had to sell to buy – or at least, players have forced their own exits, and the money raised was used to buy new players; in recent years Liverpool have sold extremely well, and bought *even better.*

In Germany, Jürgen Klopp took charge of a nearly bankrupt Borussia Dortmund and led them not only to a highly unlikely title, but then *another* title, and then a Champions League final. To criticise someone like Klopp for then losing that final, as well as other finals with Liverpool, is to enter into a strange – but readily accessible – world where overachieving only to stumble at the last hurdle is in some way inferior to never having been at the races at all. (This is the whole "Spursy" phenomenon with Tottenham Hotspur, where just falling short, on a relatively small budget, is mocked in a way that quietly finishing 5th or 6th – in line with their financial wealth – never was. To lose a final or a title race is apparently to "lack bottle"; to have never been in contention is often quietly ignored.)

In 2004, FSG ended an 86-year wait for the World Series pennant in baseball – Boston's infamous "curse of the Bambino", which had dated back to the First World War. If Liverpool fans thought 29 years – now extended to at least 30 – was tough to bear, being a Red Sox fan was much harder. (Also, Liverpool had the utter glory of Istanbul halfway through the fallow league spell, and now has the magic of Madrid. Football does not give out just one major prize. Arguably the Reds' greatest single achievement came during the title-less decades, whilst this season's confirmation of a sixth European crown is up there with it, too.)

So how did they do it?

There Was No Curse

In 2002, John W Henry and co. had taken control of the Boston Red Sox, and two years later they had won their first World Series crown in nine decades. Liverpool's wait for a league title thankfully hasn't been as long as that, though there are clear parallels between two storied, well supported – and, well, *red* – sporting institutions residing in historic stadia which had seen better days, alongside their supporters' insatiable thirst for glory.

Sports fans also have a thirst for explanation, for something to blame and cling to as to why their heroes failed. In Boston, it was the 'Curse Of The Bambino'. While the curse itself was not taken too seriously by most, the Red Sox' title drought began around the time they sold Babe Ruth to their bitter rivals, the New York Yankees. Yet as any rational person will say – unless they're distraught by the failings of their sports team – there's no such thing as a curse. Writing in the book *Mind Game*, Steven Goldman stated:

"There was no curse. There was just a tradition of incompetence and mismanagement going back to 1919. In short, the Red Sox finally got smart and won themselves a championship."

And yet, it nearly didn't happen. The Sox had lost the first three games of the best-of-seven American League Championship Series – in football parlance, the semi-final stage ahead of the World Series final – and were 4-3 down in the bottom of the ninth (final) inning in game four. No team had ever come from 3-0 down in a seven game series (which sounds suspiciously like Liverpool against Barcelona). Boston's hopes hung by a thread, and to make matters worse, it was the Yankees who were on the brink of humiliating them.

The prologue of *Mind Game* notes, "It was a desperate moment, but nonetheless a moment that had been planned for. Every problem is a lock looking for a key. The Reds Sox had spent decades half-asleep, oblivious to the locks, never mind looking for the keys."

After failing to secure the services of Billy Beane (the star of *Moneyball*) to be his general manager, John Henry set about picking baseball's locks by appointing Theo Epstein to the role. In July 2004, Epstein, a 28-year-old 'applied performance analysis' expert, traded a minor league outfielder in exchange for a player called Dave Roberts. By December of that year Roberts had moved on to San Diego, but before leaving he wrote his name into Red Sox folklore. That's because Dave Roberts was *quick*. And with Boston a run down in the final inning of that vital match against the Yankees, having a swift man on the field who could steal a base might prove priceless. Which it did. Roberts was sent on as a pinch runner; essentially a substitute runner for someone else who bats. He may have only been on the field for a total of nine pitches that night, but in that time he did what he needed to.

Roberts stole a base, then got home to score a run, and took the match into extra innings. Boston went on to win that match, then their next three to see off the Yankees, then the first four in the World Series to take the crown at the expense of the St. Louis Cardinals. Cue bedlam across Beantown.

It would be lovely if there were a plethora of parallels we could draw between Boston's 2004 team and the current Liverpool side. Just as the human mind tries to dismiss negative events by blaming curses, so it looks for patterns and links – the phenomenon known as pareidolia – to explain things, to offer hope and explanation where there may in reality be none. Even so, as much as baseball and football are clearly very different sports, when reading about the Red Sox' journey to lifting the 2004 World Series there were undoubtedly elements which seem to reflect what has happened in Liverpool.

The season before their glorious triumph, Boston scored a MLB-leading 961 runs, which was at least 54 more than every other team. But they also had problems with their pitching, allowing 809 runs to their opponents. While it was only the 11th-worst defensive tally from the 30 teams, it was more runs than any of the other seven who made it to the postseason conceded. A lethal attack but with a suspect defence – which certainly seems familiar with the Reds' first title charge of the FSG era, in 2013/14.

The main issue was with their relief pitchers – the substitutes who take over when the starting pitcher is worn out – so they improved their bullpen options. Keith Foulke led the American League for saves – preserving a lead at the end of a tight game – in 2003 with the Oakland A's, and was available as a free agent. The Sox snapped him up. Their relief pitchers went from collectively allowing the fifth-most runs in 2003 to the joint-fourth fewest the following year. And further defensive reinforcements were to come before the trading deadline in 2004 too.

Out went the popular yet often injured and disgruntled shortstop, Nomar Garciaparra, and in came players who weren't as strong as him offensively but were better at preventing opposition runs. It almost sounds a bit like selling a want-away attacking midfielder and buying some better defensive options with the money, doesn't it?

Having won 56 and lost 46 of their matches prior to the transfer deadline, the Red Sox won 42 of their final 60 regular season games thereafter. Smart transfer business, with Epstein playing a role later essentially taken by Michael Edwards at Liverpool, allied to a fabulous team chemistry carried Boston to their own holy land.

Under FSG's stewardship, the Red Sox have since added a further *three* pennants; on a large budget, but not necessarily the *largest*. Getting that first World Series opened the floodgates. A lot was made of *Moneyball* back in 2010, when John W Henry and co. took charge of Liverpool Football Club; Henry even briefly appearing in the book and film about the Oakland A's rise to prominence on the back of statistical innovation (albeit without that relatively small franchise ever winning the crown), and how the Red Sox took this a stage further. Moneyball as a concept was largely misunderstood and misquoted. Liverpool were mocked for their foolishness in thinking that trying to be clever was a *good thing*; cleverness is just being too clever by half when it comes to English football. This is a warrior football nation, built on heart and hoofing, rather than intelligence and insight. But if you can ally smart thinking with the kind of commitment that winners need, wouldn't that be beneficial?

Liverpool cannot be richer than Manchester United, with their years of commercial power turning them into a financial behemoth (albeit one partly crippled by the interest on their leveraged buyout), or Manchester City, with their petrostate backing. So Liverpool have to be *smarter.* The notion of marginal gains is not fatuous: any little thing you can improve upon can lead to a greater overall result.

And of course, if being smarter makes you better, being better makes you richer. Then the financial benefits can be brought into play, as long as getting richer doesn't make a club stupid. In the last few years, in contrast to Liverpool, Man United have been like a wealthy person obsessed with status and bling, rather than quality and taste. Liverpool are now at the forefront of football smarts.

Speaking to *The Financial Times* in March 2019, Ignacio Palacios-Huerta, a director of the football club Athletic Bilbao and a professor at the London School of Economics, said of football data analytics: "There is clear leadership by one club: Liverpool. They have a group of four or five PhDs in maths and physics, and they know football."

It's all part of trying to think about things that bit more deeply, to find any edge, any advantage. And so, not only do Liverpool employ a core of analysts with maths and physics doctorates, the backroom team also includes someone who first measured the subatomic Higgs boson particle. Any notion that Liverpool's increasing success these past two seasons is *just* down to luck, money or a world-class manager should be dispelled at the level of thought the club is giving to *getting better.*

Lots of Smart People in the Room

In late May 2019 Bruce Schoenfeld of the *New York Times* wrote about the time Ian Graham – one of Liverpool FC's aforementioned PhDs, with a doctorate in theoretical physics from Cambridge – first met Jürgen Klopp.

"Jürgen Klopp was in his third week as Liverpool's manager, in November 2015, when the team's director of research, Ian Graham, arrived at his office carrying computer printouts. Graham wanted to show Klopp, whom he hadn't yet met, what his work could do. Then he hoped to persuade Klopp to actually use it.

"Graham spread out his papers on the table in front of him. He began talking about a game that Borussia Dortmund, the German club that Klopp coached before joining Liverpool, had played the previous season. He noted that Dortmund had numerous chances against the lightly regarded Mainz, a smaller club that would end up finishing in 11th place. Yet Klopp's team lost, 2-0. Graham was starting to explain what his printouts showed when Klopp's face lit up. "Ah, you saw that game," he said. 'It was crazy. We killed them. You saw it!'

"Graham had not seen the game," Schoenfeld notes. "But earlier that fall, as Liverpool was deciding who should replace the manager it was about to fire, Graham fed a numerical rendering of every attempted pass, shot and tackle by Dortmund's players during Klopp's tenure into a mathematical model he had constructed. Then he evaluated each of Dortmund's games based on how his calculations assessed the players' performances that day. The difference was striking. Dortmund had finished seventh during Klopp's last season at the club, but the model determined that it should have finished second. Graham's conclusion was that the disappointing season had nothing to do with Klopp, though his reputation had suffered because of it. He just happened to be coaching one of the unluckiest teams in recent history."

Schoenfeld details how, in that first meeting, Graham spoke to Klopp about various games where Dortmund had lost, but on pretty much every measurable aspect, deserved to win. Klopp, who had not studied data at Dortmund, was converted to these new ideas. Indeed, Klopp observed that it was Ian Graham who got him the job at Liverpool in the first place (although Graham was just part of the process).

"'I don't like video,' Graham – a Liverpool fan born in Wales in the 1970s – told Schoenfeld. "'It biases you.' Graham wants the club that he works for to win, but he also wants his judgments to be validated. 'All of these players, there has been discussion of their relative merits,' he said. 'If they do badly, I take it as sort of a personal affront. If I think someone is a good player, I really, really want them to do well.'"

Schoenfeld explained that Graham often eschews the most basic, widely-available stats in favour of his own models. As explained in the mammoth *New York Times* article, one such model calculated "the chance each team had of scoring a goal before any given action — a pass, a missed shot, a slide tackle — and then what chance it had immediately after that action. Using his model, he can quantify how much each player affected his team's chance of winning during the game. Inevitably, some of the players who come out best in the familiar statistics end up at the top of Graham's list. But others end up at the bottom."

Despite what might be inferred from the *New York Times* article, Liverpool do not treat Graham's model as an omnipotent god, to which they are subservient; they still use traditional scouting, in person and on video, to assess players. Graham's model is an incredibly important tool in the process, but it's just one facet of the operation.

Graham himself would not like to think that he is the secret to the Reds' success – as that would go against the club's ethic of teamwork and humility, as well as not being strictly true. Right now, the club has so many vital cogs, rather than one genius or magical computer model running the show. (But the idea of a magical computer model makes for better copy.)

Graham, like Michael Edwards, was working at Spurs a decade ago. Two of the smartest English clubs – both outside the top three £XI rankings – made it all the way to a Champions League final; Spurs for the first time ever, Liverpool for their ninth across the renamed major European competition (five as the European Cup, four as the Champions League). As you might have noticed, Liverpool won, to land 'Old Big Ears' for a sixth time.

Ahead of the final, Comolli told *The Independent*: "I met Ian when he was working for Decision Technology," Comolli says. "I appointed them as our data providers, data analysts at Spurs. So I go back a long time with all those people.

"… We took two of the most advanced individuals in terms of analytics in the Premier League, if not the world of football, in Ian Graham and Michael Edwards. I knew they were incredibly smart, and they could take any clubs to the next level. Ian and Decision Technology helped Spurs get there and they are obviously doing it at Liverpool as well."

In his *New York Times* article, Bruce Schoenfeld detailed the group of men who could probably start a fight over who is the smartest in the room, were they so inclined. "Tim Waskett, who studied astrophysics, sits to Graham's left. Nearby is Dafydd Steele, a former junior chess champion with a graduate math degree who previously worked in the energy industry. The background of the most recent analyst to be hired, Will Spearman, is even less conventional. Spearman grew up in Texas, a professor's son. He completed a doctorate in high-energy physics at Harvard. Then he worked at CERN, in Geneva, where scientists verified the existence of the subatomic Higgs boson. His dissertation provided the first direct measurement of the particle's width, and one of the first of its mass. Another club might conceivably hire an analyst like Graham, or Steele, or Waskett, and maybe even Spearman. But it's almost impossible to imagine any but Liverpool hiring all of them."

Spearman's job, however, is not to analyse Liverpool's football; it's to try and think of a totally new way to play football. As such, his results – if successful – could still be years away.

Kyle Wallbanks was one of the unsung heroes of the scouting department pointed out to me in the aftermath of Madrid. Wallbanks is in charge of video analysis for the scouting department, and creates the full summaries the club uses (with a minimum of fifteen games covered in the reviews) to showcase a targeted player to the rest of the club. He is also responsible for the videos that are used to sell Liverpool Football Club *to* a transfer target: to show them how much the club knows about them as players and as people, as well as showcasing the club and city.

It then occurred to those in charge of Liverpool FC that Wallbanks would have some new material to add to the showreels, with Jordan Henderson lifting the Champions League trophy and the best part of a million people lining the streets of the city for the open-top bus parade. Already an easy-sell to players, the club is now in an even better position to seduce potential signings.

New Ideas

The idea of particle physicists at Liverpool would probably give certain ex-pros the shakes, not least as the reaction to something far more perfunctory early on in 2018/19 was pure mockery and disdain. Some of the reaction from the old guard was laughably irate when the Reds appointed Danish throw-in specialist Thomas Grønnemark in September 2018. Grønnemark – the world-record holder with a throw-in measured at 51.33 metres – joined the Reds' staff after making his name with his native FC Midtjylland, who famously punched well above their weight with two league titles and a run to the last 32 of the Europa League, which included a 2-1 home victory over Manchester United.

"When I heard about Thomas," Klopp said, "it was clear to me I wanted to meet him; when I met him, it was 100 per cent clear I wanted to employ him. Now he is here and we work on that from time to time.

"You cannot have enough specialists around you. I must always be the guy who makes the decisions on when we use all these specialists but you cannot have enough. We have the fitness, medical department, we have the nutrition, and now we have somebody for throw-ins."

Andy Gray, presumably speaking from beneath a slimy rock for *beIN SPORTS*, said of Grønnemark's appointment: "I know how you can take advantage of a situation, throw it to one of your own players. That would be No.1 … No.2. Keep hold of the ball. Maybe we are going to see Andy Robertson do a headstand and take it. Here is a lesson. Pick the ball up, take it behind your head, throw it to a teammate and keep both feet on the ground … I have got a new one. I want to be the first kick-off coach."

The ignorance would be staggering, if it wasn't coming from a disgraced dinosaur sent packing by *Sky Sports*, to a part of the world where harassing women, it seems, is not such a big deal. (The disgraceful way Gray regularly spoke about Rafa Benítez off-air during his time as Liverpool boss – according to one of *Sky's* cameramen – is part of the reason I'd rather never hear about him again, although the Scot's "insights" can prove amusing.) The idea that anything you can gain from a throw-in is essentially worthless ignores the astonishing extra distance Joe Gomez was able to add in just a short space of time, to the point where his jaw-dropping long-throw for England against Croatia resulted in them scoring a *vital* Nations League goal to take them to the finals; although Gomez – who will be less likely to utilise the skill from centre-back – had his leg broken before he could add much value for Liverpool in that area.

"Gomez's throw-in against Croatia showed it is a dangerous weapon for Liverpool and England," Grønnemark later told *BBC Sport.* "I think it won't be used very often, but the opponents have to think twice before they put the ball out of play."

It's not just the long throw into the box where benefits could be found. An advantage can be gained in throwing further and faster to enable breakaway goals, not least as, along with a goalkick, the only way a forward "pass" can be made to someone standing beyond the opposition defence without it being offside is from a throw. Therefore, if you can throw it as far as someone else can *kick* it, you have an advantage. And any full-back who can throw a ball just five yards further than before, after specialist work, would have a greater opportunity to avoid being hemmed in by the opposition, and a greater chance of turning defence into attack; with 'transitions', after all, so much of what modern football is about. And that's before looking into specific ways to work on pre-planned moves, to make use of any space that may be unprotected by the opposition.

A Personal Glimpse Into the Workings of Liverpool FC

In October 2010 I received a strange Facebook friend request, from someone with just a dozen friends, claiming to be a certain John W Henry. *Obviously* I ignored it, thinking it to be yet another hoaxer. (I once had an argument with someone on a Liverpool forum *who was claiming to be me*. That's pretty meta.) Days later I received an email, and, now convinced I was talking to the real deal, there followed an invitation to meet with the new Liverpool owner in the city, for a one-on-one lunch. At that meeting – which was briefly interrupted by Roy Hodgson on the phone when things ran longer than planned – Henry informed me that he had read some of my books before buying the club, having looked online to conduct his research. I was invited by Henry to sit beside him at Anfield, to help explain the game, but I declined, in part due to my chronic health issues, and in part due to not wanting to get that involved.

This came a year after Rafa Benítez invited me to Melwood, to become the first person to sit down with him (for what turned out to be the best part of a day), and talk football, after over five years in the role. Other invitations have come my way, some of which I have accepted, but for the most part I try to stay out of club politics, given how badly it ended with Liverpool's previous owners, with whom I'd never met or spoken, but who had hoodwinked me with positive PR like they had others. (And also given how political it got around Benítez towards the end, who to me remains a genuinely lovely man – but football often sees you pushed to one side of the fence, in the need to take sides; sometimes for the greater good, other times in the partisan separation between *Us* and *Them*.)

Also, given that I see myself as a football writer/analyst rather than a trained journalist who is on the hunt for news, I'm not looking to establish relationships, but prefer to keep a more distanced eye on things – as a supporter of the club, but not a supporter of bad ideas. The problem with that is that you don't get fed a steady stream of insider info, and that insider knowledge can help you understand things that bit better; so I am definitely not always 'in the know'. Equally, close relationships with the protagonists can allow them to pull the wool over your eyes, if they are so inclined; or provoke the need to be too kind to them, in order to please. Even so, I have met and/or spoken to various key people currently at Liverpool FC (always at their behest), so I am not without any insight into the workings of the club. I have a sense of what those people are about, and their drive for success – as told to me – but equally, these are people I would only go *so far* to defend, given that I only know them superficially.

That said, I've always seen FSG as very different from their predecessors, who first started to worry me when they began courting Jürgen Klinsmann behind Benítez's back. At that time Liverpool had just reached two Champions League finals in three seasons, and Klinsmann, though an interesting character, was a novice. That dalliance came to nothing, but the warning signs were already brightly lit. (And as such I immediately cancelled a reprint of what was then my fourth Liverpool book, *Above Us Only Sky*, and with it, lost quite a lot of money. It was, I felt, a decent book, ruined by a lack of due diligence towards the "cowboy" owners.)

Within three years their whole ownership had crashed and burned. As such, FSG – despite saving the club from administration – were quickly tarred with the same brush: American owners, out to make a quick buck. The reality was very different, although it remains hard to praise FSG too freely, because of the lingering sense of "fool me once" that hangs over from their predecessors.

(That said, in an unusually long and sincere letter of thanks on the day he left Liverpool FC, Daniel Sturridge took the time to praise the owners, as well as the manager and his teammates: "To FSG, you guys have done everything in your power to ensure the club has gotten back to the top and it's been an absolute pleasure to work with you. Special mention for Mike Gordon who was more than just one of the owners but a mentor who has given me advice in and out of football. Tom Werner you're an absolute boss and I'm still waiting on my cameo in a movie, John W Henry thank you so much for being incredible with me through my tenure at Liverpool. Lastly Mike Edwards who was a big part in recruiting me to the club. Had some great banter with you over the years.")

In time FSG may indeed make a lot of money on the back of Liverpool Football Club, but after nine years (and counting) it won't be a *quick* buck, flipping the club for profit with no care for how the team performs. And, having twice narrowly missed out on the league title, in 2019 they were able to finally achieve something undeniably huge, when Liverpool won the Champions League.

There is also the scepticism that dates back to Bill Shankly, where the legendary founder of the modern Liverpool FC stated that owners and directors were there just to sign the cheques for players. As with a lot of Shankly's quotes, it was perhaps apposite in its time and context, but the nature of club ownership has changed; as have many other aspects of the game. Whether for better or worse, owners now wield great influence. While the manager is still vital – especially at Liverpool – there is such a greater backroom infrastructure now, with so many key departments. (Although one of the things I love about the original bootroom boys from the 1960s and '70s is how they meticulously detailed every aspect of each training session. They were, in their own ways, pioneers of data in football.)

Jeff Reed, a veteran US sports fanatic, and a Liverpool fan since visiting the city and seeing the Reds play in the 1960s, recently told me: "I have noted any number of times, you were the *only* and I mean *only* person I could find online who paid any attention to what I knew was the reality of Tom Hicks and the Texas Rangers and the only person who actually wanted to know something about the record of FSG in Boston with the Red Sox."

And yet all I did was listen to someone who seemed to have something interesting to say – and who included links to various articles from local American newspapers that were not easy to find via a quick google. Jeff watches more football than almost anyone else I know (across all the major European leagues), was very influential in my beliefs that FSG/NESV were no cowboys. By October 2010, Liverpool were a total shambles, as Jeff had predicted. The warring owners of Tom Hicks and George Gillett were not going to go without a fight; looking to derail the takeover from Boston, and there was the bizarre day in court which was live-tweeted like a Champions League final. The club looked like it could fall into administration. It had a mediocre, ill-fitting manager and a mediocre, ill-fitting squad; and it was in serious debt. On October 13th the High Court ruled against Hicks and Gillett's attempt to block the sale of Liverpool FC by the Royal Bank of Scotland to NESV. Liverpool had *won*; won their freedom from awful owners who had borrowed money to buy the club, and then, after a brief spell of investment, began to starve it dry.

The purchase of the club by NESV was high drama. As *The Guardian* said in its liveblog: "8.37pm: As John W Henry strode into the building, *Sky Sports News* reporter Bryan Swanson asked him how confident he was about the takeover. 'Pretty confident,' replied Henry. 'And how do you feel about owning Liverpool?' Swanson pressed. Thumbs up from Henry."

A few weeks later I was sitting in a high-class Liverpool steakhouse as nervous waiters and kitchen staff came to the table and asked for autographs. (Henry's, not mine – *obviously*.) By then, Damien Comolli had been brought in from Spurs as Director of Football, with the little-known Michael Edwards in tow. Roy Hodgson was still in the Liverpool dugout, despite my protestations to the new owner; but there would be no hurried decisions, and that was in itself encouraging, even if it meant retaining a manager who just looked horribly out of his depth, beyond his comfort zone, incapable of forming a bond with the fans, and intent on deploying a style of football that felt 20 years out of date. Their intention was not to keep chopping and changing managers, even if they themselves were not convinced by Hodgson. At this juncture the new owners probably didn't understand that unique, *necessary* bond between Liverpool fans and their manager; although they had been warned by various people at the club, at the point of their takeover, that Benítez – who did share that bond, and who still had enemies in place – should not be brought back. The desire for someone the fans could connect with would be realised when Kenny Dalglish was appointed from the cold, to replace Hodgson; 'King Kenny' moving from the club's academy – having been brought back to the club by Benítez (with Hodgson then, according to those closest to Dalglish that I spoke with at the time, essentially ostracising him).

Dalglish and Benítez *got* Liverpool; Hodgson did not. And at that stage, the group who became FSG probably didn't either. After all, it's not easy for anyone to fully understand a club that they hadn't even heard of months earlier, in a sport with which they were totally unfamiliar. But Benítez had burnt bridges – even if many of those he'd locked horns with were no longer required, or sacked for offences like handing out a lucrative two-year contract to veterans just as the takeover was taking place, against the explicit wishes of the owners. Dalglish, by contrast to the Spaniard, was no longer a cutting-edge manager, but he was a far better *fit* than Hodgson. The Scot had the expected impact and lifted the whole place; the club rising from the bottom half of the table to 6th in the second half of the season, playing some great football.

But it didn't last. A bit like Manchester United in 2018/19 – as if they were not watching Liverpool in 2011 – the feel-good factor and bounce quickly evaporated once Dalglish and his assistant Steve Clarke were appointed on a permanent basis. The Reds instantly lost the final two games of the season, immediately after Dalglish was given a longer-term contract, having won four of the previous five. The league form refused to be sufficiently revived in 2011/12, although two fine domestic cup runs were undertaken, with two finals: one won, against Cardiff, the other lost, against Chelsea. (In stark contrast to Manchester City this season, both cup campaigns included several very tough fixtures.) Liverpool's football wasn't as easy on the eye as it had been in the second half of the previous season, although they hit the woodwork twice as many times as they normally would in any other season – to suggest that maybe the margins between success and failure were extremely narrow.

A bit like the Ole Gunnar Solskjær situation almost a decade later, the freedom of being rid of a hugely unpopular manager who deployed dull tactics – and the hugely positive *reaction* to it – was not the time to make sweeping assessments; but when you've brought back a club icon and he has done well it's almost impossible to then ignore his claims for a permanent role. FSG had little choice but to give it a go, but at this stage it was almost crisis management, lurching from firefighting to more firefighting, with no time, and no emotional clean slate, to plan for a total overhaul. Their biggest appointment – Comolli – also seemed to backfire, as money was spent on several players (raised in part from the sale of Fernando Torres to Chelsea), but with few immediate successes. The two who would abide – Luis Suárez and Jordan Henderson – were both slow starters; Suárez new to English football and, though clearly a real talent, initially very wasteful in front of goal, and Henderson only 21, and deployed on the right of midfield (with his performances confusing the owners). There were *ideas*, but there was no clear overarching vision.

Towards the end of 2011/12 I received a phone call at home at 6pm on a Sunday evening from John Henry, who wanted to talk about potential directors of football – although I wasn't much help, with a limited knowledge on who might be suitable, due to my main focus being English football (and therefore there were whole continents of great people out there that I was not aware of). In conversations with other people in the game, FSG had been advised on finding a figurehead like Louis van Gaal or Johan Cruyff, to oversee a footballing identity, if not those exact "difficult" characters; although I had assumed this meant Comolli would be retained as a transfer strategist, albeit with the worry it would be adding yet another layer in the chain of command. Days later Comolli was gone.

As I understood it, FSG were more concerned with employing someone who could lead the direction of the club from the top, and so when Dalglish was sacked in the summer, and the young and relatively inexperienced Brendan Rodgers was appointed, my assumption was that it would be to work under an established figurehead. There was talk that this was still the case when Rodgers, upon his unveiling, announced that he most certainly would *not* be working under any director of football. Whether this was a change of approach by the club, or Rodgers torpedoing the plans in a very public fashion, remains unclear to me. But what ensued was yet more chaos, possibly caused by the manager going rogue. That summer's transfer business was a disaster, with both ins and outs causing concerns (as well as further potential *ins* raising alarm).

At this stage the club had transfer analysts, but as yet, not the infamous transfer *committee*. There was talk of Rodgers refusing to take Daniel Sturridge that summer, instead bringing in two players he worked with at Swansea, and attempting to bring in some more, including the ageing Ashley Williams. The elephant in the box – Andy Carroll – was immediately and publicly told by Rodgers that he was no longer required, which undermined the striker's value; Carroll was offloaded on loan before any replacement could be found, and so the

Reds went into the season a striker light. Jordan Henderson was offered to Fulham in a swap deal for journeyman 29-year-old American striker Clint Dempsey, but Henderson did not want to leave, and so, thankfully, Dempsey (albeit on the back of a good season) did not arrive. Rodgers was happy to let Henderson leave, but in fairness, happy to allow him to stay if he didn't want to go.

It was chaos. As such, and ahead of the January window, the transfer gurus were given all the power, with the formation of the committee, and they instantly hit pay-dirt with Sturridge – now that they had the power to pursue him – and Philippe Coutinho. But the situation remained tense, as I will discuss in more depth later in this book, when analysing the shift in the club's transfer strategy to the point where it has become the most envied in the world. To make matters worse for FSG and Rodgers, a lot of this was being filmed for the fly-on-the-wall documentary television series *Being:Liverpool*. In essence, the club was undertaking a big PR exercise at a time when it was not yet in a fit state to expose itself to a global audience. (This past season would have been a much better candidate to document.) Rodgers, in his first really big role in football and under the spotlight, often didn't do himself any favours either, albeit in difficult circumstances.

At this stage it would be fair to say that FSG appeared anything but the smartest men in the room. Caught up in the chaos of one bad decision forcing further bad decisions – and/or compromises – it would take them another three years to finally start to get everything in place. In that time there was an unlikely shot at the league title – for which Rodgers deserves plenty of credit – before things rapidly fell away; a clear false dawn if ever there was one. But it was only when Jürgen Klopp was appointed, and Michael Edwards promoted, and FSG's Mike Gordon (who has the greatest football knowledge amid the owners, and who once told me that his "desire for objectivity borders on the obsessive") took a firmer role – and, a little further down the line, the excellent Liverpudlian businessman Peter Moore appointed as CEO – that Liverpool went from also-rans to the champions of Europe. Even appointing the hugely successful and popular Liverpudlian journalist Tony Barrett in the fairly low-key role of Head of Club and Supporter Liaison was an inspired step, showing joined-up thinking in all areas.

Liverpool Football Club needed all the right people, pulling in the same direction. Arguably for the first time in decades, it had just that.

Autumn and Winter – A Title Race and a European Revival

The ball, badly skewed and wildly spinning, looped up into the floodlights and, Virgil van Dijk assumed, into Row 10 of the Kop. In disgust he turned away, having thrown away the Reds' last chance to grab two further points against bitter rivals Everton, with the final whistle due to sound at any moment.

Seconds later Jürgen Klopp *found himself* – and it did look like some kind of out-of-body experience, over which he had little control – galloping and galumphing onto the pitch in trainers, gangly and splay-footed to get purchase on the slippery pitch without the aid of studs, a grin as wide as the Mersey as he rushed to embrace Alisson, his goalkeeper. The match *wasn't even over*.

But between van Dijk slicing his shot and the moment Klopp entered the pitch something truly remarkable happened.

The Reds Roll On

By the autumn Liverpool were still joint-top of the league, but had fallen behind Man City to the tune of an eight goal differential. The Reds had just struggled to overcome Huddersfield away, after the international break, but won through a Mo Salah goal; in xG terms, one of very few undeserved wins of the season, with the hosts also hitting the post – although the stats still suggested a draw would have been the fairest result. Next, Cardiff were despatched 4-1 at Anfield, albeit in weird circumstances, with Neil Warnock's men pulling a goal back to make it 2-1 through Callum Paterson, who, in an offside position – and from what was Cardiff's first meaningful attack – scored from close range with 13 minutes left. But Xherdan Shaqiri concocted a lovely solo goal to make it 3-1 on 85 minutes – Salah playing the Swiss in on goal with two defenders still to beat, but a drop of the shoulder and they were sent packing and his left-foot did the rest. Sadio Mané, again latching onto a Salah assist, confirmed the win two minutes later with a dink over the keeper after a phenomenal burst of pace to seal a 4-1 scoreline.

In between these games Liverpool thrashed Red Star Belgrade 4-0, with all the goals shared between the first-choice front three. The first goal came from Shaqiri winning the ball back in midfield, and then playing a lovely ball to dissect centre-back and right-back to the advancing Andy Robertson. His cross found Roberto Firmino, who shimmied his marker before his deflected shot flew past the keeper. Shaqiri then assisted Salah, who scored with a right-foot shot. Liverpool also won two penalties that just wouldn't have been given to them in the Premier League, even though both were legitimate – albeit a bit soft (certainly not *stonewallers*), and at the Kop end. After all, it's been one Kop-end penalty in the Premier League in two years (38 games), and here it was *two in one half*; and again, it's two years since Liverpool won a handball penalty in the league, but here was one in 45 minutes. Salah scored his, but Mané's effort, after Salah was taken off, was tipped onto the bar by the keeper. However, soon after Daniel Sturridge slid in a nicely weighted pass for Mané to atone, and stab home.

Jürgen Klopp was pleased that his strikers were starting to find the back of the net after several low-scoring games. "It was just a good football game and they could finish the situations because we had the right movements in the right moment, we had the right passes, we had the right formation. The first two goals were after a counter-pressing situation, which is brilliant and very important."

After four goals against Red Star and Cardiff, the Reds could only manage a 1-1 draw away at Arsenal. Like Chelsea when Klopp's men went there, the Gunners were in rampant form. The game was in early November, and Arsenal hadn't lost since *August*. The Reds weren't helped by the way Fabinho, in a rare start, looked a bit overawed and overrun, but his adaptation to the English game, and Liverpool's style, could not happen only in training. One of the downsides of new signings is the time it takes to acclimatise; something Man City and Spurs weren't really having to deal with. This was a tough lesson for the Brazilian, who hadn't even made the squad earlier in the season, but the Reds did take the lead, through James Milner with a rare open-play goal, before Alexandre Lacazette equalised with eight minutes remaining.

As with the draw at Chelsea, and the later draws at Old Trafford and Goodison Park, this is a point that would be seen as a good result in any other season, but these four games comprised exactly half the league matches the Reds failed to win. It was probably a bad time to play *any* of these away games: Chelsea were flying high at the time, as were Arsenal; while Everton had finally won a game to end a losing run the week before facing the Reds (in the game that was played in a gale), while Man United were riding the HGV with Ole behind the wheel, before the wheels spectacularly fell off and the juggernaut lost its jugger and became a mere *nought*.

Another European away game followed just days after the Arsenal 'Big Six' clash, and again Liverpool were off the pace, losing 2-0 to Red Star. With the Reds then losing 2-1 in Paris – a James Milner penalty not enough to save Klopp's men, in the face of some outrageous theatrics from the home side – it looked like Liverpool's Champions League dreams were over. With three defeats and just two victories the Reds had to beat Napoli in the final group match to proceed.

Before then, Liverpool eked out a 2-0 victory over Fulham, which opened with a controversial goal: Aleksandar Mitrović was marginally offside when scoring to put Fulham in front and, with the goal correctly disallowed, Alisson took a quick free-kick just before the ball stopped rolling – but the ref saw no problem, and seconds later Mo Salah was racing away and putting the ball in the back of the net, to change the complexion of the match just before half-time. Soon after the break Xherdan Shaqiri added another – with a quite sumptuous instep-volley from a deep Andy Robertson cross – to seal the win. Next, the Reds kept possession and plugged away at Watford for 67 minutes, before Salah, Trent Alexander-Arnold (direct from a free-kick) and Firmino finally saw Liverpool's possession-based dominance reflected in the scoreline; even after Jordan Henderson was sent off for a second yellow with just under ten minutes to play. It meant that for the first time ever Liverpool had 33 points after 13 league games.

"It's nice," Klopp said after the game. "33 points are brilliant, outstanding. The goal difference is really good, so I like all that. In this fantastic, big club with the outstanding teams of the past, that this group of players can get this record is nice. We all know the season is not finished and it doesn't bring anything, but if somebody wants to have this record in the future they must beat this team. So, that's good, not bad, but of course we will carry on. It's just a nice moment. A clean sheet, after being 2-0 up you not only want to win but you want to keep a clean sheet as well. It's not usual you have these two things in your mind, usually you only think about winning. So, all good and I really think the players deserve it. Today they did a really good job and I like this game a lot because it was so difficult."

Next up in the league? Everton at Anfield.

The Best Month In Liverpool FC's History
While other months – particularly a whole host of Aprils and Mays – saw the Reds win trophies, no calendar month in the club's entire history had seen the team win seven league matches; and to boot, there was a vital victory over Carlo Ancelotti's Napoli (with Ancelotti, of course, a veteran of Liverpool's best ever Mays) to seal qualification for

the knockout stages of the Champions League. Add that the month included dramatic victories over Everton and Manchester United – always hugely welcome – as well as a 5-1 drubbing of Arsenal, and you could also make a case for this being up there with the club's best-ever months in terms of the teams beaten, too.

It also happened to be the month where Manchester City had their one and only major wobble, losing not once, not twice but *three* times. It was a month when Liverpool finally started to win some league penalties, and the Reds made the most of them across the whole season, with a 100% conversion record in the league.

Feeling Blue

Jürgen Klopp, with the game still ongoing, had his arms around his goalkeeper, Alisson. The Brazilian no.1 had won the admiration of his manager by rushing out to take a free-kick near the halfway line, albeit with a short pass to Trent Alexander-Arnold. With Everton having literally everyone back it allowed the full-back to advance another 20 yards before sending the ball into the visitors' box. The gigantic Colombian Yerry Mina headed it clear, but only to Virgil van Dijk, one colossal centre-back to another. Van Dijk – who had recently volleyed a vital goal for Holland – got his shot horribly wrong, and the ball sailed up in the air and, apparently, over the bar.

But Jordan Pickford was on hand, literally, to intervene.

Pickford had earlier denied Xherdan Shaqiri with a smart save. Going back even further, to earlier in the season, he'd also said that he wouldn't be like Alisson and attempt a Cruyff turn. Not only had he done just that for England against Spain in a recent Nations League match, and found himself lucky not to be sent off as he grabbed the striker he'd just presented with the ball, he was now making the mother of all errors right in front of the Kop. And just minutes before Pickford's last-gasp intervention he had watched Divock Origi – playing his first six minutes of league football of the season – stretch to stab a close-range shot past him, but which cannoned back off the bar.

This time Pickford turned provider for Liverpool as, with van Dijk's shot likely to come down on the wrong side of the bar, he jumped to parry it back into play. Origi was the only player on the pitch to think that the ball wasn't dead, and, as it remarkably came his way, he stooped to head past the crestfallen Pickford. To make matters all the more surreal, Origi then ran and picked the ball up to hurriedly restart the game – as if his head had totally gone and his team still needed two more goals, rather than to just kill the final seconds. But even with him helping Everton to get the game underway again, there wasn't time for any kind of reply.

With hindsight there are myriad moments in a league season when you could say *that* – that right there! – was the exact instant when the title was won or lost. But had Liverpool won the title, then aside from the game where it was clinched, this would have seemed the most obvious moment. It was just too illogical and surreal to be any *normal* goal, any normal win.

Klopp was quick to apologise to Everton for entering the fray. "I've said it now a few times in a few interviews, but immediately after the game I apologised to Marco Silva [for my celebration]; we spoke to each other, I told him how much I respect his work because it is incredible what he has done with that team. They are just an outstanding side. It was a really difficult game today - derbies are always difficult but today it was a completely different difficult to the last few years. What can I say about it? I didn't want to run [when Origi scored], it was not my plan, I didn't want to run to Ali and I couldn't stop. It's not cool, but it happened. More important things happened during the 95 minutes. All my respect for Everton, they were really good. Both teams delivered a proper fight, a proper derby from the first second."

And it wouldn't be Origi's last big moment of the season; further *immensely* important goals would follow. Klopp took time to draw parallels to the moment Origi's blossoming career at Liverpool had been derailed in 2016 by Everton defender Ramiro Funes Mori, with a sickening challenge that resulted in a red card for Funes Mori, and hospital for Origi. While Origi returned the following season to score 11 goals, he was never a regular again; but in the 13 days up to and including that Everton game he'd scored away at Borussia Dortmund, twice against Stoke (as a sub), at home to Borussia Dortmund (another vital goal in his own personal folklore) and then in the 4-0 victory over the local rival. He was on fire.

Of that incident in 2016, Klopp said: "I said it to him on the pitch actually. I had it in my mind and never forgot it. Fouls happen, harsh tackles happen and in his case it was so obvious it was a break in his development because at that time he was outstanding. After that he needed a long time before he felt absolutely nothing. For the Europa League final he was somehow ready but not completely pain-free, and there was a tournament [Euro 2016] and he couldn't really show up there. That all changed a little bit, you lose confidence... at that time when Div played, he was an unbelievable threat: speed, physically strong, I remember the Dortmund game and stuff like that. So it was always in my mind when I thought about Div, that night. Coming on tonight, now he can finish that book and from now on everything will be fine again."

The next win came away at Burnley, although it involved a loss of a kind: Joe Gomez's leg broken in a hefty challenge on him; easily not the worst challenge of the match on a Liverpool player, but the most costly. And a more literal kind of loss appeared on the cards when Burnley took the lead in the 54th minute. After the derby, and with games coming thick and fast, Klopp had to rotate his team, and for a while it appeared to backfire. However, James Milner drove in an effort from just outside the box to equalise just eight minutes later. That brought about the introduction of Mo Salah and Roberto Firmino, and minutes later the latter was tapping in from a clever free-kick routine that put Virgil van Dijk free on the far post, to slide and square the ball in one elegant moment. Naby Keïta, enjoying his best game in a Liverpool shirt, hit the post and had another effort cleared off the line. The game was heading for injury time when Alisson pulled off a remarkable save to tip the ball onto the woodwork, after which he ran out to somehow stop the ball going over the line for a corner. His quick throw then reached Daniel Sturridge, whose lofted pass found Salah on the break; and the Egyptian's outside-of-the-boot centre fell invitingly for Xherdan Shaqiri to blast past Joe Hart.

Klopp explained the changes he made to his XI. "I said to the boys in the meeting: I have done the job now for a while and if somebody would have told me 15 years ago I could change seven positions and have a line-up like that, I would have said it was not possible ... There's always a reason. But, in the end, you cannot only change; you have to make sure that it fits, that it's tuned."

Days later the Reds won 4-0 at Bournemouth, thanks to a Salah hat-trick and a Steve Cook own goal. Cook was absolutely bamboozled by Salah all match, and a cynical hack at the Egyptian's ankles was not enough to stop the striker. Salah lost momentum in his run, and had it been a quicker defender, might also have lost the ball too. But even after struggling to stay upright – and had Cook caught up with him it would have been another example of why strikers do go to ground under contact – he kept running and found the back of the net. A lot was made about Salah's first goal being marginally offside, but this came days after Burnley scored an offside goal against the Reds; these things don't always balance out, but equally, a lot was made all season of Liverpool scoring offside goals and not always much of the offside goals they conceded, or those they wrongly had chalked off.

Napoli arrived at Anfield days later, with a team full of quality but with an average age of 29. The Reds had to win to qualify from the group, and one goal was enough to seal it; although Klopp's men could have scored many more (missing each of their four big chances). The winner came when Salah dropped his shoulder to ghost past the otherwise impressive Kalidou Koulibaly, and as he was doing so frequently at the time, the Liverpool no.11 used the space he had created by going onto his right side – when everyone expected him to cut inside – to drill home with his weaker foot. While cutting inside will always allow him to hit better shots, it often also means running into traffic; and the time and space going outside affords him just means any kind of shot on target is difficult for the keeper to deal with.

Chances for Liverpool were coming thick and fast after the goal, without any of them being put away. Then, out of nothing – and in the 92nd minute – Arkadiusz Milik found himself goalside of the Liverpool defence from a set-piece and, just seven yards out, blasted at goal. It looked all the world the equaliser to send the Italians through and Liverpool crashing out, but Alisson's reactions were like lightning to close Milik down, and present himself as big a barrier as possible. With his whole body spread out, the ball cannoned back off his thigh. Liverpool cleared, Salah sent Mané through on goal but, on a bad night for the Senegalese, he dragged his shot on the one-on-one wide. Napoli had just enough time to launch the ball upfield and, lost in the final whistle that immediately followed, Koulibaly jumped into Joël Matip, with his 15-stone frame, and Matip crumpled with a broken collarbone. In just a few days, Liverpool had lost two centre-backs to broken limbs from overly forceful challenges. (Again, a lot was made of Man City's injuries, but these were costly for Liverpool.) However, the games were won; Liverpool were in a title race, and now still in with a chance of a second Champions League final.

Klopp was still totally pumped up after the match. "I'm still full of adrenaline. This game was just amazing, it was outstanding… unbelievable. The boys played with their whole heart on the pitch; with each part of their body they were in that game. Our offensive defending, our offensive pressing was some of the best I ever saw. We played football and the direction we played with – the intensity we played with – was just difficult to deal with … And the save Ali made, I have no words for that. That was a life-saver tonight. I'm really proud of what the boys did tonight."

Sadio Mané had already missed two excellent chances in the second half before that late, hearts-in-mouth moment from Milik – and then the third miss of his own. But Mané was simply keeping his powder dry for the visit of Jose Mourinho's Manchester United – on the final occasion, it transpired, that they could be called *Jose Mourinho's Manchester United.*

Shots! Shots! Shots!

You'd be hard pressed to find a game between Liverpool and Manchester United where one of the sides had 30 more shots than the other; particular in games where it remained eleven versus eleven. Now, plenty of Liverpool's shots in the 3-1 victory were speculative, and two deflected goals ended up winning the game for Jürgen Klopp's men. Indeed, 36 shots was the most taken by one side in any Premier League game up to that juncture, which was approaching the halfway point of the season; with the next-highest number of shots faced by teams like Huddersfield, Burnley, Brighton and Fulham. And it was also the most shots United had faced in a single Premier League game since Opta began recording shot data at the beginning of the 2003. On top of the deluge of shots, it took 13 Liverpool corners before United had one of their own. This was an absolute *mauling.* Even so, it needed the introduction of Xherdan Shaqiri to make the clear dominance count.

Sadio Mané put his glaring misses against Napoli behind him when, after the Reds failed to score with a blitz of early pressure, he took Fabinho's lovely lofted pass down on his chest following a diagonal run into the area, and rifled a low half-volley under the body of David de Gea in one seamless movement. But in less than ten minutes, United equalised out of nothing, Jesse Lingard gesturing to the Kop after he slid in to turn home a cross that Alisson had fumbled. (In the keeper's defence, he took the ball cleanly but then, as he landed on the turf, the ball struck his knee and rolled free.) Lingard, running in front of the Kop, formed his fingers into a 'W' as he turned towards the Liverpool fans, when in truth he should instead have created a gigantic 'L'. In the second half the word 'loser' was confirmed when Shaqiri latched onto the loose ball on the edge of the area after a dazzling run by Mané, and with the aid of a slight deflection, scored with a shot that, with added aesthetic grace, hit the underside of the bar with a wallop and went in. The little Swiss sub's second goal – to kill the game – relied on a bigger deflection, but after all the pressure and chances the Reds had created, it was no less than they deserved.

After the game Klopp was asked if Andy Robertson was emblematic of the progress Liverpool have made. "If you want, yes. So what we did today was change it a little bit. We brought Sadio on the right side and Naby was in the half-space, so that's how we opened [the game]. Man United was playing rather man-orientated, and that's why

Robbo had the space and he obviously used that really well. He's in a good moment, honestly, and that helps as well."

Even Mourinho, shortly before getting the sack, was impressed, noting that Liverpool "… are fast, they are intense, they are aggressive, they are physical, they are objective. They play 200 miles per hour with and without the ball. I am still tired just looking at Robertson. He makes 100-metre sprints every minute, absolutely incredible, and these are qualities."

Liverpool then went to Wolves, who were developing a habit of taking points from the Big Six. The standout moment was the Wolves' sprinter Adama Traoré trying to do Virgil van Dijk for pace, and the big Dutchman's reactions – mopping up without breaking sweat – suggesting it was not such a good idea. An early Mo Salah strike – a lovely outside-of-the-foot finish after some sterling foraging by Fabinho – set the Reds on the way to victory, and the points were made safe by none other than van Dijk, stretching to volley, with a side-foot finish, Salah's inviting cross. If there was one area where van Dijk had proved disappointing it was in his goalscoring, given his physical gifts and technical excellence – not least after he scored the winner against Everton on his debut – but this was the start of a six-month spell where he scored almost at the rate of a box-to-box midfielder.

Newcastle were brushed aside 4-0, in a game notable for a rare – but nonetheless fairly spectacular – goal from Dejan Lovren (rifled on the half-volley into the roof of the net), a soft penalty for a pull on Salah's shoulder (which *was* still a foul), and the first Liverpool goal for Fabinho (a close-range header) to end the scoring, five minutes after yet another Shaqiri goal – his 6th in just two months, but somewhat surprisingly, his last for the campaign, as he fell out of favour in the second half of the season, after initially being sidelined with a muscle injury.

Three days later came another home game. Such was the destruction of Arsenal after they – like Burnley – took a rare lead against Liverpool that it's easy to overlook how the Gunners had had a strong first half to the league season, and arrived just six points behind Man City, who had themselves fallen to third after three defeats in four games. The Reds were seven points clear of City at this stage, and after that early scare, put Arsenal to the sword; but City had recovered some composure to grab a win at Southampton and keep the title race alive.

Arsenal's early goal through Ainsley Maitland-Niles was quickly cancelled out by a fast move with skilful interplay between Firmino and Salah somehow ending with the ball back at the Brazilian's feet after Arsenal's awful attempts at clearing the danger – a double deflection falling extremely kindly to the Reds. Yards out, and beyond Bernd Leno, Firmino – in trademark fashion – looked away as he prodded the ball home. It was his first Anfield league goal in eight months, but as so often happens, the floodgates opened; and his next goal was *remarkable*.

Again Arsenal defenders didn't cover themselves in glory, but after Mané pressed to win the ball back just inside the opposition half, Firmino strode forward with the ball. He shimmied to the right of the hapless Shkodran Mustafi, then jinked left past Sokratis Papastathopoulos – with both Arsenal players making despairing tackles that got nowhere near either ball nor man. Then, to add to the optics, Lucas Torreira fell while sliding in to block the shot – which Firmino delayed for a split second – and it meant three Arsenal players ended up on their arses as the firm left-footed finish hit the back of the net. The visitors had taken the lead in the 11th minute, and by the 16th minute they were 2-1 down.

Sadio Mané made it 3-1 – side-footing high into the net from a Salah cross – and right at the end of the half Sokratis tripped Salah on the second or third attempt to clip his ankles, and the Reds' no.11 made no mistake with the penalty, drilled hard down the middle. The move had started with a sublime Alisson side-on drop-kick to Firmino on the wing, to once against demonstrate the new dimensions the keeper had given the Reds, not just in stopping shots but the speed and quality of his distribution.

This was the 389th time that the Reds had led a league game at Anfield by at least two goals at half-time, and as in the other 388, they did not lose. Indeed, it was the 158th time they had led a league game at Anfield by *three* goals at the break, and this marked the 158th victory. It took yet another penalty – the one and only league spot kick at the Kop end for the Reds between May 2017 and at least August 2019 (when the new season kicks off) – to add further merited gloss to the scoreline. With his teammate on a hattrick, Salah handed the ball to Firmino, and he duly obliged.

Klopp was suitably impressed. "Look, it worked and it's one of the nicest things I ever saw in my life. Really, I don't know a lot of players who would do that. When I saw him then celebrating with Bobby it was just wow, just outstanding. So far, the gesture of the season. Really, really nice."

Indeed, it was the second-most generous thing seen at the Kop end in the season thus far, after the gift from Pickford.

However, five days later Liverpool's luck ran out, on their visit to the Etihad. The atrocious refereeing is covered elsewhere in this book, as is the fact that the referee was from Manchester. At 0-0, not only was Vincent Kompany not sent off for one of the worst challenges of the entire season, but Liverpool hit the woodwork, through Mané, and the rebound appeared to fall to Salah, but John Stones cleared off the line, with the ball all but 11mm across. Then Sergio Agüero fired City in front from close range, and Leroy Sané's luck with the post saw his shot roll in, rather than out. Firmino headed in from close range in between, to draw the Reds level, but despite "winning" the game on xG, the visitors could not put their chances away; Kompany, obviously, on hand to clear one situation off the line. Had Liverpool won they'd have gone ten points clear, and the sense was that City would have been done. But instead the gap was just four points.

Klopp chose to remain positive, and he had every right to after the performance. "In the second half, we had really big chances with no counter-attacks involved pretty much – Mo with a very good finish but a fantastic save from Ederson, Gini and Bobby Firmino chances and all these things. Quite often, they had to make sliding tackles and blocks in their six-yard box and that doesn't happen too often for City I would say, so that is credit to my boys that we did that. In the end, we lost it and we take that – it is not the first game we lost in our lives. It's not really cool, but it's one of the three results that could have happened and it's the one we didn't want, but we have to take it. Now let's keep on moving."

The Reds bounced back with a 1-0 win at Brighton, thanks to another controversial Mo Salah penalty that appeared to be controversial only because it was Salah, given that he was fouled three times by Pascal Groß. Liverpool remained imperious – and unbeaten – throughout the rest of the league season, but the force had swung City's way after their fortunate victory over the Reds.

PART TWO

How Liverpool Reversed a Decade of Inadequate Transfer Dealings To Become Leaders in the Field

Following the very successful summer transfer window of 2007 and prior to the summer of 2016, Liverpool Football Club bought *some* outstanding players. However, the overall balance in that time was well below the level required to take the team back to the top of English – or indeed, *European* football; especially given that the amount spent – while considerable – still lagged behind that shelled out by Chelsea, Manchester City and Manchester United. Despite talk of 'Moneyball', FSG and the club were simply not getting value for money.

Up to and including the summer of 2007, Rafa Benítez's transfer dealings had been sensational, and his purchases underpinned the runs to two Champions League finals. (Sound familiar?) A lot – in fact, a ludicrous amount – was made in terms of criticism of cheap duds like Antonio Nunez and Josemi, but between 2004 and the start of the 2007/08 seasons, Liverpool signed Xabi Alonso, Luis Garcia, Pepe Reina, Dirk Kuyt, Fábio Aurélio, Álvaro Arbeloa, Fernando Torres, Daniel Agger, Lucas Leiva, Yossi Benayoun and, on loan initially, Javier Mascherano; as well as more temporary successes that offered something different for a shorter period of time, such as Momo Sissoko, Peter Crouch and a returning Robbie Fowler.

The only really expensive flop in those initial three years was Ryan Babel (£53.8m after inflation), although he did have a promising first season (ten goals, often adding real impact from the bench), before dropping off the radar, in part because of a refusal to track back, as if he was too good for that; his argument, espoused on Twitter, being that Cristiano Ronaldo didn't have to track back for Real Madrid – which was a bit rich considering that the Dutch winger didn't even get close to *half* Ronaldo's output. (In fairness, Babel's total of 146 appearances for the Reds is 50% more than the average figure for all signings by the club between 2004 and 2019; so he wasn't a *disaster*, but more a case of wasted potential, and he wasn't exactly cheap.)

And there were some young bargains, too, in Benítez's time, even if they didn't quite make the grade at Liverpool. Emiliano Insúa was a cheap young player who also arrived during that period, and went on to have a top-level career across several strong European leagues, and play for Argentina; fellow young Argentine centre-back Gabriel Paletta went on to have a successful career in Italy and, after nationalising, became an Italian international; Antonio Barragan has had a successful top-flight career in Spain, where he still plays in *La Liga*, after a year in the Premier League with Middlesbrough; Mikel San José has played almost 400 games for *La Liga* perennials Athletic Bilbao; and Miki Roque was making waves in his homeland with Betis before his tragic death from pelvic cancer. (And although he never made the grade at Liverpool, how shocking and bizarre that fellow Academy import Besian Idrizaj *also* died, in his case from a heart attack in his sleep.) Even Nabil El Zhar has gone on to play well over 100 games in *La Liga* (where he too still plays.)

If there's a criticism of Benítez's transfer record between 2004 and 2007 it's perhaps one of too much churn; too many cheap punts to bolster the ranks. But in this time, no players of sufficient quality were emerging from the club's youth Academy. It's easy to say that the Spaniard did not give them a chance, instead preferring to import young compatriots or kids from South America, but Insúa, Paletta, Suso and San José were all eventually capped several times by major football nations, and most of the younger players named above are still in the top divisions of top European leagues at the time of writing. However, before moving onto the first-team players signed over the years, it's worth revisiting what the club was producing from its own ranks at the time, because – as seen with Man United in the 1990s – how much you spend on players is in part determined by how much you can save by producing your own.

Indeed, there was another promising foreign youngster who arrived in 2007: then 16-year-old winger Alexander Kačaniklić, who went on to make 47 Premier League appearances for Fulham, and play 28 times in *Ligue Une* for Nantes; and who, to date, has scored three goals in 19 internationals for Sweden. Three years later, upon taking over from Rafa Benítez, not only did Roy Hodgson give away one of Liverpool's most promising teenagers when buying the turkey that proved to be Paul Konchesky, but later Kačaniklić revealed that

Hodgson had given away the *wrong* Alex. "It was a bit difficult for Liverpool to replace me," Kačaniklić told the *Fotbollskanalen* podcast In 2019, "but when I was in Fulham and before I signed up, I had a conversation with Roy Hodgson on the phone, where we found out that he had chosen the wrong Alex. In his head, he thought he had sold *another* Alex for Konchesky. But then it was too late. It's a little fun! Then he just told me I was welcome back in Liverpool with open arms, but … by then I had already made my mind up and was very excited about coming to Fulham."

It's really hard to imagine such staggering levels of incompetence. (If nothing else, you'd think Liverpool's current transfer team could at least not confuse the names of their own players.)

Between 2004 and 2010, the best kids to come through the Liverpool Academy were Stephen Darby, who sadly had to retire in 2018 at the age of 29 after being diagnosed with motor neurone disease (another cursed by the "born in 1987-1988" misfortune, following the aforementioned deaths of two others), albeit without ever playing a top-flight game after leaving Liverpool, and spending almost his entire career in League One; and Jay Spearing, who had a few seasons in the Championship but has spent the last few years in League One, with Blackpool. Adam Hammill played 19 Premier League games in two top-flight seasons with Wolverhampton Wanderers, but has largely spent his career as a maverick journeyman, offering great talent but not the consistency or work-rate required for elite football. Martin Kelly emerged late in the Spaniard's tenure, to eventually play a total of 33 Premier League games for Liverpool – and a further 100, to date, at Crystal Palace – as he brings up a decade in the top flight, mostly as a squad man; and unlike the others, he did get to play for his country, albeit just once. Nathan Eccleston emerged in 2009, but didn't make the grade, and went on to play mostly in League One and in the Scottish Premiership.

Then there's Jack Robinson: a left-back, who was given his debut at 16 in what proved Benítez's final game as Liverpool manager, away at Hull City. (Robinson emerged just before Jon Flanagan, who made his debut a year later, and who played 46 times in the Premier League for Liverpool and Burnley.) But it would not lead to a top-flight career for Robinson, thus far at least; aged 25 he has played over 100 Championship games, which is pretty decent – but perhaps not the heights you'd expect from a player to gain a debut for a big club while essentially still at school. Weirdly, the similar sounding and vaguely similar looking Andy Robertson – also 25, and virtually the same height and build – has become a Liverpool star, via that same Hull City pitch. At the point when *Robin*son was getting a big break with Liverpool, *Robert*son was a trainee with Scottish club Queen's Park, where, a further two years later, he made his debut in the Scottish Third Division (which, one assumes, must be a *horribly* low standard, given that even the top tier isn't that great these days). In this case, Robinson was the hare, Robertson the tortoise.

Some English youngsters purchased during Benítez's time also had decent careers, including Jack Hobbs and Paul Anderson; plenty of games in the Championship, where Hobbs still plays, without ever rising to the top flight. And of course, although he was only 15 and too young to play for the Reds at the time, Raheem Sterling arrived from QPR shortly before the Spaniard was sacked.

Interestingly, another youngster to arrive just before Benítez left was the Spanish 16-year-old, Suso, who has gone on to make almost 200 appearances across the Premier League, *La Liga* and *Serie A* by the age of 25, and gain four caps for Spain since 2017. Both Sterling and Suso have gone on to have careers far superior to any of Liverpool's homegrown youngsters who emerged between 2004 and 2010. And of course, Benítez also signed Jonjo Shelvey, a future England international who would go on to make almost 200 Premier League appearances by the age of 27 – but the manager was sacked in 2010 before the player arrived. (The two were finally united at Newcastle, no pun intended.) These three teenagers alone have played far more top-flight football than any of the properly homegrown kids to graduate the Liverpool academy from 2004-2010 *combined*.

(Indeed, you could expand that to the whole decade between 2000-2010: Stephen Warnock, Jay Spearing, Martin Kelly, Richie Partridge, John Welsh, Jon Otsemobor, Zak Whitbread, Lee Peltier, Danny Guthrie, David Raven, Darren Potter, Adam Hammill, Stephen Darby and Neil Mellor played a total of 549 Premier League games, mostly for clubs other than Liverpool; Suso, Shelvey and Sterling, still in their mid-20s, have already played more than 570 in the Premier League, *La Liga* and *Serie A*.)

Stephen Warnock, inherited by Benítez when the player was 22, proved a useful left-back for a while, and went on to have the best career at the top level from the Reds' entire 2000-2010 academy graduates, with 212 top-flight games into total. Darren Potter, with just two league games for the Reds, has gone on to make over 400 appearances across the three lower professional leagues, 166 of them in the Championship.

There were some other less-heralded youngsters at Liverpool during Benítez's time who have gone on to have pretty good careers.

Danny Guthrie became a surprise hit at Bolton and Newcastle, with four seasons in the Premier League between 2007 and 2013, before becoming a Championship player in his mid-20s and, most recently, moving to Indonesian club Mitra Kukar (who sound like a 1990s' indie band) at the age of 29. Lee Peltier finally became a Premier League player this season, at the age of 31 with Cardiff City, after almost 400 league games in the lower divisions, to where he has now returned. Neither of these have been anywhere close to being England players. Ryan Flynn had a long spell in League One with Sheffield United, and, aged 30, is now in the Scottish top flight with St Mirren. Jimmy Ryan has played almost 400 games in the lower two tiers of English professional football. Other young hopefuls, like Craig Lindfield and Robbie Threlfall, flitted between the lower leagues and non-league football. Perhaps some of these players may have profited from training regularly at Melwood, and improving as a result; and then being given match experience, and again, improving as a result. That will have to remain an unknown. What is know is that none of those homegrown players went away and made a mockery of the decision to release them, or move them on.

So it's hard to argue that Benítez underplayed any of these homegrown players, or take the view – popular at times between 2008-2013 – that Jay Spearing was a better footballer than Lucas Leiva (nearly 300 league appearances in the Premier League and *Serie A*, and 24 caps for Brazil).

And yet Liverpool won the FA Youth Cup in 2006 and 2007. Why did that not lead to more success?

As an interesting parallel, Ajax rejuvenated their approach to youth football in 2011, spearheaded by Wim Jonk and Ruben Jongkind. Years before the stunning first-team emergence of several young players in 2018/19 (whom they will of course struggle to hold onto, but whose market value is immense), they realised that too many coaches wanted to win youth trophies rather than develop elite players. "We did not want the results to be important," Jongkind said in 2017. "There is only one team that needs to win and that is the first team. A youth game is the same as training. It is a means to an end not an end in itself. It is a tool."

Indeed, this is now replicated at Liverpool. In an interview conducted in May 2019 by *Goal's* Neil Jones (a former contributor to *The Tomkins Times* and journalist at *The Liverpool Echo*) with Alex Inglethorpe, Liverpool's Academy director, the comparison was clear.

"I don't look at league tables," Inglethorpe said, "because I think it alters the opinion you have and the decision-making process.

"I'm very lucky. The owners, Mike Gordon, Michael Edwards – they will never ask me where we are in the league. If we are top of the league or we win the Youth Cup, I'm never going to get a text or an email or a phone call saying 'well done'. The only question I get asked consistently is 'who's next?'

"We could win the Youth Cup for the next 10 years running, and if there's no player coming through to the first-team then I am out of a job, and rightly so." (Indeed, Chelsea and Man City have enjoyed incredible success in various youth competitions this past decade, but promotion to the first team has been rare.)

Of course, at the time of the interview with Inglethorpe, Liverpool had indeed just won the FA Youth Cup for the first time in over a decade, with Paul Glatzel and Bobby Duncan the two standout strikers in an impressive team. But it is clearly not seen as an important achievement by those in senior positions at the club. It is, however, a good experience for the players; a chance to taste some success, and get a sense of what it takes to be part of a team that wins things; and the delirium with which they celebrated their penalty shootout win over Manchester City was a joy to behold. But the aim from a club's point of view is 'which ones will make the first team?'.

Inglethorpe – another who, along with Damien Comolli, Michael Edwards and Ian Graham, moved from Spurs to Liverpool at the start of the decade – explained to Neil Jones how he'd overseen a streamlining of the academy, with 40% fewer trainees, and, with a conscious reduction in the wages handed out in contracts; not to penny-pinch, but to avoid sating young players' hunger. The top pay packets being handed out to the most promising stars upon signing their first professional deals are now around £40,000 per year, much less than in the past.

Inglethorpe noted, "… you have to remember, you're dealing with children. I don't know how you were at 17? I was quite sensible and not too flash or ostentatious, but give me X-thousand pound a week and I am not sure I could have coped. It would have changed me.

"I've seen players paid an awful lot when they're young, and I can't think of too many examples where they have fulfilled their potential.

"But I've seen players paid enough to live on, wages which kept them humble and hungry. Those players, I have quite a long list of the ones who came through. They were players who weren't given too much too young, who weren't paid to fail. There are enough examples in the game now of players who have been kept hungry."

This ties in with the first-team philosophy implemented by FSG: no huge contracts to new players, but instead, incentivised deals, and with a quick renegotiation of terms if the player impresses (and then, of course, a further year or two can be added to the contract). That way, the wage structure isn't broken, and the new player has to prove himself *at Liverpool*. Then, and only then, will the financial rewards accrue. Contrast this with Alexis Sánchez at Manchester United: brought in aged 29 as the club's most expensively paid player (around £500,000 per week), on wages £200,000 higher than the biggest name at the club (Paul Pogba) and several times what the *best* player in recent seasons, David de Gea, was earning. Then, when Sánchez was execrably bad, even fringe players earning a tenth of what the Chilean was paid would be asking about the disparity. Not only that, but Sánchez appeared to have been bought to stop him going to Man City, to capture a marquee signing from a rival, with no idea of what to actually do with him. So it's interesting to see that, even at youth level, Liverpool are adhering to strict principles.

The impression I got almost 15 years ago, and wrote about at the time, was that Liverpool were producing strong-minded "winning" U18 sides with little *outstanding* talent. A winning mentality is essential in sport, and talent can be overrated; but does winning at all costs have to be present at such tender ages? Ajax, qualifying from the Champions League group for the first time since 2006 (having lost in the pre-group playoffs many times) and a little unlucky to go out in the semi-finals to Spurs – having not even made the quarter-finals in 16 years – obviously thought not when, with the help of Johan Cruyff, they began reinvigorating the youth setup eight years ago. (It's also interesting how youth-system overhauls often take up to a decade to bear fruit; Matthijs de Ligt is rumoured to be joining fellow teammate Frenkie de Jong at Barcelona this summer in deals that, combined, could be worth over £150m; and with players from the same age group – 19-21 – including Kasper Dolberg and Donny van de Beek, playing for their national sides; while Justin Kluivert – a Dutch international at 18 – moved to Roma in 2018. Additionally of course, Ajax lost a certain Ki-Jana Hoever to Liverpool at the age of 16 in 2018; with Ajax reported to be "devastated" over his departure.)

Liverpool's best homegrown players of the past 30 years – Robbie Fowler, Michael Owen, Jamie Carragher, Steven Gerrard and Raheem Sterling (albeit bought in from QPR aged 15) – mostly came through without any youth cup success; although Owen and Carragher won the trophy in 1996. But someone like Jay Spearing won as many FA Youth Cups as Fowler, Owen, Carragher and Gerrard *combined*.

And none of this is to denigrate Spearing, who was a useful squad player for a couple of seasons, which is the least you'd want from your academy. Players like Jack Hobbs and Godwin Antwi were incredibly physically robust as teenagers, but often that advantage gets cancelled out once they move into men's football. While Spearing was perhaps too small to have an elite career – players have to be technically special to thrive at 5'6" – Fowler and Owen, by contrast, shone at a young age because of talent and/or pace, not physique or stature.

The Great British Swindle
There have been some wonderful British players over the years, many of whom have worn the red of Liverpool. However, even though the English game has obviously always been populated with homegrown players, the ratio of those born in this country is now down to about one-third. While homegrown players obviously have an innate understanding of the idiosyncrasies and culture of English football (including the weather, the types of pitches, the style of refereeing, and in most cases the language), it seems logical to suggest that at least 95% of the best players in the world will exist within the remaining 99% of the planet's population.

There's a clear lesson in the data since 2004: buy talented young British kids for nominal fees, by all means (it can be hugely profitable in all senses), and if possible, *develop your own*; but beware the overinflated British transfer fee once players are aged 20 and above. And, given that British players generally present much poorer value to Premier League clubs than foreign players, beware appointing a British manager – as they are far more prone to be drawn towards the British player.

(As a really weird aside here, the only clear benefit I can find is that Liverpool win more penalties when the side is populated by a higher number of Brits and has a British manager. In ten seasons for Benítez and Klopp, the Reds never once ranked higher in terms of penalties won than league position; so for example, in 2009/10, Liverpool finished 7th in the league but ranked 17th for penalties won, and in 2017/18, the Reds finished 4th but were ranked way down at 9th for penalties won (while this season saw the Reds finish 2nd but rank 5th for penalties won). Weirdly, while the foreign managers have had nine out of ten seasons where the penalty rank was below the league position – with one neutral – the British trio of Roy Hodgson, Kenny Dalglish and Brendan Rodgers *never finished as high in the table as their league penalty rank*; so, when the Reds finished 2nd in 2013/14, they ranked #1 in penalties won, and when Dalglish's team finished 8th in 2012, they ranked 6th for penalties. Overall, with Klopp and Benítez the Reds rank a shocking 9th on penalties won, but with a British manager this averages out at just 4th, even though the two managers with the best league win percentage for the Reds are Klopp and Benítez. The main difference is the number of British players those British managers fielded, and the pattern is also true of Gérard Houllier, who, while foreign, fielded a large number of Brits – regulars such as Owen, Carragher, Gerrard, Emile Heskey and Danny Murphy – and won a large quantity of penalties. And the top penalty-winners in the Premier League in recent times are almost all British or British nationalised too – the likes of Jamie Vardy, Raheem Sterling, Wilfried Zaha, Glenn Murray, et al. This appears to be the only obvious benefit to buying British, if all other things are equal. That said, the current crop of teenage English players appears to be about as promising as any generation.)

Right now Liverpool have a good balance between British and foreign. James Milner and Jordan Henderson are essentially the glue in the Liverpool squad in 2019, Andy Robertson has become one of the world's best full-backs, and Trent Alexander-Arnold has been outstanding as a young local right-back – but too much money was wasted by Liverpool on players born in Britain and Ireland since 2004. The contrast in value is stark.

While Liverpool's transfer dealings have largely been the domain of the manager, that hasn't *always* been the case in the last 15 years. For the purposes of this section I've split the Brendan Rodgers-era signings into either his or the committee's deals, as there was a clear distinction. A couple of the signings may therefore be wrongly attributed; while some examples may be evidence of those rare occasions when both manager and transfer team were in agreement. The differentiation is due to the fact that Rodgers is the only Liverpool manager to start buying his own players and then essentially have transfers *taken off him*; only to then be given them back, albeit only partially. It makes for a little bit of a guessing game, but on the whole it's fairly clear who Rodgers wanted by how he then treated the players in question.

To remember just how fractured the transfer situation was, as soon as Rodgers was sacked in early October 2015, Neil Ashton, writing for *The Daily Mail*, published a bizarre attack piece on Edwards – headlined "Liverpool's head of technical performance Michael Edwards is the laptop guru who did a number on Brendan Rodgers" – that, as told to me by a national journalist who knows Ashton, had the ring of a Rodgers briefing.

One key nugget was: "The committee have yet to explain how they came up with the figure of £29million to sign Brazilian forward Roberto Firmino from Hoffenheim, who finished eighth in the *Bundesliga* last season."

It's a wonderful piece of evidence to highlight just how unwanted Firmino was by Rodgers, and also of the scepticism towards the committee from a British manager and his friends in the media. I mean, imagine buying a player from a club who finished 8th in the *Bundesliga*?

Presumably, Liverpool have been foolish in the three subsequent seasons to buy players from relegated clubs, as if Andy Robertson would be a dud because Hull suffered the drop, and Gini Wijnaldum and Xherdan Shaqiri were not good enough to play for Liverpool because their clubs went down, too? And let's not forget, Southampton were in a relegation battle in 2017/18, so presumably Virgil van Dijk would be a bad buy based on such logic?

And another player lambasted in the article? Divock Origi. Whatever happened to him? Even in an age of increasingly bizarre tabloid journalism and clickbait this article – which essentially attacks Edwards for the "crime" of being in touch with his bosses – still stands out as a shocker.

Football365 published an article the next day on their *Mediawatch* section that countered Ashton's claims, and also further detailed the players who Rodgers bought, and those driven by the committee.

"After reading Ashton's hatchet job on the geek with the laptop, *Mediawatch* consulted James Pearce in the *Liverpool Echo* for a breakdown of Liverpool's signings and just how many of them were driven by somebody other than Rodgers … According to Pearce: 'Rodgers was the driving force behind signing the likes of Fabio Borini, Joe Allen, Adam Lallana, Dejan Lovren, Rickie Lambert, Danny Ings, James Milner and Christian Benteke, while the other members of the committee championed the suitability of players such as Daniel Sturridge, Philippe Coutinho, [Mamadou] Sakho, Emre Can, [Alberto] Moreno, Luis Alberto, Iago Aspas, Lazar Marković, Divock Origi and Roberto Firmino.'"

Football365's retort was essentially a call and response.

Ashton: "After each Liverpool game Edwards emails analysis and data to the club's owners in America, detailing where the match was won and lost."

Football365: "Sounds useful."

Ashton: "Edwards and his team of analysts have invented a new language for football. Strikers are all about goal expectancy, chances created and the percentage of successful passes in the final third. Old-school managers just want to know if the boy can put the ball in the net. Defensive midfielders are judged on interceptions and the number of challenges won in the centre of the pitch."

Football365: "Firstly, we're pretty sure that Edwards did not invent those words. And secondly, what do 'old school managers' judge defensive midfielders on if not tackles? The muckiness of their shorts? The blood on their testicles?"

Ashton: "He [Edwards] constantly monitors the opposition, providing detail about playing positions, style, routines, set-pieces and other important matchday information'."

Football365: "Again, sounds useful."

Ashton didn't stop there. "The increasing influence of analysts, young men who have no experience of scouting or recruiting players, has meant the end of the road for good football men such as Mel Johnson. He was the scout who recommended Liverpool sign talented young winger Jordon Ibe from Wycombe but was sacked, shamefully, in November 2014."

(As an aside here, if Jordon Ibe, getting publicity for playing for Wycombe aged 15, is your only claim to fame, then time suggests that's not such a great thing to boast about. Ibe is still a Premier League player, but at the time of writing, not a success at Bournemouth.)

Ashton: "Former academy director Frank McParland has also left … Instead a new breed sits in air-conditioned offices, cutting up videos from matches all over the world and burying their heads in the stats."

Football365: "Proper football men hate air-conditioned offices."

And of course, you can only "bury your head" in stats, like an ostrich does in the sand, and not use them for any kind of *enlightenment*. If only Liverpool had stopped with all this transfer nonsense in 2015 and employed only "good football men".

Part of the issue is clearly that men like Edwards, and also Mike Gordon, the president of FSG who has most active involvement with the club, eschew publicity, and don't tend to grant interviews. As such that may make them seem in some way duplicitous – as if they are anonymous men who, unlike someone like Rodgers, never have to face up to the media, and that this is somehow underhand. It enables paranoia to propagate. If a manager chooses to work with them, as Klopp does, it spreads the knowledge bank, and forms a kind of brains trust, peopled by those with varied skillsets, working towards a common goal. But if a manager works against them, they become shadowy figures, to blame for the boss' own downfall; somehow going behind the manager's back to the owners, when their job is to keep their bosses in the loop and provide detailed assessments.

Again, time has not been kind to Ashton's piece of 'journalism', just as it hasn't been kind to 'good football men', which increasingly seems a euphemism for the old-boys' network. The phenomenon could also be seen in 2019, when Sam Allardyce appeared with fellow hairy-knuckled fossils Andy Gray and Richard Keys on BeIn Sports to say "I'm not a fan of the way the Premier League's going at all" – around the time all six English clubs had qualified for the quarter-finals of European competitions (and, months later, England provided *all four* European finalists, the first time any country had achieved that feat). Allardyce makes the classic mistake of saying that he doesn't get the same buzz of excitement, which is essentially nostalgia; almost *nothing* is ever as heady as the first time you experience it. There was a reason *BBC Radio One* stopped playing Status Quo records in the 1990s, much to the old rockers' outrage – life moves on, and the elder statesmen and women in any field have to adapt or become relics. The onus is on you to step aside if you can't keep up. Equally, when you are good at something, and doing well, it's exciting; when your skillset is out of date, the fun naturally stops. You can't control things anymore, and you feel left behind by the next generation. That's how life is supposed to work; but the best adapt, and move with the times. Alex Ferguson didn't spend almost three decades at Manchester United with the same coaching staff playing the same brand of football – he evolved, and delegated, and switched things up. He never lost his trust in young players, which suggests he could still relate to them; unlike other managers.

It's entirely fair to say that time has been far kinder to Michael Edwards' work at Liverpool than it has to Brendan Rodgers'. The game has moved on, and Liverpool are benefiting from not being stuck in the past. Rodgers is hardly a relic, and his style of football (even if it was often hard to discern at times at Liverpool) is certainly modern enough; but he wanted the old-school style of management: total control. The biggest clubs have had to move away from that, for good reason.

Obviously the transfer committee's role altered after the arrival of Jürgen Klopp, with Edwards promoted to Sporting Director, and where the deals still had to be agreed by the manager; with the respect the two men share absolutely apparent in how well they work together and their collegiate approach. However, for the purposes of this section, when analysing specific deals, I will put the "shared" signings down to Klopp, but the obvious asterisk is for Edwards' contribution, along with the senior scouting and analytics team he heads. (And as was confirmed to me by one of them, everyone works together, and everyone has to be in agreement.)

Excluded from the study I am about to discuss are kids bought for nominal fees unless they played for the first team more than a few times, and also reserve goalkeepers, who almost always spend their entire careers warming the bench, as a kind of insurance that is almost always never needed.

What's interesting is that Rafa Benítez, Jürgen Klopp and the committee all bought very few British players; each at under 20% of their overall total. (Benítez 19%, the committee 15%, Klopp 14%). Yet Roy Hodgson, Kenny Dalglish and Brendan Rodgers all made *more than half of their signings* homegrown players: 60% of Hodgson's (if you don't include the re-signing of Fabio Aurelio, who never actually left the club when his contract expired), 54% of Dalglish's, and 60% of Rodgers'.

Benítez and Klopp clearly *played* British players; Jamie Carragher and Steven Gerrard were mainstays for the former (and spells in the side were given to Stephen Warnock, Robbie Fowler, Jermaine Pennant and Peter Crouch, amongst others), and Henderson, Milner, Alexander-Arnold, Adam Lallana and Andy Robertson, plus Joe Gomez and Alex Oxlade-Chamberlain (before injury) are/were all key players for the latter. But neither manager was prone to regular big splashes of cash on British players.

Indeed, it was only at the *end* of Benítez's tenure that he made two expensive British/Irish signings, and neither Robbie Keane nor Glen Johnson worked out as hoped.

The Great British Hope

If buying Brits can be an overpriced hazard, selling them is often a profitable business. Raheem Sterling, Jordon Ibe and Dominic Solanke all made sizeable inflation-adjusted profits for Liverpool Football Club, albeit with only Sterling (thus far) becoming a real star for their new side. Joe Gomez, like Sterling, was signed on the cheap as a teenager, and has seen his value increase to tens of millions. Jonjo Shelvey, 18, and Scott Carson, 19, also made inflation-adjusted profits.

As a note here, our Transfer Price Index inflation-adjusted profits naturally take into account the market in which the player was bought and also the one in which he was sold; after all, you could buy a player for £1m and in five years sell him for £2m, but if, in that time, transfer prices have generally quadrupled – meaning the purchase fee would now be adjusted to £4m – you're actually making an inflation-adjusted loss. (This is not to be confused with accounting terms like book value and amortisation.)

Between 2004 and 2019, Liverpool signed 21 British (or Irish) non-teenagers for the first team squad. The average age was just under 26, and the average cost, adjusted for inflation, was £39m per player. By contrast, the overseas signings aged 20 or over – 59 in total – averaged an age of 24.4 (a year and a half younger), and cost £33m, making them 18% cheaper. The average number of games played for Liverpool across all competitions is 92 for the Brits, 90 for the imports; so, 18% extra paid for an extra 2% in appearances.

Of course, as 2018/19 draws to a close, the current squad still includes British (non-teenage) signings Jordan Henderson, James Milner, Alex Oxlade-Chamberlain, Adam Lallana and Andy Robertson, as well as over a dozen foreign players. So if they're still at the club in August, all of these players can add to the average number of appearances. (Daniel Sturridge departed in June, with his contract expiring).

If you look at how much the foreign signings were later sold for (adjusted for inflation), or how much they are now valued at (the latter taking *transfermartk.com*'s somewhat conservative values, and only in some cases adding a bit more; such as to counter their weird valuation of Virgil van Dijk at *less* than what Liverpool actually paid), you will get an average recouping of £31.6m per signing, an inflated loss of just £1m. But if you look at the British signings, it's £19.3m recouped, or potentially recoupable, and £19.8m lost, or roughly 50% of the money effectively down the drain.

Interestingly, both the British and overseas deals involve 14% free transfers – so the transfer figures are not skewed towards either category by Bosman deals. A bigger part of the problem with the signings born in these shores is almost certainly the age, with, as noted above, the British players averaging out at 26; meaning that even just two years spent at Anfield would see their values plummet, and four years would see their value drop massively. The best signings from the homegrown category are Henderson (over 300 games for the Reds), Sturridge (superb until injuries struck), Robertson and Milner; and only one of those – the last – was aged over 23 at the time. (Oxlade-Chamberlain was 24 when signed and was doing very well when injury struck in the 2018 Champions League semi-final.)

But there is also a distinct lack of *total game-changers* within the homegrown buys. The honest grit of players like Henderson and

Milner is absolutely vital (and they are more than technically proficient), but Sturridge (initially) and Robertson aside, none of the signings were necessarily *transcendental*. Meanwhile, Andy Carroll and Stewart Downing were the biggest flops, with the Reds losing a staggering £79.2m and £66.9m respectively after their inflation-adjusted sale fees were removed from their inflation-adjusted purchase fees. (Carroll cost a staggering £121.8m.) Equally, while Joe Cole was a free transfer, wages of £100,000-a-week almost a decade ago would be more like £300,000-a-week now (although this is an estimate, as we don't track wage inflation). James Milner was another who arrived for free, but on big wages, although he, at least, has proved worthy of his pay packet. (And on a personal note, I had some doubts in 2015 that he would be a success after looking a bit too slow in a ponderous team, but has got better and better with age, as better players have arrived to play alongside him.)

And of course, Rafa Benítez's two big *British Isles* signings didn't work out. (Robbie Keane included on account of Ireland's geographical location and closeness to the UK's football culture.) Keane was offloaded within mere months, at 75% of the fee paid, but Glen Johnson's value dwindled to nothing, after a £75.7m transfer fee in today's money. Johnson was not the most popular player with the fans, but he did play exactly 200 games for the Reds. Perhaps he just arrived at the wrong time – when the club was mired in internal wars ahead of four poor or relatively poor seasons. Interestingly, he would be perfect for Jürgen Klopp's use of full-backs as quasi-wingers, but of course, Trent Alexander-Arnold is heading towards 100 games for the Reds at the age of just 20, and has a bit more fire in his belly than the sometimes casual Johnson.

Alexander-Arnold is more proof of how bringing through homegrown kids – even if it involves purchasing them for the youth team – is far more profitable, in all senses, than buying ready-made Brits. Adding together the nominal fees paid for Raheem Sterling, Jordon Ibe, Joe Gomez, Jonjo Shelvey, Danny Wilson, Dominic Solanke and Scott Carson – the seven first-team British teenagers signed in the time period in question – amounts to just £52m in current money (so, less than the total spent on Joe Allen after inflation), and if you take Gomez's value at a conservative £50m, that would mean £223m in transfer fees recouped or transfer values in 2019 from those signings.

Alexander-Arnold could join Jamie Carragher, Steven Gerrard, Michael Owen, Robbie Fowler and Steve McManaman in playing hundreds of games for the Reds, and pretty much all of those players were *definitely* transcendental. But as noted earlier, none of the British *buys* were ever at that level. (Gomez could yet be.)

From the overseas buys since 2004, some have been big successes, but arguably a dozen – Xabi Alonso, Pepe Reina, Javier Mascherano, Fernando Torres, Luis Suárez, Philippe Coutinho, Virgil van Dijk, Mo Salah, Roberto Firmino and Sadio Mané (plus possibly Alisson and Fabinho, if they continue their promising starts) – have that X-factor quality.

Daniel Agger could – and maybe should – have joined the list but picked up too many injuries, while Dirk Kuyt, Gini Wijnaldum and Emre Can were/are more of the Henderson-type of ultra-reliable and resilient signings; and of course, Luis Garcia and Yossi Benayoun were fleeting magicians who didn't hit the heights consistently but were excellent value for money. Others were good value, too – Arbeloa, Aurelio, Škrtel, *et al.* (Wijnaldum is an absolutely fantastic player, discussed elsewhere in the book, but he can be undervalued, given the subtlety of his play. He does occasionally fail to impose himself on a game, as in the Champions League final in Madrid, but a lot of what he does goes unnoticed – albeit with the added bonus that when Liverpool need a goal and no one else is providing it, he often steps up.)

The standout dozen continental buys average out at £62m per purchase in current day money, at a total of £751m; but they were sold, or could be sold, for £1.25*billion*, or an average of just over £100m per player. Anyone saying that you must sign only experienced, proven players should note that their average age was just 23, and that these players were not considered trustworthy by a lot of major clubs at the time, with some of them at unfashionable clubs, and some (such as Mascherano and Coutinho) rotting in reserve teams.

Of course, this is cherry-picking the best signings, and ignoring foreign flops like Alberto Aquilani, Christian Benteke and Lazar Marković, but just as there are also expensive British Isle flops (Carroll, Downing, Keane), my point is that there just aren't many *transformative* British Isle players signed in recent years. That could of course change, with the emergence of elite young British players, but of course, they are likely to cost more than the equivalent overseas players.

So one part of the Reds' renaissance under Klopp and Edwards has to be connected to a willingness to trust *some* homegrown players, and not to overspend on overpriced Brits. Perhaps interestingly, a high proportion of Klopp's buys have come from within the Premier League – including overseas players Mané, van Dijk, Wijnaldum and Shaqiri – while Mo Salah had previously spent 18 months at Chelsea. In addition to the Brits – Oxlade-Chamberlain, Robertson and Solanke – there are two other types of Klopp signing: the very cheap deals from Germany – Loris Karius, Ragnar Klavan, Joël Matip – and just three major, expensive brand-new imports: Alisson Becker, Naby Keïta and Fabinho.

The following figures are from 2004-2019, before the focus shifts to the period between 2007-2016.

Total Spent (Gross) After Inflation

Benítez – £1,178,576,606 – 42 players

Dalglish – £454,275,562 – 10 players

Klopp – £439,283,987 – 14 players

Committee – £411,303,400 – 13 players

Rodgers – £382,260,739 – 11 players

Hodgson – £70,287,418 – 5 players

Average Fee Per Player, After Inflation

Dalglish – £45,427,556

Rodgers – £34,750,976

Committee – £31,638,723

Klopp – £31,377,428

Benítez – £28,061,348

Hodgson – £11,714,570

2007-2016

Of the aforementioned "golden dozen" – Xabi Alonso, Pepe Reina, Javier Mascherano, Fernando Torres, Luis Suárez, Philippe Coutinho, Virgil van Dijk, Mo Salah, Roberto Firmino and Sadio Mané (plus Alisson and Fabinho) – only two (Suárez and Coutinho) were signed between the end of the summer of 2007 and the end of the 2014/15 season. The other nine were signed in a total of just six seasons, three either side of that fairly consistently (but not *exclusively*) low point in the history of Liverpool Football Club.

So, were Liverpool simply buying the wrong players between 2007 and 2016?

A big part of the problem had to be the lack of elite coaching between 2010 and 2015, and the internal problems at the club between 2007 and 2010; plus, tensions behind the scenes in one form or another between 2007 and 2015.

For instance, Roberto Firmino did not look destined for greatness until Klopp took charge, with Rodgers not sure what to do with a player he did not seem to especially want. Iago Aspas was something of a joke figure during his season with the Reds, but has gone on to have an excellent career in *La Liga* (over 75 goals in five seasons with unfashionable clubs) and even play for the Spanish national side, scoring one international goal in 2016, two in 2017 and three in 2018; although in fairness to Rodgers, in 2013/14 Luis Suárez and Daniel Sturridge were the obvious first-choice attackers.

(That said, there can be no underestimating the impact Aspas has had back in Spain, and this partially validates the committee's decision to recruit him. "There may be no single player in Spain as significant for his team," Spanish football expert Sid Lowe wrote in *The Guardian* in April 2019. "What has happened this season – what happened on Saturday [when he came back to score two goals] – underlines that, although it goes back even further. Of the 27 games that Celta have played without Aspas in *Primera* while he has been at the club, they have won just five and lost 18; in that time, they have scored three times as many goals with him as without him. Going into the match against Barcelona just before Christmas this season, Celta were ninth, had 21 points and were three points off Europe. Oh, and seven points and nine places above the relegation zone." Aspas got injured, and, without him, Celta ended up fighting relegation. But as Sid Lowe notes, he came back towards the end of the season and, with yet another goal against Barcelona, when they rested their entire team ahead of the Liverpool game, Aspas effectively sealed their safety.)

Luis Alberto has shone in *Serie A*, and has also made his debut for Spain. Mario Balotelli was a phenomenal talent, but just seemed to have several screws loose. Alberto Aquilani was an undoubtedly gifted player, who played almost 30 more games for Italy *after* leaving Liverpool in various loans and then on a permanent basis (no, it seems he *can't* be recalled), but arrived at Liverpool with a big price tag, huge boots to fill (Alonso's) at a time when the team was floundering, and a serious ankle injury that refused to heal as expected. With a bit more luck these players could have flourished, but equally, some – like

Aquilani, Marković and Babel – also didn't quite seem cut out for the mental and/or physical side of playing in the Premier League.

Several changes of manager between 2010 and 2015 meant the new boss always wanted his own new players, and so out went others who may have succeeded with some time and nurturing. As well as the cost of sacking existing managers and their coaching staff, managerial churn leads to player churn. (Manchester United appear locked in the cycle of appointing the wrong manager who then buys the wrong players, and who then gets sacked, only to be replaced by a new manager who is not a good fit for the club, and who then buys his own players, until the squad is an absolute dog's dinner. Which, of course, is yet further evidence of why a director of football can be such a good idea.)

And in the case of Brendan Rodgers and his own personal picks, the signings just appeared too uninspiring, often going back to his old clubs – which all managers do – to plunder; but where his old club was at a much lower level than Liverpool, and the talent pool much narrower. Joe Allen was technically accomplished but did not make the impact a £60m (TPI) signing should make; Fabio Borini was average at best; Kolo Touré was old; Christian Benteke looked overawed and lacking the pace of old; Nathaniel Clyne, Adam Lallana, Dejan Lovren and Danny Ings were good but not *sensational;* and often inconsistent, albeit with injuries playing a big part in halting their progress. Only James Milner remains as a near-guaranteed first-XI player, with Lovren – after improving under Klopp – having lost out to Joe Gomez and Joël Matip.

The only really transformative players to arrive during Rodgers' tenure and to look special during his time in charge were Sturridge and Coutinho, both signed by the committee at the time when Rodgers lost all influence in such matters (before regaining some say after the unexpected success of 2013/14); whilst fellow committee-picks Can and Firmino thrived under Klopp, before the former – surely worth at least £50m on the open market – chose to move to Juventus on a free transfer. (Incidentally, Juventus were reported to have paid Can €16m to complete his signing, and with his contract containing a €50m release clause – applicable only to clubs outside Italy and commencing in 2020; apparently the first time Juventus had ever allowed any type of escape clause. One of the few mistakes made by Liverpool FC in recent years was allowing Can – who made 167 appearances for the club – to enter the final years of his contract; but equally, his form only really spiked in the final season – by which time he rejected all the club's offers. And, as good as he was, he hasn't been missed.)

Buy A Player's Future, Not His Past

A general opinion seems to be that Liverpool have switched in the last few years from signing 'potential' to signing 'proven talent', but it's only a slight switch. The only player aged over 26 to arrive in the Klopp era has been (although not quite a *has-been*) Ragnar Klavan, who valiantly plugged a hole for a couple of seasons. Rodgers signed Kolo Touré, James Milner and Rickie Lambert, while Adam Lallana proved expensive at the age of 26. Include Marko Grujić and the average age of first-team squad players to arrive since Rodgers was sacked is 24, the exact same average age as all of Rafa Benítez's signings.

But in Rodgers' time, the committee-led signings averaged an age of just 21.7; whereas Rodgers' own signings averaged out at 25.6. So there was clearly a schism. And if you go back a few more years to Roy Hodgson, you get a British manager bringing in players with an astonishing average age of 28.8; and weirdly, 28 (or *less than a full season*) is the average number of games they played for the club – as you'd expect from such short-term thinking. Klopp, the committee and Benítez all bought younger, on average, than Rodgers and Hodgson; with Kenny Dalglish in between, at an average age of 24.3. (And again, Rodgers also wanted to bring in Clint Dempsey and Ashley Williams, two other older players. The mind boggles.)

But has age made a huge difference to the success rates of transfers? In previous books I've talked about how the average age of Bob Paisley's transfers was extremely low – averaging out at 22, and topping out with only a couple of 25/26-year-olds (Kenny Dalglish and Graeme Souness); and how Rafa Benítez brought in so many elite players aged 22-23 (Xabi Alonso, Pepe Reina, Javier Mascherano, Fernando Torres, et al). With hindsight it becomes easy to see the Spaniard's best buys as established, ready-made players, but at their times of arrival there were plenty of doubts (Alonso was apparently too slow, Torres was seen as flaky, Mascherano was in the reserves at West Ham, and so on).

If we go back to 2012, when Edwards joined Liverpool, the best signing in the five years beforehand had been Luis Suárez, aged 23 – masterminded by Damien Comolli, the man who also brought Edwards and Ian Graham to Liverpool; while the only other successful signing from that period, Jordan Henderson, was just 21, but in addition to now having played well over 300 games for Liverpool, has reached 50 for his country too (and as such, even his many detractors have to admit those are excellent returns on any investment. By contrast, Phil Jones, who moved to Manchester United at the same time, for a similar fee – and who was widely touted as the future of English football – has played just 159 league games for United, and 211 overall; and just 27 times for England. Plus, of course, Henderson just captained Liverpool to Champions League glory).

Indeed, Jack Pitt-Brooke interviewed Comolli for *The Independent*, when it became clear that his two former clubs were meeting in the Champions League final. The French former Director of Football at Liverpool explained the process behind signing Jordan Henderson, even if the player's relative failure in his first season – in the eyes of the owners – apparently cost Comolli his job.

"It was a mix of four different factors," Comolli said, as to why the young Wearsider was bought. "The first one: when we looked at his fitness data it was absolutely out of this world. That was very important, to know that he could match the intensity that physically Liverpool should play at. Secondly, when we looked at his technical and tactical data, he was doing things at Sunderland that were as good as some of the top midfielders in the Premier League. The third aspect was live scouting, we all watched him, all came back very enthusiastic about what we saw. And the fourth aspect is the personality. We made a lot of enquiries about what type of individual he was, his behaviour, his obsession for improvement. They talk about marginal gains, with Jordan every day it is 'how can I improve, how can I gain 5% of marginal gains?' The other aspect of his personality, when you spend a bit of time with him, you can straightaway tell about his leadership skills, his determination, his commitment. Everything you see on the pitch."

Comolli then reflected on how he believed the signing got him the sack. "I remember the day I was sacked, the owners told me, Jordan Henderson what a massive mistake it was. That was about the only thing they told me."

(As mentioned earlier in the book, I can partially confirm this. John Henry phoned me from Boston days before Comolli was sacked in 2012, and one of the only things he asked my opinion on, aside from who could be brought in as a figurehead to give the club real direction and a proper footballing identity, was what I felt Henderson offered. Henry asked for advice on creating digital chalkboards for the player's actions – crosses, shots, etc. – on *The Guardian* website, and in reply I made the case for the young midfielder as someone who would in time migrate back to the centre of the pitch, but who, as a relative rookie, was playing on the right of midfield to balance out with the pure winger, Stewart Downing, on the other flank. I could see Henderson's potential, but also why people might not "get" what he did. That said, I'm pretty sure everyone at FSG now knows the value of Jordan Henderson. However, Comolli's lack of internal communication was raised as an issue – the way I interpreted it, he wasn't explaining the decision-making to the owners, so his sacking wasn't just about Henderson.)

Since 2012 – when Comolli went and Edwards arrived – Liverpool have signed no fewer than 47 players, and taken a handful of others in on loan. Of those 47, I would say that 14 have been *undeniable* successes; which isn't to say that the other 33 were all flops – some have done well enough for the Reds, but may have been lacking in overall value, while others are still young, and a few are still only in their first season at the club. In descending age order at the time of signing, the 14 standouts have been: Milner, van Dijk, Wijnaldum, Salah, Alisson, Mané, Oxlade-Chamberlain, Fabinho, Sturridge, Firmino, Robertson, Coutinho, Can and Gomez. Of these, only one was a Brendan Rodgers signing, whilst the committee either totally led, or influenced, 13 of the others.

Perhaps this is a little generous on Oxlade-Chamberlain, but he was doing particularly well before getting injured; and it's still early days for Fabinho and Alisson, although like Oxlade-Chamberlain a year earlier they ended their first seasons as obvious successes.

The average age of the 14 clear successes, at the point when signed, was just 23.5, and as of April 2019 they had made a combined 757 league appearances for the club, with only Can and Coutinho not set to add to that tally; but where Coutinho brought in an absolute ton of cash, the amount of which paid *exactly* – almost to the penny – for van Dijk and Alisson.

We can talk about signing only fully-established quality, but even van Dijk was *only* at Southampton, and at the time still had less than 20 caps for Holland. People were astonished when £50m was first mentioned two summers ago, let alone the £75m it became. Three of the list were signed from relegated clubs, and eyebrows were raised at paying even £8m for Andy Robertson. Coutinho was in Inter's reserves; a bit like Mascherano at West Ham all those years earlier. Sturridge, like Wijnaldum, was seen as too inconsistent; Salah, like Sturridge, was a Chelsea "flop"; while Oxlade-Chamberlain's career appeared to have long-since stalled. And of course, all that apparent disbelief from some quarters regarding Liverpool handing £29m to Hoffenheim for Roberto Firmino, as discussed earlier. Alisson had just two seasons in European football with Roma, but only played in the second of those, while Joe Gomez and Emre Can were promising players that most people in England hadn't heard of when they arrived. As with Alonso and Torres, and even Suárez, it's easy to say *much later* that these were all no-brainers, or that they were fully proven players. And as noted, the average age was *just 23.5*.

Of those players, van Dijk is now without question the best centre-back in the world; Coutinho moved to Barcelona for a near-world record fee; Sturridge was as good as any striker in England before injuries took their toll; Can was headhunted by the biggest and most successful club in Italy; Robertson has been called the best left-back in Europe; Mo Salah has become the fastest ever Liverpool player to 50 league goals (and the third-fastest at any club in the Premier League era); Roberto Firmino has joined Alisson in being a first-choice player for Brazil, and one of the best in his position in the Premier League; Mané has been largely sensational, and is starting to develop a 20-goals-a-season record from the wide attacking area – and joined Salah in winning the Golden Boot this past season with 22 league goals; Joe Gomez could rival Matthijs de Ligt as possibly the best young defender in the world, if he can stay fit after some terrible luck with injuries; and the others are all key players for Liverpool. And many of those were behind Liverpool's incredible Champions League success and record-breaking league form.

You can argue that Divock Origi, at 19, wasn't ready, and therefore indicative of the folly of buying *potential*. But Rickie Lambert, at 32, *was* – at least in terms of being old enough, if not in terms of actually being *too* old. However, Origi has 28 goals in 98 games for the club, and Lambert got just three in 36 – and in a further 26 games for West Brom, after being moved on (20 of them in the Premier League, six in the cups), scored just one goal. Then there's the staggering value of Origi's goals, that have earned the club millions and won vital games, including the Champions League semi-final and final; so even if he still doesn't look the finished article, and at times looks a bit confused as to what he's supposed to be doing, he has repaid his transfer fee several times over in terms of pounds of prize money garnered, and above all else, the *priceless* trophy in Madrid.

Bob Paisley famously used to let his players "lose their legs on someone else's pitch", and Lambert – as with the *annus horribilis* of Roy Hodgson – was yet another example of buying someone based on their past, not their future. It could also be argued that Dominic Solanke's goals return at Liverpool was not too dissimilar to Lambert's, but Solanke was sold for three times what was paid, with a largely-unreported buyback clause should the young striker develop, as many at Liverpool think he still can.

What has become of Rodgers' other signings? Well, James Milner has been a resounding success at Liverpool, while Adam Lallana and Dejan Lovren have been decidedly mixed bags at the club, but continue to be part of the matchday 18, when fit (although towards the end of the season Lallana struggled to even make the matchday squad). Otherwise, Fabio Borini, after various poor stints at clubs, is at a big club in AC Milan, but as a full-back. Joe Allen is perhaps too good for the Championship, but that's the level at which he's played for the past year, and unless he moves club, he will remain at that level with Stoke. Kolo Touré, like Lambert, has retired.

Mario Balotelli has been a big success in France, but has had no fewer than four seasons since his breakthrough at Manchester City where one league goal has been his *best* tally (one at Liverpool, and one on loan at AC Milan; plus what are actually two half seasons, his final six months at Man City and similarly at Nice in 2018/19, before he was offloaded). That leaves Nathaniel Clyne, a good defensive full-back who cannot attack, and Danny Ings, a likeable striker with two cruciate knee ligament injuries; both of whom ended the season on loan at smaller Premier League clubs, with Ings set to complete a £20m full-time switch to Southampton, and Clyne likely to leave in the summer. And at the time of writing, Christian Benteke has scored a pitiful three goals in his last 46 games for Crystal Palace.

So not only did Rodgers' signings have a pretty poor return at Liverpool, most have moved on to much smaller clubs, and often failed to shine there, too. And with not a lot of resale value left on Milner, Lallana and Lovren, the total losses on the players to have departed, after inflation, is some £127m – on just seven players. For a manager to leave a club and, just three years later, for only one of his signings to still be an important player – and the others to represent a big financial loss – is pretty damning.

And, indeed, the reason why Liverpool now rely on experts like Edwards, Ian Graham, Barry Hunter and Dave Fallows to get the right players into the club.

Why Are Liverpool's Signings *Suddenly* So Successful?

First of all, it's fair to say that Jürgen Klopp is clearly a better manager than Brendan Rodgers; even if, as of October 2017, there were still persistent protests about how the German's win-rate at Liverpool was no better than the Ulsterman's. (Which still didn't explain away all Klopp's *phenomenal* success in Germany.) Hopefully I've now proven the case beyond doubt, although this does not mean that Rodgers cannot improve, and *hasn't* improved; people can get better at what they do through testing experience and practice. And, after doing very well at Celtic (in what had admittedly become a one-team league, where the Hoops had three times the budget of the next-richest club), Rodgers has taken on a young and exciting team at Leicester City. It's a chance for him to manage a bigger club than Swansea, but a smaller one than Liverpool.

But even allowing for Klopp's stronger tactical ideas, his more inspirational manner and his greater collegiate sense of leadership, one issue I keep returning to is *fitness*. Now, it's become almost a cliché for a new manager to arrive and provide extra training sessions, to get the squad up to his required physical standards. But this is often more true of the modern, hard-pressing-style of manager, like Klopp, Mauricio Pochettino, Maurizio Sarri, Unai Emery, Pep Guardiola and Ralph Hasenhüttl.

Indeed, if you ever need proof of how vital now fitness is, see the Champions League final. While both teams' distance-covered stats were well down on their usual high totals, this was of course in part due to a three-week break and the tropical heat in Madrid. However, the two players who were most off the pace were Harry Kane and Roberto Firmino, shadows of their usual selves after missing the final part of the regular season. That extra 10-20% makes all the difference in getting away from defenders, something neither could manage to do.

As the game has moved towards such managers, the more sedate style of someone like Arsène Wenger began to seem archaic. Fifteen years ago Wenger's team were the gold standard for skill mixed with physicality; as he imported fitness ideas that absolutely revolutionised the English game in 1996, while his team peaked in 2003/04, with the 'Invincibles'. Then came Jose Mourinho, whose Chelsea side – aided by the kind of spending never before seen in England – took that physical standard to the next level, taking the Blues to what was a league points record – 95 – before Guardiola's City rewrote the rulebook on what was possible. (And, of course, Liverpool this past season.) But by 2018, both Wenger and Mourinho seemed outdated. In late 2015 I gave a rare presentation at a London football data conference on the Transfer Price Index, and afterwards was approached by some people working within the game, including analysts at Premier League clubs. One independent fitness expert wandered over, and noted – almost three years before the Frenchman was sacked, and before the club had slid out of their perennial top-four finishing positions – that Wenger's methods were outdated. His players simply weren't fit enough.

If innovators are not of a sufficiently growth-related mindset they may stick with the tried and tested, as new innovators overtake them. And perhaps even the best innovators just run out of energy or ideas further down the line.

In December 2018, following the Portuguese's dismissal, *The Times* ran a piece about how Mourinho's United were simply not as fit as other teams. United ranked 16th out of 20 for total kilometres covered, and 16th again for total sprints. Going back a few years to the end of the Rodgers era, it felt like Liverpool – certainly after Luis Suárez left – were not as hard-working as a team, nor as likely to make over a hundred sprints per game (although the data for this is hard to research, outside of what might get published on a specific one-off occasion; unlike a lot of metrics, running and sprint data are not usually available to outsiders to peruse at any given time.)

So, someone like Adam Lallana arrived fresh from hard-pressing Pochettino's Southampton. But under Rodgers at Liverpool he looked laboured, albeit a situation often not helped by persistent niggling injuries. His intense pressing only really became a feature of his game again under Klopp, who turned a mediocre buy into a *good* buy. Klopp's preseasons are infamous for how hard the players have to work. The drop in Lallana's quality under Rodgers could be related to the fact that he was probably no longer as fit, although the pressure of playing for Liverpool and the large price tag for the time maybe added to a difficult transition.

We tend to think of players in terms of talent – and that their talent is "fixed" – but a player who is suddenly 10% fitter can get to the ball a fraction quicker, run a little longer, retain strength to shoot after a mazy dribble, or chase back after losing the ball. The difficulty is in assessing how much fitness work becomes too much; players get bored of all the running if a ball is not involved, and if a team does triple training sessions the day before a match then the manager will have eleven tired players in the team. Research has shown that players cannot run as far, nor make as many sprints – and are more prone to injury – two or three days after a game, with five days seen as the standard "turnaround" time for a player to be at his optimum level. The ignorant type of fan tends to say "but they're *professional athletes*", missing the point that even the best marathon runner in the world might be able to complete another marathon later on the very same day, if a gun was held to his or her head, but they wouldn't be anywhere near as quick. Being a *professional* doesn't make a sportsperson superhuman. Energy reserves are finite.

Unlike Olympic runners, for example, footballers have to work on myriad, varied technical and tactical issues, which take up time in training. There are only so many hours in a week between games, and recovery periods have to be built in. That said, there has to be an envelope whose limits many managers don't get close enough to pushing.

Managers like Klopp, Pochettino and Guardiola have gone into clubs and improved countless players. It can't be a coincidence that their styles involve intense training and hard pressing. Unless overworking them to the point of exhaustion, making players fitter has to make them *better*.

At first, Klopp arrived in England accompanied by quotes from his time in Germany where, with Mainz, he set the team a challenge to run 120kms per game; whereas a lot of teams averaged between 100-110kms. But this was Mainz, with no budget to buy players. Klopp knew that, lacking quality, they had to overcome that with effort.

In 2015, former Mainz defender Tim Hoogland told *FourFourTwo* magazine that players would be set specific running targets by their manager. "You have to run. That's it," Hoogland said. "I think this is one of the important things you have to know about him. The whole team has to run 120 km collectively every game. 120km minimum."

Patrick Owomoyela, who spent five years under Klopp at Borussia Dortmund, reasserted Hoogland's claims, and said players would be given rewards if they hit their individual targets. "In his first year he said he wouldn't guarantee anything apart from that when we reached 120km per game then it would be much harder for us to lose," he said. "He actually offered us a day off when we reached that target. He thought that if we reached that then we would win the game. And from then on it became easy because we understood that his plan would work."

With no players of any real note, and the smallest budget in the 2nd-tier of German football, Klopp had to make Mainz *fitter* than anyone else. More than a decade later – in which time he led Borussia Dortmund to two league titles and a Champions League final, and Liverpool to one of their best-ever all-round seasons – Klopp's style of play has evolved away from just *gegenpressing* (although with Dortmund's increasing quality during his tenure, they too were more than just hard-running lunatics). But the evidence of Klopp improving players can also been seen in the regression of several stars to have left his teams.

Indeed, Nuri Şahin transferred from Dortmund to Real Madrid, then to Liverpool on loan in Rodgers' first season, but never looked the same player; and never hit the same heights again when back at Dortmund. Shinji Kagawa was another who was exceptional under Klopp, mediocre at Man United, before returning to the Westfalenhallen. (Interestingly, when not under Klopp's guidance, Kagawa scored goals at half the rate compared to when he was one of Klopp's key men; and his most prolific spell for Japan also came between 2010-2012, when under the German's fitness regimen.) Mario Götze was outrageously good under Klopp; and he too later returned to Dortmund a pale shadow of his former self, albeit with illness playing a part. And of course, Dortmund as a team have never been quite the same since. Neven Subotić – a regular centre-back for the club under Klopp aged just 20, and part of all their glorious successes – was an outcast by the age of 28, loaned to Cologne and then sold to Saint-Étienne in France. Arguably only Robert Lewandowski, Mats Hummels and İlkay Gündoğan have gone on to better things, although Gündoğan has been more of a fine squad-man at Manchester City than a pivotal player. In 2018/19 Marco Reus finally returned to the levels he'd been at under Klopp at the Westfalenstadion. Indeed, by the time Lewandowski, Götze and Hummels moved to Bayern Munich, Bayern had realised that, as well as snaffling Dortmund's players, they made a conscious effort to move towards ultra-fit, hard-pressing football.

Interestingly, Philippe Coutinho is another Klopp success – where the Brazilian played his best football under the German (his goals-per-game doubled in his final 18 months at the club) – who left and saw his career stall. Coutinho went to Barcelona in January 2018 and scored 10 goals in 22 games for the remainder of that season; but he scored just 11 in *53 games* in 2018/19 – including an anonymous reappearance at Anfield – leading to talk of the Catalans cutting some substantial losses. Could it be that Coutinho went to Spain with "Liverpool fitness", but by the start of his first *full* season, was not coming off the back of a Klopp preseason? Interestingly, Coutinho's best football (five goals in 16 games) before Liverpool came at Espanyol, when managed by … Pochettino. And while often very good under Rodgers, his best football at Liverpool was under Klopp. These may all be coincidences, but if you take a player into a new environment and, amongst other things, provide different physical conditioning, it's unlikely that he will be the exact same player.

Players will almost always become different propositions when shifted to new environments, different countries, to play with different teammates, under different levels of pressure (which can be increased by a transfer fee that now hangs over their head), to be deployed in different tactical systems. But more players have seemed to improve under Klopp than regress – unless, such as in the case of Daniel Sturridge, they have been dogged by injuries and/or cannot easily maintain the requisite high-energy fitness levels – and more players have seemed to fall off a cliff at clubs when he has departed, or they have moved to pastures new. These are not just the players aged 19 who found themselves *naturally* better by the age of 22, given that you'd expect some kind of improvement between those ages.

In the aforementioned *Times* article from December 2018, Liverpool found themselves ranking "only" 8th for total kilometres covered, at 1,905, which was 53kms behind the top-ranked runners, Arsenal. But while it may have been important for Mainz and then Dortmund, total distance covered is not the key metric. Far more importantly, at the near-midway point of the season Liverpool were well clear in terms of *sprints* – 2,080 after 17 Premier League games of the season, some 54 sprints more than the team ranked 2nd. Indeed, the top seven clubs for sprints were all having good seasons, relative to expectations.

What's interesting is that the 2nd-placed team for sprints was Manchester City, and that City were just behind Liverpool in mid-table for total kilometres run. As such, both shared almost identical profiles, with Liverpool running a little bit more than their closest rivals, and also sprinting a little bit more. As Liverpool have increased their share of possession in recent times under Klopp, less pressing is to be expected. But the sprints are *telling* – the ability to bomb forward and get back. Indeed, in the game at Stamford Bridge the Reds put in over 150 sprints, when a lot of teams clock under 100 per game, and the usual Liverpool average (based on the figures that are public) varies between 100 and 120 sprints per match. It was no wonder the Reds looked uncharacteristically sluggish just four days later in Italy, when losing 1-0 to Napoli in the Champions League. That kind of exertion is way beyond the normal level a football team will usually ever reach.

As of March, 2019, Liverpool still led the way on most sprints in the Premier League; by stark contrast, in 2014/15, under Rodgers, the Reds ranked 14th. (The more statistics that crop up about 2014/15, the worse it looks.) Liverpool used to average just 103kms run per game under Rodgers, some 10kms per game down on what Klopp's side was achieving in 2018/19; so the side in 2014/15 was neither covering much distance, nor sprinting hard – in addition to (or perhaps leading to) poor defending and poor attacking.

Indeed, after 31 games in the Premier League this season *Sky Sports* ran a piece showing that the Reds had made 3,794 sprints, or an average of just over 122 per game; the exact same average as after game 17. So as the Reds entered the run-in there was no slacking off in their high-energy bursts, and had risen from 8th to 5th in total distance covered. In December, Man City were more or less matching the Reds for sprints, at 119, but by March they were down to 115.6 per game. Between December and March Liverpool had increased their distance covered from exactly 112kms per game to closer to 113km; while Man City were at exactly 112kms. (And in the period between game 17 and game 30, City's sprints had dropped to just 111 per game, a fall of 7%.)

An academic study conducted seven years ago showed just how important sprinting was in football (Oliver Faude, Thorsten Koch & Tim Meyer, 2012: "Straight sprinting is the most frequent action in goal situations in professional football", Journal of Sports Science), and with a handful of PhDs on the backroom staff, Liverpool would expect to know this kind of thing. (As well as a whole lot more than those of us on the outside trying to figure all this out.)

Indeed, the top sprinters in the Premier League as the season approached its conclusion included several of the top scorers: Mo Salah ranking 2nd in the entire league for sprints, with a phenomenal 547 (Andy Robertson was 3rd, with 531); Raheem Sterling 4th, with 513; and Pierre-Emerick Aubameyang 5th, with 482. (Ben Chilwell of Leicester – a former target of the Reds' committee – had the most sprints, at an eye-watering 609, and has been widely linked with a move to Man City). While *Sky* only published the top seven for total sprints in their article, Salah was almost 100 sprints ahead of the player ranked 7th (Andros Townsend), which seems utterly ridiculous given that there are more than 500 players in the league (albeit many of whom don't play that often). While Salah could at times look selfish when it came to taking too many shots, his work-rate could not be in doubt; indeed, in the game at Fulham, when Ryan Babel – the winger who famously hated tracking back – was breaking from the halfway line, it was Salah who got back to be the last line of defence.

Another area of improvement by the Reds can be seen in the fact that, as told to me by a sports scientist, there was a 24% injury rate under Rodgers, but that it was down to just 9% towards the end of this season under Klopp (and players like Matip and Gomez missed games not due to muscle injuries but broken limbs from overzealous challenges, which cannot be mitigated against). Ex-Bayern Munich fitness coach, Andreas Kornmayer, arrived at Liverpool in 2016, since which time the German – with some resemblance to Klopp himself –

has taken the physical conditioning of players to the elite level. "Korny is kind of the drill sergeant here," Klopp said in August 2017. "He needs to be. We make the decisions what he has to do and he gives the advice of which specific areas we can improve. He needs to be the 'bad boy' from time to time because players don't like running. 'That's Korny's idea, if you ask me you can have a day off, but *Korny* said you have to!'" Mona Nemmer, Bayern's head of nutrition, followed Kornmayer to Liverpool that same summer, to resume her work with specialised diets – this time to help Klopp, rather than thwart him.

And of course, improvement by players is also due to elite coaching, not just better fitness regimens. And if a handful of players are improved, and a club can then buy some additional high-level players, then they will all improve each other via the social multiplier effect.

The Social Multiplier Effect and How Klopp Improves Players

In Scotland, Virgil van Dijk used to train on a daily basis against Teemu Pukki and Georgios Samaras, while the top scorers outside Celtic – the strikers he faced on matchday – were Kris Boyd, John Sutton, Billy Mckay, Adam Rooney, Nadir Çiftçi, Anthony Andreu, Greg Stewart and Niall McGinn. It's clear from that list of mostly *who the hell are theys* that this was hardly the most testing of environments for the giant Dutchman, with such players unlikely to be household names outside of Scotland. (Occasionally van Dijk may have played against a team like Barcelona, but they'd ship seven goals in a serious mismatch – even if, as an individual, he'd win plaudits.)

To assume that van Dijk is just some amazing natural talent is to ignore that he only became a regular at a fairly small Dutch top-division club, Groningen, at the age of 21, and left for a small fee to join Celtic at the age of 22; first playing for the Dutch national side a few months before turning 24, ahead of a move to mid-ranking Premier League club Southampton. Up until he joined the south coast side, he would rarely have faced anything like an elite striker – occasionally in Holland, never in Scotland – nor trained against one every day during the week. He shone north of the border, without question, but his technique will have been honed by two seasons at Southampton – still not training *with* elite players but certainly playing against them – and now, aged 27 and approaching 28, he continues to improve to the point where he's regarded as the best centre-back in the world.

The fact that he *looks* like such a natural should actually serve as a warning to anyone that this is a process of improvement, and not a case of an overnight sensation.

Indeed, van Dijk told the peerless interviewer Donald McRae of *The Guardian* ahead of the Champions League final in Madrid that he had been impatient as a young player, and it took time for him to make his mark.

"I wanted things very quickly. When I went to Groningen I started in the under-23s and I was on the bench. I was like: 'What's going on here?' I went to the manager Dick Lukkien and I was arguing with him back and forth, saying: 'How is this possible?' But I learned so much from that period. I grew as a human being.

"It was the first time I was on my own and I had to learn to deal with not getting my way. I went to training on a bicycle. It was the same the next season. Luckily, I kept working hard, kept improving, and I'm still in contact with Dick who is the head coach of FC Emmen now. He's a fantastic coach and got the best out of me. He pushed me because he knew I could be a bit lazy. He knew my mentality then was to do just enough to win challenges. He kept pushing me and made me angry at times. It was tough but it worked. Before the end of the season I made my debut in the first team. I'm so grateful to Dick."

Similarly, Mo Salah, Roberto Firmino and Sadio Mané – up there with the best front-threes in world football over the past decade (with Salah and Mané the first pair of Liverpool strikers in over 30 years to score 20+ goals two seasons running) – were all unremarkable players aged 21; at smaller clubs or in smaller leagues – minnows in relative backwaters. Similarly, Fabinho at age 20 was a merely promising right-back, loaned from Rio Ave in Brazil to Real Madrid's 2nd team, then on to Monaco – who, at the time, had just been promoted from the French 2nd-tier. Aged 21, Andy Robertson was an unremarkable player in Scottish football, and Alisson Becker only became a regular for Brazilian club Internacional at the age of 22; and after his move to Roma, only made his league debut in a big European league in 2017, aged 25. Elsewhere in Liverpool's squad, Adam Lallana played nothing but lower division football until the age of 24, and Dejan Lovren only left Dinamo Zagreb for France at the age of 21.

So it's fair to say that almost half of Liverpool's first-team squad – including several of the best players – were not teenage prodigies, nor "naturally gifted" wunderkinds (at least when compared to many of their peers at the same age).

The players who *were* teenage sensations – to varying degrees, and with differing styles of play – were Alex Oxlade-Chamberlain,

James Milner, Jordan Henderson, Divock Origi, Daniel Sturridge, Joël Matip, Simon Mignolet, Joe Gomez, Naby Keïta, Alberto Moreno, Trent Alexander-Arnold, Xherdan Shaqiri and Gini Wijnaldum; all playing top-level, top-flight and/or international football in their teens, with many also racking up a string of U21 caps for their countries (although some largely bypassed that level to go straight into the senior team). A lot were playing at a high level aged 17.

Both sets of players contain men key to Liverpool's ambitions in recent seasons – and indeed, future ambitions – but also contain plenty of fringe players. If anything, you'd probably say that the group containing Salah, Firmino, Mané, van Dijk, Alisson, Fabinho and Robertson would be more vital to the Reds than the generally (but not exclusively) more workmanlike selection that includes Milner and Henderson, but where, equally, those players are not to be underrated.

But why have those players in the first group improved so markedly? They were certainly well behind the second group at the age of 19 or 20 in terms of career progress and experience. If ability was a fixed concept, then they would never have become what most people would label 'world-class' players. In March, former Manchester United and Everton defender Phil Neville called Andy Robertson "the best left-back in Europe". Claude Puel and Mats Hummels were just two of the voices labelling Van Dijk the best centre-back in the world prior to the end of the season, at which point the consensus spread; as of March, van Dijk the defender hadn't lost an aerial duel at Anfield in *months*. Despite almost managing it in the Champions League final, Son Heung-min failed to become the first player in 64 Liverpool games to dribble past the giant Dutchman; as noted in *The Times*, each of the other centre-backs on the pitch had been dribbled past 20-30 times that season alone.

And that's before getting onto the accolades accumulated by Salah, in particular, but also the growing admiration for Mané and Firmino.

Daniel Sturridge's career has stalled mainly due to physical issues, but the rest of the early bloomers don't appear to be hampered by long-term issues beyond a current injury layoff. Divock Origi saw injury halt his own progress in 2016, but unlike Sturridge – whose pace never resurfaced – he returned to his peak physical condition but, due to a spell on the sidelines, had lost his place in the team to new arrivals, and then went out on loan (although he has recently revived his career in spectacular fashion as a Liverpool sub/stand-in). It would be wrong to say that the early-bloomers lack hunger on the whole, especially when you look at what Milner, Henderson and Wijnaldum give in terms of professionalism and kilometres covered in the later stages of their careers. But Xherdan Shaqiri's career hasn't quite lived up to the early promise – although it's still been full of success – and Alberto Moreno certainly didn't build on the bright beginnings of a career he had with Sevilla, which ultimately led to him leaving Liverpool this summer.

Sturridge is perhaps one of the most interesting examples, not least because his justification of his delight at winning the Champions League – with seven appearances in the competition on the way to Madrid (before remaining an unused sub) – highlighted the importance of squad harmony, the role squad-men play, but also, in its way, the social multiplier effect.

"I contributed and even the players who haven't played a minute [did so too]. There are guys who have been on the bench and haven't played a single minute but have been a part of it: from training, to acting like the opposition that we have been playing against, to doing a job, to sacrificing themselves and the way they play just to do a job on the training field."

Virgil van Dijk has spent the last 18 months defending against Sturridge's sharp and clever turns in training; Alisson the past 10 months trying to save his shots. Younger players – as pointed out by Klopp, when saying farewell to the striker – were taken under Sturridge's wing; Rhian Brewster will have learnt from the man he may essentially replace in the match-day squad next season.

For all the benefits of elite coaching and the social multiplier effect in training, some players will lose a bit of confidence and maybe, in some cases, some hunger as the years unfold; while the accumulation of injuries – or one serious snap of tendon or bone – derail others.

But those who do improve will often do so by being surrounded by better players. While some players will be too intimidated to play alongside the biggest names (going back to the 1980s, Michael Robinson admitted he felt something of a fraud to be at Liverpool), those who can handle the pressure will be raised to a new level, if they have better luck than Sturridge and avoid serious injuries, while retaining their focus.

The Flynn Effect

In 1998, New Zealander James R. Flynn, an Emeritus Professor of Political Studies at the University of Otago, noted that the IQs of certain societies improve due to the way knowledge is shared, and which was duly dubbed The Flynn Effect.

This has essentially become the basis for what's also known as the social multiplier effect.

An example Flynn used in his work related to basketball, and how the sport changed rapidly with the onset of regular televised games. It led to an increase in kids playing the sport, and of course, they would try to emulate what they were seeing on television. As Angela Duckworth notes in her excellent book *Grit: Why Passion And Resilience Are The Secrets To Success*, "The kids started trying left-handed layups, crossover dribbles, graceful hook shots, and other skills that were routine for the star players on TV".

As each individual improved, so did those they played with and against. But – crucially – the greater the challenge, the greater the improvement; playing with those who are exclusively worse than you may help those players to raise their quality, but it will not help you raise yours. To play against better and/or older players as a youngster can often speed development.

Let me take you back to Klopp's Dortmund, via Raphael Honigstein's essential biography of the manager, *Bring the Noise* (which will surely be even better with an update after the season the Reds have just had), in which the author speaks to Klopp's erstwhile centre-back prodigy Neven Subotić, who followed the German from Mainz to Dortmund.

"In the first year, it was rather normal football," Subotić told Honigstein, "with a pinch of Klopp tactics. In the second year, it got spicier. In the third year: boom! We reached a whole new level, because all twenty-five players now truly got it. Training felt like war. The starting eleven playing v subs. By the middle of the week, you sort of knew the line-ups. You can't imagine how difficult these games were. You were used to having a bit of space and air to breathe but that was all gone. Everyone attacked the ball, everyone defended. Everyone pressed. These games were as hard as the real ones, perhaps even harder."

While a lot has been made over the years of the 10,000-hour rule – the time it apparently takes when practicing to become an expert or elite athlete – the rule only really applies to *testing* training. As soon as anyone stays within their comfort zone they stop improving.

In Germany Klopp refused to take players who admitted they'd happily coast through training if they believed they could bang in a couple of goals at the weekend. Klopp simply wasn't interested; it was non-negotiable. And when applied to the Flynn/social multiplier effect, he is right; after all, *how does that improve everyone else?* Yes, they may score goals for the team on the weekend, but not only are they providing a bad attitude, they are not contributing to the overall expansion of abilities that takes place *between* games. And they are not *improving themselves*.

When scouting players, Klopp and his assistants have always insisted on a "no dickheads" policy; an approach that may have helped Liverpool avoid some obvious mistakes between 2007 and 2016. Players like Mario Balotelli (£40.6m) and Lazar Marković (£50.2m) – both of whom were known to be poor trainers – and someone like Mamadou Sakho (£51.1m), who had plenty of off-field disciplinary issues from his time in France (a bit like Balotelli in various countries) – may have been avoided. Sakho was a good – if not *sensational* – player at Liverpool, but Klopp lost patience with the Frenchman over a series of misdemeanours.

Indeed, this is perhaps where the transfer committee probably needed Klopp's extra input – to look much more deeply beyond the numbers and into the players' mentality and commitment. Which isn't to say scouting players' personalities wasn't part of the process – it very much is – but it seemed more hit-and-miss in the past, with a few undesirables slipping through the net. With 14 years' experience as a manager in Germany, and his own unique way of dealing with people, Klopp is perhaps the ideal gatekeeper at the end of the process to decide who has what it takes, *as a person*, to play for his team. (It seems that when he met Virgil van Dijk in Blackpool in 2017, as alleged by Southampton, both player and manager knew they were right for one another, and the move happened six months later.) And of course, Klopp has to feel he can get on with the players, who become part of a family-like setup.

Xherdan Shaqiri is another example, where the insider knowledge of the ex-Bayern staff attested to his excellent character, which was in stark contrast to the public persona – driven largely by British players who seemed to be shifting the blame for Stoke's relegation. Like Sturridge, Oxlade-Chamberlain and others who must have been frustrated at not getting on in the final, his delirium in the post-match celebrations showed that he has fully bought in to the group ethic; indeed, all season long he was one of the most enthusiastic celebrators of goals, on the pitch and on the subs' bench. "I'm at Liverpool FC, the best club in Europe," Shaqiri told *Goal* after the final. "The manager has many good options and has to decide who can play. I knew before my transfer that the competition here is very tough. I have a long-term contract and I definitely will stay."

As such, he has been a dream signing.

The manager is also the person who has to deal with the players *after* they are signed. The analytics team can scout and identify talent, with video clips, statistics, as well as being in the stands at games, but they cannot go to the training ground every day to drill the players on tactics and fitness, nor can they give them motivational or calming pep-talks in the changing rooms before kick-off and at half-time. They can't speak to players to assess injuries, or deal with issues in their personal lives. The talent they identify is vital; but it succeeds or fails *due to the manager*. The manager, in turn, cannot get anywhere remotely close to identifying and analysing enough players, in detail, in a global market.

Klopp's assistant, Peter Krawietz, told Honigstein that the coaching staff insisted on an informal but binding contract between all the players: everyone must do their share of the work and close down as demanded. First, because it doesn't work as well if only one man presses (it's easy to bypass), and second, because everyone is equal. No one is too good to do his share.

Rodgers' overall issue with his own transfer demands was less about signing 'dickheads', and simply just not signing players who were good enough – and/or who couldn't be sufficiently improved; looking too narrowly at the pool of players he had previously worked with, and those from within the Premier League. Indeed, Christian Benteke could represent the classic mistake of a manager buying someone who terrorises his own team, when that sample size is not representative of what the player achieved on the whole. (Obviously Benteke had scored goals against other teams, but Liverpool were his favourite opponents, it seemed. Equally, Benteke's best form came before an achilles tendon rupture in April 2014, which perhaps robbed him of some of his pace, as can happen with such injuries; John Barnes, for instance, was never the same player after the injury to his in 1991. Arguably Liverpool were not buying the Benteke who scored 23 goals in 2012/13, but the one who topped out at only 10-15 after that point, and whose best international stats were from 2012, two years prior to the injury. Indeed, there were also question marks from Belgium before his move to Merseyside about his mentality, and if he had enough self-belief.) It seems that there was no great imagination in Rodgers' transfer policy; it felt too insular and uninspiring – certainly by *elite* standards.

Another factor Klopp and his team look for is versatility. While van Dijk plays purely as a centre-back on the team sheet, he can move into midfield with the ball, and in the opposition box can score goals that a lot of centre-forwards would be proud of (he has scored ten goals for club and country since the end of March 2018, as he starts to bang them in for Holland and Liverpool, having taken ages to get going; at the time of writing – just ahead of the Nations League finals – he has four goals in his last seven games for the Dutch). Andy Robertson essentially plays as a winger *who sometimes has to defend*. Fabinho started life as a right-back, but has all the tools to deputise at centre-back, which is what he did with such aplomb against Bayern Munich at home in the Champions League. Both Mané and Salah played games this season at centre-forward, as well as in wide positions. Oxlade-Chamberlain has been a forward, a winger and a midfielder, as well as a wing-back at Arsenal (which suggests he could ably deputise at right-back in the future). Meanwhile, across his career, Gini Wijnaldum has played almost *everywhere*: as a winger, second-striker, midfielder and even in a back-three away at Brighton in 2017/18; most often playing for Klopp as a possession-retaining midfielder who, at the age of 28, has scored over 100 goals – which is something you won't see from the likes of an expert holding midfielder like N'Golo Kanté (19 career goals to date, aged 27). In Germany, Matip sometimes played as a defensive midfielder, and is superb at bringing the ball out from the back, and his calm pass to Divock Origi in the final (his first assist for Liverpool) showed his quality. Even Alisson wouldn't look out of place as an outfield player.

Indeed, almost every player Klopp and Edwards as a team have signed has spent some time as a midfielder in their career – whether they now play up front or in defence – to fit with the notion that the midfielder, while not necessarily the most *gifted*, often has to be the most rounded of players. Logically, a midfielder has to be able to do *some* defending and *some* attacking, even if they are better at one than the other.

As well as this versatility enabling the team to be more fluid during games, it also means that these signings get additional chances to get into the team; Fabinho, for instance, can be trusted at centre-back in a big Champions League game during an injury crisis, ahead of a youngster without any first-team experience, who may not be ready; and Wijnaldum can fit in so many different positions that he might be preferred over a more one-dimensional specialist.

Squad Harmony

It isn't just about buying players who will fit in with the squad ethos – no outsized egos need apply – but also the way a team harmonises *over time*.

For well over a decade, I've been talking about what I call Shaun Wright-Phillips Syndrome, where a player is taken out of one comfortable environment (where he has had time to grow and develop, in stages, without any intense pressure) and put into an uncomfortable one – in his case, complete with massive price tag at Chelsea – and he looks a totally different player. I may not be the first to have made this observation, but it's interesting that the influential author Malcolm Gladwell is now focusing on this phenomenon, albeit with a different sport as an example. In a 2018 interview with organisational psychologist Adam Grant, which appeared on both men's podcasts, Gladwell discussed the issue of 'fit' – as in *suitability*, rather than physical fitness.

"I wanted to talk about basketball," Gladwell told Grant, "because right now the NBA is a lovely little case study in 'fit'. To backtrack, the intuitive position on basketball is that it's the sport where talent matters the most and coaching matters the least. If you put LeBron [James] on a team of also-rans you can basically guarantee you make the play-offs; in fact, he has made the final at times with *teams* of also-rans.

"It doesn't really matter who is with LeBron, you can put a bunch of stiffs with him and it's fine, right? In fact, the two greatest basketball teams of all-time: the mid-'90s Chicago Bulls – who had three superstars and then two very ordinary players with the fifth guy being a slow, white guy from Australia; and if you look at the Warriors of two years ago they had three superstars, two ordinary players and the fifth was a slow, lumbering white guy from Australia.

"What's happening now in basketball is a few instances of going against that. One is: this season one of the best guards in the game, Victor Oladipo, was considered a disaster, and by [him] simply moving teams, to a better environment, with a different coach, he's gone from being considered as a bust … into suddenly a superstar who is playing transcendently.

"The reverse is also true: the best coach in the league is probably Brad Stevens of the Boston Celtics and every time a very promising player from the Celtics is traded away, they turn out to be terrible.

"Jae Crowder is a good example because when he left them everyone was 'Oh god, they traded Crowder, I don't know if they can survive without him' and yet he moves to the Cavaliers and then people realise 'Oh, Jay Crowder isn't that good, he just was good on Boston.'

"Is this always true in basketball? I don't know. But certainly at this moment it feels very, very coach-dependent. And once you've seen a few examples, you start to wonder how many players on basketball teams – who we consider mediocre – are actually really good but just in the wrong environment. Is Victor Oladipo the exception or is he part of a larger trend? I'm increasingly of the opinion that there must be many more Oladipos."

In reply, Grant said: "I think there are, and not just in basketball. So it makes me think of a study of cardiac surgeons where you track their performance across the day and the question is: how many surgeries do they have to perform with minimally invasive robot technology to the point where they are up the learning curve? Practice has no effect whatsoever in this context, they are as deadly on number 100 and 1,000 as they were on number one. This is weird right? Because we are supposed to learn from experience. And so what [Robert] Huckman and [Gary] Pisano did was break down the data by which hospital they were performing surgery and they said: what is the difference in results and practice between Hospital A and Hospital B? And they found that surgeries were hospital-specific, so that every surgery performed at Hospital A reduced the patient mortality rate by about 1% but then later that afternoon the surgeon would go and perform in Hospital B and it's like they are starting over and have none of the experience – and the reason for different performances is the different team who knows my strengths and weaknesses who have developed a set of effective routines. That kind of suggests that performance, skill and expertise is team-specific and context-specific. You see the same thing in financial services companies."

Grant continued: "… over 75% of airline accidents happen the first time a crew flies together; and the evidence goes so far on this that NASA did a simulation showing that if you a had a crew that was well rested and flying together for the first time they made more errors than a sleep-deprived crew who had just pulled an all-nighter but flown together before."

But the benefits of being a settled team has limits, too.

Grant: "The other challenge which in some ways is bigger, is *too much* shared experience, so in the NBA teams max-out on probability of success around three or four years together and then once they have more than four years of shared experience their odds of winning go down."

In the summer of 2018, when previewing the new season, I wrote on *The Tomkins Times* that: "My guess at Liverpool's best XI this season (if everyone plays as expected), if not necessarily my *preferred* side, would have the following full years spent at the club or full seasons in the first-team setup: Alisson (0), Alexander-Arnold (1), Lovren (4), Van Dijk (0.5), Robertson (1), Fabinho (0), Henderson (7), Keïta (0), Mané (2), Salah (1) and Firmino (3).

"That's an average of just 1.8 seasons at the club. It could be seen as a concern in some ways, in that it's not a lot of time to get bonded and onto each other's wavelengths, but one thing Klopp has done at Liverpool is to quickly integrate players, and to create a unified mentality. Indeed, it's been a defining characteristic: specific new signings slipping seamlessly into the team (while others have a bedding-in period), although my theory on the success of this is that, allied to excellent scouting and analytics – as well as Klopp's ability to know what he wants (and convey that to the player) – there's also not been a great deal of churn at any one single moment in time [in recent seasons].

"Liverpool added four players in the summer of 2017 (and one in January 2018), and so far, just four players this summer. But as I noted last week, only Mo Salah went straight into the team last summer, while Andrew Robertson, Alex Oxlade-Chamberlain and Dominic Solanke were gradually phased in; and only after that, Virgil van Dijk went straight into the XI. It seems that of the four new buys, only Alisson Becker and Naby Keïta are certainties for the XI in the early part of the season.

"Added to the low average age – albeit rising by one year on 2017/18, given that most of the team remains the same (and the replacements are mostly mid-20s) – the lack of 'team boredom' (or, that this is the *start* of a cycle, not the end) suggests that if things go well this season, this could only be the beginning.

"The rest of the squad has, on average, had a longer average period at the club than the probable "best" XI: 2.3 years versus 1.8, and an average age of 26 versus 25.6. The average for the Premier League champions is 26.8, with seven having an average age between 25 and 26. (City in 2017/18 being the 2nd-youngest yet; oddly, Mourinho's 2004/05 team remain the youngest champions – which is strange given his current penchant for older players.)"

If anything, the team performed even better than I expected in 2018/19; with my thoughts a year ago that 90 points would perhaps be the upper limit, especially if there was another long run in the Champions League. To end up with 97 points when reaching – and then winning – the Champions League final is well beyond what I thought possible. It's up there with the greatest seasons in English football history, as a whole.

In 2018/19 there was a clear distinction between Man City and Liverpool in terms of how long the teams had been together. Going into the final weeks of the season, City had 19 players who had played over 700 minutes in the Premier League, whereas Liverpool had just

15. The average time spent at the club for those 19 City players, as the season drew to an end, was 3.9 years; for Liverpool's 15, it was just 2.8. What's fascinating is that the five senior Liverpool players who played fewer than 700 minutes – and at that point Adam Lallana, with just 465 minutes, was top of this group – had almost six years at Liverpool (5.6), with Nathaniel Clyne, who was loaned out in the second half of the season, a sixth player (in his case, he had four years at the club, and played less than 200 minutes this season before being loaned out).

Lallana, Sturridge, Origi, Alberto Moreno, Simon Mignolet and Clyne were all inherited by Klopp, and all featured heavily in his first season; but these were gradually "weeded out" of the XI, as it were, when better players were bought or when their powers began to wane. The only long-serving player in Liverpool's top 15 appearance-makers (in terms of minutes played in 2018/19) was Jordan Henderson, completing his 8th full season. Contrast that to Man City: in the top eight appearance makers for the club were Fernandinho, Raheem Sterling, David Silva and Sergio Agüero, with a combined seven year average at the Etihad; while Vincent Kompany, with eleven seasons at City, was able to play as many minutes as Lallana and Sturridge combined – despite ranking 18th on City's appearance list – when Lallana and Sturridge ranked 16th and 17th on Liverpool's. (And how vital was Kompany's experience in the run-in?)

This all shows that Pep Guardiola was able to rotate more than Klopp, because his squad was that bit deeper at the edges. And he was able to call on more experience – City's average age going into the final week of the season was 27.2 (the 9th-oldest team in the Premier League, identical to Spurs), compared with Liverpool's 26.5 (which ranked 16th) – but City, like Spurs, had a far longer-established "fit".

What does this mean for the future? Well, given that Fernandinho, Kompany, David Silva, Agüero and Nicolás Otamendi will be aged between 31 and 34 next season, you'd expect some serious melting, and maybe some retirement. (Indeed, Kompany has now moved back to Belgium to manage Anderlecht.) Three of these players were amongst City's top-eight most used (four from the top-13 used), and two of them comprise half of their centre-back options.

City will obviously hope to see more of the injury-prone Kevin de Bruyne and Benjamin Mendy in 2019/20 than in 2018/19, and several of their key creative and attacking players are still under 25 – Sterling, Bernardo Silva, Gabriel Jesus, Leroy Sané (albeit linked with an exit) and the emerging but not-quite-yet-proven Phil Foden – and Riyad Mahrez is still young enough to have a few seasons left, aged 28. Also aged 28 when the season starts will be de Bruyne. But

Fernandinho, Kompany, David Silva, Agüero and Otamendi may take some replacing, as senior players who have been at the club a long time, and whose leadership was called upon in the face of the stern test Liverpool applied. While City's team has evolved over the years, it is now at the upper limit of the four-year "fit" rule, and several key players are in the twilight of their careers. They will have to spend money, and spend it wisely – and hope that the new signings hit the ground running – to compensate for the stars who are surely on their last legs. It's unlike that they will collapse in 2019/20, but the first part of the season may be a test, and if it's a tight title-race they won't have all of the established old guard to call upon.

This could lead to dropping points, in the way that Liverpool would probably have got a better result at Arsenal, in particular, earlier in 2018/19, but also away at Chelsea and home to Man City (and perhaps away), had Fabinho been up to speed. It was only really in the second half of the season that he became a real force.

To put this into context, Fabinho's presence in the team made a significant difference to the Reds' Premier League results. While 'with or without' stats may be something Bono of U2 likes to think about, they're not always the most reliable, due to small sample sizes; and can be skewed if a player only features in the easier or tougher games. However, in the 28 league games in which Fabinho featured, the Reds' points per game would extrapolate to 100 points over a 38-game season. More startling is the fact that, including only his 21 *starts*, the pro-rata points tally would be *an absolutely staggering 103*. He started against Arsenal home and away, Chelsea (home), Manchester United home and away, Tottenham (home) and Everton home and away; so it wasn't a case of only starting the easier games.

Indeed, across the 12 "toughest" games – the Big Six, plus the derbies – Liverpool won 2.25 points per game with Fabinho in the starting XI, and just 1.25ppg when he wasn't; with those four earlier games falling between September and January (Spurs away, City at home, Chelsea away and City away), when he was still acclimatising. Perhaps those four games are more difficult on paper than the aforementioned eight tough games he started, but the sense is that, had he been integrated at that earlier stage, with the form from once he got used to the English game (and Liverpool's tactics), results could have been *even better*. And of course, he played against Spurs in the final and helped keep them at bay. Ditto Naby Keïta, whose best form came in the final month of the season, before a serious groin injury curtailed his clear progress; and who again, wasn't on the losing side for Liverpool in the league.

By contrast to City's age concerns, Liverpool have few such worries – and also have their own returning stars. Both Alex Oxlade-Chamberlain and highly-rated young striker Rhian Brewster effectively missed almost every minute of the season, while Joe Gomez's leg was broken at Burnley in December when he'd been arguably the Reds' best defender up to that point; the team conceding just six goals in the 15 league games up to his injury, and 14 in the 23 that followed – so, from conceding a goal, on average, in just a third of games, to conceding an average of a goal in almost two-thirds of games (which is still admittedly impressive).

Aside from the evergreen James Milner, no Liverpool player who played more than 500 minutes in 2018/19 was in his 30s; and as of the start of 2019/20, only Dejan Lovren from the current squad, should he still be at the club, is set to join that list; and he ranked 15th (and last), in the list of those who played 700 or more minutes. Lovren starred in the previous Champions League final, but is arguably Liverpool's 4th-choice centre-back now, in part due to persistent injuries and bouts of illness.

In March 2019, after eliminating Bayern Munich, Jürgen Klopp expressed his desire to keep the team together; not to sell key assets, but also, not to generate more churn. "I don't want to talk exactly what we will do, but I don't think this is a team at the moment where we have to spend the big money, or whatever … The best way to do it is bring together a group of players, try to develop them all together and then stay together for a while. And that was maybe the main problem of Liverpool for the last decade. When they had a good team after a season they went all over the world. That will not happen this year for sure."

With the age of all *key* players bar James Milner under the age of 30 – and often *well under* 30 – there's no need to be replacing ageing legs, and vitally, there are no key players nearing the end of their contracts. This is another area where Michael Edwards has been sharp, with talk of a year added to Oxlade-Chamberlain's deal to replace the year he lost to injury. (While it was confirmed to me as club policy to not let any promising youngsters go out on loan unless they are tied to a longer deal.) Emre Can remains the only first-XI player to "get away" on a Bosman deal in recent times; while fringe players, with low sell-on values, are kept to the end of their deals and then happily released.

And so there will certainly be some *squad* players who leave the club in the summer, due to contracts expiring, or departing in the search for regular first-team football; with players like, Lallana and Origi seemingly uncertain of their futures at the time of writing, although the latter is reported to have been offered a new contract; while Sturridge and Moreno have been released at the end of their contracts.

In some ways it could be a problem to lose *all* these players, as the best ways to create "squad players" is often to buy better first-XI players, and then the back-ups are already established at the club, and often eager to try and win their places back; new players who don't get to play very often may struggle to feel integrated, and they offer none of the "fit" that pre-existing players naturally bring. But there are no hard and fast rules.

However, some of these will probably be replaced by players already at – or owned by – the club: Rhian Brewster, Harry Wilson and Marko Grujić being the standout contenders for promotion to become squad players (unless they want to leave for regular football), while Kamil Grabara or Caoimhin Kelleher may usurp Simon Mignolet. These existing players do not need to adjust to Liverpool Football Club, the area, culture or the language; albeit Grujić has spent the last year on loan in Germany, and Grabara on loan in Denmark (but both these European-born players have spent at least two years on Merseyside, and have sufficient experience of English football, if not necessarily the Premier League).

Other youngsters may make a quick burst of progress, and find themselves in the senior ranks on a regular basis, with Rafa Camacho, Ki-Jana Hoever and Curtis Jones three teenagers already to have played for the first team, while Adam Lewis is an impressive left-footed player tipped for a bright future. There's also the two young centre-forwards, Bobby Duncan and Paul Glatzel, each of whom bagged more than 20 goals in U18s football; but like Ovie Ejaria and Harry Wilson, these may all need a year or two on loan to finish their footballing educations, given that Under 23 football is not as testing as it should be. Others, such as Ben Woodburn and Sheyi Ojo, seem to have fallen off the radar a little (Ojo not really making an impact out on loan in France, Woodburn returning early from an unsuccessful loan at Sheffield United), but 22 seems to remain the magic age for a young footballer to be *finally* judged; even if any player can of course continue to improve thereafter. By 22 they should be sufficiently physically developed – to have "filled out" – and it's also the first time when all areas of the brain are at full adult maturity. (Recent research has shown that the prefrontal cortex – the region that has deals with planning complex cognitive behaviour, personality expression, decision making and moderating social behaviour – is not fully developed until the age of 21. Which is why so many teenagers make bad decisions.)

Woodburn is still only 19, and at the same age players like Paul Scholes and David Beckham were not in the Man United first team, as usually it's only the super-quick and/or athletic youngsters who break through earlier. Even Harry Wilson was 20/21 when he first started making waves on loan at Hull, before establishing himself as a top Championship player with Derby County; his prior loans far less successful.

Liverpool's policy is make sure any promising youngsters going out on a developmental loan are tied to long-term deals; if they want to taste regular first-team football at a slightly lower level they will be allowed to do so, but there's no point in watching them become a sensation only to then be free to leave at the end of it, or a year later. A small detail, perhaps – but obvious, and logical, and yet such clear thinking is not always present at big football clubs.

Joined-Up Thinking

So Liverpool's transfer success of the past three or four seasons could be put down to a mix of several factors: elite scouting, including analytics but also checks on mentality, especially to exclude "dickheads"; focusing on players at a good age, with plenty of hunger – and stamina – remaining, and no one purchased simply for past glories; a refusal to overpay for, or overstock on, British signings – but where Premier League experience is often helpful in terms of the speed at which a player is integrated; a refusal to rush everyone into the side, which can create a team on totally different wavelengths; a culture that improves players once they arrive; and in the case of Virgil van Dijk, a refusal to compromise with far inferior alternatives when the centre-back had his heart set on joining Klopp at Liverpool, despite everyone saying that it was absolutely crazy not to sign a different defender in the summer of 2017 when the deal originally fell through.

After the scattergun and at times reckless approaches in several seasons between 2007 and 2016, this has to be a core reason why Liverpool became challengers for the Champions League and Premier League crowns.

Indeed, how Liverpool operate now – aside from the different nationalities involved – is very similar to how Bob Paisley turned the Reds into the best team in Europe in the late 1970s: not too much player churn; few signings over the age of 24, and no "superstars" signed; not *automatically* throwing everyone into the first team, unless they were too outstanding to ignore; and finding hungry players who could develop and improve as part of a dynamic, competitive squad.

Then, as now, Liverpool know *exactly* what they are doing.

Unravelling? The Mildest of Slumps

Having managed to get eliminated from all domestic cups to good Premier League opposition – which felt like a good thing, given the injuries and fixture congestion other teams were experiencing (and the tough draws handed to Klopp in the past two seasons) – Liverpool chose to take a warm-weather break to Dubai; an obvious solution at the time of year. Unfortunately it seems to have backfired in spectacular fashion.

It wasn't widely reported that the trip was allegedly cut short a day early, as several players went down with food poisoning; those believed to be affected were Virgil van Dijk, Fabinho, James Milner, Simon Mignolet and Andy Robertson, with assistant manager Pep Lijnders also taken ill. Reserve keeper aside, all of the players looked well short of their best in the two games that followed, and three formed the defence against West Ham.

The sense of *force majeure* was carried back to England where, half an hour before the kick-off against Leicester, an almighty hail storm, in addition to snow, turned the pitch into a mix of unmelted ice and patches of waterlogged, sludgy grass where the ball held up; destroying the Reds' passing rhythm.

Already carrying several injuries in the defence, at the time of the West Ham game days later players were *still* ill or recovering from the upset; Milner had to travel to London by train, away from the rest of the squad, and Klopp admitted that van Dijk had "lost three or four kilos" in the past week. To make matters worse, the Reds trained with one midfield and then, on the eve of the match, lost Jordan Henderson and Gini Wijnaldum to short-term injuries; and so, at the last minute, the formation had to be changed. "There would have been three different players in the team," the manager admitted.

Presumably Fabinho (left out against Leicester due to the bug) and Milner would have been omitted, but the injuries meant those unwell simply had to play. In the end, three of the Reds' back four were victims of the gastric catastrophe.

In came Adam Lallana, to join Fabinho and Naby Keïta in the middle of the park. At times it looked like three strangers in midfield at the London Stadium, and that's essentially what they were six months earlier, with Lallana also a relative stranger to first-team football since May 2017. Lallana had a hand in the Reds' goal – Milner a yard offside when receiving the ball to set up Mané – but often looked understandably off the pace, and Fabinho, already unwell, struggled in the different system. Keïta was caught out defensively at times, but was majestic in his forward running and probing with the ball; almost a coming-of-age performance from the Guinean, to follow a similarly impressive showing away at Burnley.

The "blip" began against Leicester at home, albeit without people realising the illness decimating the Reds' squad. A blistering start lit up a pitch that looked positively post-blizzard – but where, aside from light snowfall, it was actually a heavy hailstorm that failed to melt on the under-heated soil. Sadio Mané – a player who grew up in the opposite climate, but one where the pitches are hard and awkward for a different reason – was dancing across the surface, and lashed the Reds ahead early on, but everyone else looked spooked.

"You saw that the ball didn't roll really," said Klopp. "If you then have the ball pretty much for 70 to 80% of the time it makes life really uncomfortable. The only problem is if it [the snow] stays on the pitch, and that was actually the case."

At half-time the ground-staff cleared the final third of the pitch at the Kop end, because Klopp wanted slicker passing, with the ball holding up on the icy surface at the other end; but it seemed odd in that it left Leicester defending on a better surface, reducing the likelihood of a slip, or a stray back-pass or kick-out. In the end Liverpool created next to nothing on the slicker surface – bar a clear penalty appeal and a fine shot by Firmino – while at the other end Leicester were having a reasonable amount of joy on the slippery ground, as Liverpool's defenders struggled for their footing. (Of course, had Mo Salah been in on goal in the second half and slipped on the ice – had that end not been cleared – we could bemoan not removing the slippery covering.)

It all started so well. Sadio Mané collected the ball on the two-minute mark, and with Leicester having had only one single touch of the ball in those 120 seconds, produced an incredible feint-and-swerve to bamboozle the last defender, before tucking a firm shot under Kasper Schmeichel; the Reds' quickest league goal in almost three years (although a much faster goal still awaited in the months ahead).

Roberto Firmino went close seconds later, with a sharp turn and shot, before Mané sent a free header from a corner wide. And then ... not a lot else, against a Leicester side with a very good away record, a propensity for upsetting better teams, and a lot of raw pace, with no injuries or suspensions. Claude Puel had shut down Liverpool on half a dozen previous occasions, and yet again he worked that organisational magic.

As had Man City the previous night at Newcastle, Liverpool took an early lead, looked like racking up a cricket score, then lost their way. Unlike City the Reds didn't concede a second goal, but it was a frustrating, increasingly nervy night at Anfield.

Perhaps some of the Reds' woes can be traced back to the Crystal Palace game, where the defence – missing Trent Alexander-Arnold, Dejan Lovren and Joe Gomez, and with Joël Matip rusty after his broken collarbone – was unusually shaky. Liverpool won 4-3, but it was not a comfortable night. It could explain a little bit of the loss of defensive composure, after so many clean sheets. (And then came the illness issues.)

The Palace game was clearly the most exciting in a long while, in terms of the number of goals both teams scored, and the lateness of much of the drama. Andros Townsend put the visitors ahead, mere seconds after he handled the ball in his own area; the referee missed it, and Liverpool were left to rue the decision. The equaliser, after half-time, came from a speculative Virgil van Dijk shot – which, with echoes of earlier games, deflected to a Liverpool player; this time it was Mo Salah, who saw the ball coming down from the sky and onto his right foot. Perhaps it's a weakness of Salah's that he wasn't keen to volley it with his weaker foot, but the way he turned his back to the goal so that it now fell on his left foot was a moment of genius – as was the way he gently hooked the ball into the bottom corner of the net. There was no way for the Palace keeper, Julián Speroni, to know what Salah was going to do, as it's hard to recall ever seeing a finish quite like it; although had the Egyptian missed, you'd have had to ask why he didn't do the simple thing and just attempt any kind of volley with his right foot. Next Roberto Firmino turned and scooped a shot that deflected past Speroni and into the net. Yet the lead didn't last. Palace then scored from a corner where they set out to foul Liverpool players, but Liverpool could not be kept at bay for long; Fabinho sending a glorious cross-field pass to James Milner, who managed to a hook a cross into the danger area. As with Jordan Pickford, Speroni only made the situation worse by tipping the ball *backwards*, towards his own goalline, where Mo Salah helped it home. Milner was then correctly sent off after two yellow-card tackles on Wilfried Zaha; the referee, Jon Moss, his old P.E. teacher.

The win was sealed from yet another move starting with a smart Alisson throw, which Andy Robertson collected in the Palace half. As the ball came back to Robertson from Mané the Palace players bizarrely claimed a handball. With possession once again switching from Robertson to Mané, the Senegalese raced through and slotted past

Speroni and into the far corner. It was only much later that replays spotted Robertson had indeed handled the ball to stop it going out of play. Max Meyer side-footed home a late third for Palace, to make for a slightly nervy final minute or so, which involved emergency teenage right-back Rafael Camacho, on as a late sub for his league debut, to block in the area.

It was more like the early years under Klopp; the chaotic football. Speaking after the game he said: "Somebody asked me already what was the main feeling or emotion after the final whistle and it was relief. A game like this can go in all directions. We were extremely dominant in the first half, but we were 1-0 down. We created chances but not enough, maybe not clear enough. We didn't have enough players in the decisive areas, we had a lot of players in the preparing areas. That can happen of course, so at half-time it was clear we had to change that – we needed players in the decisive areas, more bodies in the box and all that stuff. Thank God it worked pretty well immediately. We forced these two goals to come back and everyone felt the atmosphere. Then, obviously it was not 100 per cent clear for the boys: do we control it now or do we still chase the game or whatever?

At West Ham, Sadio Mané – setting up a theme for the rest of the season – opened the scoring for the second game running – again with great footwork and a cool finish – only for the Reds to be pegged back to 1-1. In early December it was Mo Salah banging in the goals; late December it was Roberto Firmino; and from January into early February it was Mané.

But Liverpool let the lead slip, with a finely worked West Ham free-kick drawing the sides level.

After a routine 3-0 victory over Bournemouth at Anfield – memorable for a sublime Gini Wijnaldum lob – the Reds were back in action in Europe, facing the mighty Bayern Munich, who had been nine points off the pace in the Bundesliga when the draw was made in December, but were now closing the gap on Klopp's old club, Borussia Dortmund. To make matters worse for the first-leg home tie, the Reds were without the suspended Virgil van Dijk, who would otherwise play every single Premier League and Champions League game. With others out injured, it was left to Fabinho to make his first ever professional start as a centre-back, against the ruthless Robert Lewandowski (who months later would complete his fourth consecutive 40-goal season at Bayern). However, given his height, and his usual positions – holding midfielder at club-level and right-back for Brazil – it seems logical to triangulate the positioning required, and to be able to hold an offside line, than for those not used to any kind of defensive role. And so it proved: the Brazilian was excellent, and although Bayern were thought to have done well with a 0-0 draw, they were lacking that vital away goal.

Lewandowski had already moved to Bayern by the time his old team, Dortmund, arrived at Anfield in 2016, for the first of Klopp's famous European nights in front of the Kop. On that occasion the Reds had gained a 1-1 draw in Germany, but within nine minutes were 2-0 down to the yellow swarm. The Reds pulled a goal back through Divock Origi – a talisman if ever there was one – but Marco Reus made it 3-1. Liverpool looked dead and buried, needing three goals with just over 30 minutes to play, with two goals not enough due to the away goals rule; and they duly arrived, from Philippe Coutinho, Mamadou Sakho and, in injury time, Dejan Lovren.

It was one of the cornerstones for the building of this new Liverpool bastion: even though, from that team, Roberto Firmino was the only player who remains a first-XI regular from that side (and indeed, from the entire match-day 18), with James Milner the other starter who still features fairly regularly. That side was stripped down and rebuilt, pretty much lock, stock and barrel, but its achievements in reaching a European final against the odds – particularly when 3-1 down to Dortmund – set the wheels in motion.

Three years on, Bayern, on the back of six successive titles, were more formidable opponents than a good Dortmund side that, all the same, had in 2016 fallen from competing for Bundesliga. Bayern weren't at their very strongest, but they were expected to beat Liverpool on their own ground in the second leg. And yet, the Reds had been revitalised, indeed *revolutionised*.

While Mo Salah's excellent strike against Chelsea was voted the Reds' best goal of the season, the decision still seems a little bizarre when compared to the far more complex and wondrous goal Sadio Mané scored in the Allianz Arena in the 26th minute; yet more evidence of how English football values the wonder-strike ahead of something more intricate and almost unrepeatable.

From well inside his own half Virgil van Dijk hit a sumptuous long pass straight to Mané, who had spun away from his marker. The ball landed directly at Mané's right foot, and somehow he not only controlled the ball but *killed it dead*. There is not even a fraction of miscontrol, not a millimetre of movement beyond where he wanted the ball to be; remarkable seeing as his marker had got back into position during the flight of the pass and was applying pressure to Mané, shoulder to shoulder. Such was the control that the right-back, Rafinha, carried on running, as if it just wasn't possible to even consider the ball stopping dead; while Mané himself also came to a fairly abrupt halt, although his momentum took him into the box, with the ball still on the edge. Manuel Neuer, the Bayern keeper, came rushing out, and somehow Mané, with his back to goal as he regained the ball, had the presence of mind to sharply turn to his right, manipulating the ball with the outside of his right foot in a chopping motion. Suddenly Neuer was in no-man's land. Niklas Süle, the covering centre-back, and Rafinha, were still between Mané – at a fairly oblique angle – and the goal, with Neuer and Mats Hummels rushing back towards the line. Mané, on his left foot, dinked the finish with just enough height and just enough accuracy inside the far post, as Hummels entered the close-up frame just at the point where the ball crosses the line. The whole move was a work of art; an act of majesty, and beauty. While Salah's strike was stunning (and I was at the Kop end of the Lower Kenny Dalglish stand when that went in, to everyone's amazement), it was just one moment of brilliance. By contrast, this goal in Germany relied on a succession of perfect moments: pass, control, turn, finish.

Andy Robertson then went close to a second, before he was caught out in the space behind him, which he obviously has to vacate dozens of times each game; he can't be an attacking full-back and always be in position. As the cross was fizzed in, Lewandowski was on hand to finish, but Joël Matip, knowing he had to get a touch, could only divert it into his own net. The game had swung back Bayern's way, but Liverpool still held the crucial away goal.

Two-thirds of the way through the game, having just about defended a Trent Alexander-Arnold corner from their right, Bayern faced up to a James Milner out-swinger from the other flank. No one could get near van Dijk, however – despite two players attempting to – as the Liverpool defender, dead central and right on the six-yard box, powered his header past the helpless Neuer. Salah was then denied the Reds' third when he was fouled in the area, but he stayed on his feet and was duly tackled (which is just yet one more example of why strikers *have* to go down when they are *slowed down*).

Divock Origi, on as a late sub, then sprinted across the Bayern back-line with the ball in the 84th minute, before laying it out to Salah, whose sumptuous outside-of-the-foot cross to Mané was headed past Neuer, and the Reds were going through to the last eight. Not only that, but Mané had now confirmed the unleashing of his inner Duncan Ferguson, to become, at 5'9", the most dangerous striker in the air in English football in the final third of the season.

The Trio of Dutch Masters Taking Liverpool To New Heights

"Maybe Man City have more skill or are quicker, but they should never be superior in terms of team spirit, attitude or braveness."
— Pepijn Lijnders, 2019

Unlike AC Milan and Barcelona – and perhaps even Arsenal – Liverpool had never had a particularly notable Dutch tradition; the *Oranje* influence spreading to Catalonia in the 1970s (Johan Cruyff and Johan Neeskens, via managerial trailblazer Rinus Michels) and Milan in the 1980s (Frank Rijkaard, Marco van Basten and Ruud Gullit), before Denis Bergkamp and Marc Overmars steered Arsène Wenger's innovative Gunners to their own beautiful successes.

Of course, that is not to say that the Reds haven't had an *education* from Holland; the Ajax team of late 1966 providing Bill Shankly and Bob Paisley with much to think about – *en route* to the Reds' European successes a decade or so later – via the talents of Johan Cruyff and a sound 5-1 thrashing. (It's a little know fact that, to honour this, Adam Lallana is contractually obliged to attempt 15 Cruyff-turns per game.)

Prior to recent times there have been Dutch players at Liverpool, namely Dirk Kuyt, Ryan Babel, Sander Westerveld, Erik Meijer, Bolo Zenden, and that full-back from 2005/06 whose name always escapes me (a quick google reminds me it's Jan Kromkamp, but then somehow I seem to forget him once more. Dan Mugwump, or something?). Kuyt aside, all of those players were short-lived and/or fringe players at best.

But never before has Liverpool Football Club been driven by a Dutch coach, nor has it had as many influential figures from the Holland national team. In early 2019 it even found time to give a 16-year-old ex-Ajax prodigy, Ki-Jana Hoever, his debut, as if to prove the new direction was no passing fad.

During 2018/19, Virgil van Dijk and Gini Wijnaldum were voted by their peers at the club as the third- and- fourth-choice captains for the Reds, with Jordan Henderson and James Milner already established as captain and vice-captain; while at the start of the season, Pepijn Lijnders, at the age of 35, was appointed – upon rejoining the Reds – as one of Jürgen Klopp's two assistant managers, alongside the

German's erstwhile lieutenant Peter Krawietz. Lijnders' first spell at Liverpool – where he progressed from youth coach to a technical coach acting as a liaison between the academy and first-team setup – ended when he departed midway through 2017/18 to take up his inaugural managerial role, with Dutch second-tier club NEC Nijmegen. Five months later he was sacked; a fact that cannot be used to damn him, given that it is a fate to have befallen so many of the best managers in the world on their first tentative steps to stardom. (Of course, some great coaches may never be destined for the spotlight – and the different complexities – of *management*. But it's also probably true that any coach with complex ideas – certainly ideas that don't just repeat the orthodoxy – is not going to enjoy overnight success unless he also has a forceful personality and a ton of money and/or luck.)

By the time the Reds reached the Champions League final in May 2018, not only had Lijnders left, but Željko Buvač – Klopp's trusted no.2 for all 17 years of his management career – was gone, too.

While Buvač was officially said to have left for "personal reasons", his incredibly untimely departure – between the two Champions League semi-finals against Roma – happened to coincide with the exact moment Arsenal had approached Manchester City's no. 2, Mikel Arteta, and Manchester United's no.2, Rui Faria; the pattern *seeming* clear, but perhaps it was just smoke wafting from some *other* fires. (You tell me….) With Buvač on gardening leave (in which he presumably organised his azaleas into a 4-2-3-1 formation), Lijnders was invited to join the Liverpool group in Kiev, but the young Dutchman did not play an active role; and as such, the season effectively ended with half of Klopp's senior coaching staff absent.

While Buvač's departure initially appeared to be a body-blow – especially considering how highly Klopp rated him (and it certainly wasn't helpful *at the time*) – it allowed Liverpool to embark on a slightly new direction. Pepijn Lijnders is clearly having an influence on the more possession-based football the Reds are moving towards, without the team, and staff, losing the *gegenpressing* knowledge and muscle memory. Buvač was an excellent tactician, but both Klopp and Peter Krawietz had the same background and knowledge pool after 17 years together; if Buvač was the tactical genius *initially*, Klopp and Krawietz had to have already learnt a great deal from him. Lijnders, by contrast, brought a different style of football, coming up through the coaching ranks in Holland and spending seven years in Portugal. Lijnders is 22 years younger than Buvač, and 16 years younger than Klopp. He brought a fresh energy.

Before Buvač's departure, Klopp had hinted at the importance of Lijnders. "Željko is the brain, Pete [Krawietz] is the eye. Pep has become unbelievably important in a short time because he writes everything down, he is also part of 'the brain' because he is our mind to remember the things what we did in previous sessions. He brings us the next coaching generation. Pep is our connecting point to the present and the future."

As with Alex Ferguson at Man United, sometimes the best way to move into the future – to tweak and evolve – is to employ the next generation of elite coaches, whilst retaining all that wisdom – and that *aura* – as the figurehead, and to mesh the new ideas with existing tactical notions. It's not about following the latest trends just for the sake of it, but taking onboard new ideas, and gaining the kind of fresh perspective that a new generation of coaches will naturally provide.

Of course, there's one other key Dutchman on the staff: John Achterberg, the goalkeeping coach who – despite the highest possible Uefa coaching credentials – has garnered a lot of criticism over the years due to the various failures of Liverpool's goalkeepers, but where he can't necessarily be blamed for gaffes by players who were never at the really elite end of the spectrum to start with; and where playing for a club where the slightest mistake leads to hysteria, which makes the job much harder. Achterberg arrived at Liverpool in 2009 to work within the youth setup, and was promoted to first-team goalkeeping coach in 2011 by Kenny Dalglish, by which time Pepe Reina – the one world-class keeper the Reds had had in decades – had already started to lose heart, having seen his friends and compatriots leave the club, and also, having been forced to work with Roy Hodgson's elderly goalkeeping coach, Mike Kelly, with whom Reina did not seem to respect, and where the passing out from the back had to replaced with big punts upfield.

When Alisson Becker arrived, Klopp went all out to back Achterberg. "John is a goalkeeper maniac. He's working constantly," he told the *Liverpool Echo*. "It's so easy. All the people in the pubs think they know and understand football 100%. But if you asked them: 'What does a goalkeeper do?' They couldn't say more than 'catch balls'. They have no clue about goalkeeper techniques and all that stuff."

(Or in other words, classic Dunning-Kruger effect, a definition of which is: "a cognitive bias in which people mistakenly assess their cognitive ability as greater than it is. It is related to the cognitive bias of illusory superiority and comes from the inability of people to recognise their lack of ability." Or, the less you know, the less you realise that you *don't know*.)

Klopp continued: "John is the first in the building and the last to leave. No matter how early I get into Melwood, I get up the stairs and he's already there - sat there with the laptop open watching goalkeepers from the other end of the world. He's constantly in there developing, changing training programmes, working with the boys. For me, he's a fantastic goalkeeper coach. There's not any reason for criticism. He's also a fantastic lad."

Hopefully Achterberg has been vindicated by the consistent excellence of Alisson Becker, who, having already had a great season, saved the last 16 shots on target he faced this season – including *six big chances* – according to the *Anfield Index;* which, of course, covered the full Champions League games against Barcelona (at home) and Spurs in the final.

But Lijnders is arguably the *vital* Dutch coach at the club.

The Young Man

Born in Venray in the southernmost reaches of Holland, Lijnders' playing career was curtailed at the age of just 17 by the cruelest of football injuries, the cruciate ligament tear. But like many of the best coaches in the world, he used that setback to get *learning*, at an age where most footballers are wrapped up in the insular concerns of their own form and their own careers. Managers like Jürgen Klopp, Rafa Benítez and Jose Mourinho were also already studying the game in their early 20s, whilst Klopp's semi-successful playing career meant that he only did some part-time coaching, having studied sports science at the Goethe University of Frankfurt. None of these men were out buying Ferraris.

Lijnders' first role in football was chief of youth at amateur club SVEB of Broekhuizenvorst. Then, at the age of just 19, he moved to Holland's second-biggest club, PSV Eindhoven, to work with the youth team. Five years later he was at Porto, as part of their academy coaching system, and it was his work here that alerted Liverpool to his talents; with a move to Merseyside coming in 2014, to work with the Reds' U16 team, having been spotted by the then academy coach, Michael Beale (before Beale left to be Sao Paulo's assistant coach, before moving to join Steven Gerrard at Rangers). By 2015, Lijnders was liaising with the Liverpool manager and, when Klopp took charge, he instantly saw his talents harnessed by the man in charge.

It was at PSV that Lijnders was exposed to the Coerver Method of training players. Nicknamed "the Albert Einstein of Football", Wiel Coerver, won the Uefa Cup with Feyenoord in 1973/74, as well as the *Eredivisie* title that same season, and whose name was later given the Coerver Coaching Method, which was inspired by his ideas. He did not believe that talent was innate, and set in place a structure that could work on all aspects of the game, to first develop and then further hone technique. Making use of the advent of the video cassette recorder in the 1970s, he studied the skills of players Pelé, Franz Beckenbauer, Johan Cruyff, Rivelino, Ferenc Puskás, Stanley Matthews and many more; breaking down the step-overs, tricks and turns into components that could be taught, in order for players to get an advantage over opponents.

The Coerver Method involves all types of ball mastery: exercises where each player works alone with a ball performing repetitions using both feet; receiving and passing; one-v-one exercises; speed drills, to increase acceleration off the mark; innovative sessions to work on finishing; and group attacks, with combination play and an emphasis on fast break attack. To date, Arjen Robben and Bolo Zenden are two of the most famous successful students of the approach, and Lijnders is taking the principle further, to create his own 21st century ideas. In five years at PSV, his students included a young Memphis Depay, whose move to Manchester United from PSV in 2015 – on the back of an excellent season in Holland – probably came too soon, and who now, having just turned 25, has been revived at Lyon; also netting ten goals for Holland in his last 18 appearances. (At the time of writing he is being linked with a move to Liverpool, and he would certainly be an interesting option, given that he knows not only the Dutch players, but the Reds' main Dutch coach.)

Lijnders then moved to Porto, initially taking up a role in the U19s, before progressing to FC Porto B, and later the first team. The official role at all three stages with the Portuguese giants was 'technique coach'. It was a similar role that took him to Liverpool, but since then he has expanded his remit and been promoted to a hands-on role with the first-team.

Whilst at Porto, Lijnders was quoted as using the aforementioned Robben as a focal point. "I try to make our players aware how [Arjen] Robben creates space for himself ... he consciously positions himself, creating space to receive the ball and what he does with it, and how this affects team mates ... whether it is holding, moving, dropping, accelerating ... it is all about timing."

Lewis Bowers, writing for the site *In Bed With Maradona*, noted: "With claims that the players can indeed see their development stymied by a lack of freedom, Lijnders sought to recreate 'street academies'. These introduced situations such as 2v2 foot volley, six-a-side tournaments and 'challenge Thursday'. Matches would be organised between different age groups as Lijnders claimed that there is clear evidence that some players developed through playing against older, more physically imposing players."

This is essentially the social multiplier effect, as discussed elsewhere in this book; along with the research that *testing* practice improves players, in the way that *standard* practice cannot.

"Nobody knows what the future of football will look like," Lijnders is quoted as saying. "The only thing I'm sure of is that the defensive organisation of teams will be even better. They will protect the middle zone of the pitch better and defend their area better. We need to create players who can ruin this defensive organisation".

As such, it's no surprise that Jürgen Klopp was devastated to be losing Lijnders, before he knew that Željko Buvač would be following him out the door just a few months later.

"It's such a strange mix of emotions talking about Pep leaving us. Firstly, I am gutted to be losing such a valuable member of our coaching team and such a brilliant person from our group. But that is tempered by the fact I am very excited for him to have this opportunity and as much as we would have loved for him to remain with us, we cannot stand in his way for what is a fantastic opportunity.

"It is hard to undersell the role Pep played in helping us settle, educating us about football life in England and then contributing ideas to the progress and development of this team. He has such a big football brain, but it's his willingness to learn and absorb information and always look to improve and be better as a coach that makes him stand out."Of course, one of his biggest legacies at LFC will be the development and integration into the first-team squad of so many young and exciting players.

"The role he played in making us aware of these players and then helping us get the best out of them will have a lasting impact here, beyond him leaving."

But when one door closes another door opens; out went Buvač, Lijnders was sacked by NEC Nijmegen, and back came Lijnders, into Buvač's role.

A director at NEC, Wilco van Schaik, praised the then 35-year-old despite the short stay at his club.

"I have seen him do things that I've never seen in the Netherlands," Van Schaik told *ForzaNEC.nl*. "He got to experience a kind of pressure at a club that you only learn when you're standing on the pitch as a coach. I have a lot of respect for a 35-year-old man who got here at a difficult time and kept fighting until the very last match."

"I get why Liverpool hired him again, because he has some unique qualities. The whole of Dutch football can learn things from him in certain areas. He's far ahead of his time.

"Lijnders is a brilliant thinker and people like him can help Dutch football forward in certain areas. I have seen training exercises from him that players absolutely loved.

"Two of the best coaches in The Netherlands I know both say that they use Lijnders' training exercises occasionally."

Feeling Good

"I feel good. It's a role that suits me, especially next to Jürgen," Lijnders told *The Liverpool Echo*'s James Pearce in April 2019, ahead of a return to his old club, FC Porto, in the Champions League.

"He [Klopp] is the motivator, the stimulator behind every forward step we make but he gives responsibility to the ones he trusts. I'm responsible for training and giving direction towards a plan for the week that gets the most out of the team. Together with Jurgen and Pete, we decide where we want to go in our sessions and I will make sure it's getting done. Everything we do in training is related to our ideas. Every exercise is specific to what we want to build."

As it was at Dortmund, training is intensely competitive at Melwood, with the standards set to such a level that anyone not keeping up stands little or no chance of making the team. "I believe that you become what you believe so we stimulate high on and off the pitch standards," Lijnders told Pearce. "We work as hard as possible and see each training session as the game."

Indeed, it is here that Klopp's intense work ethic meets the Dutch influence, to create a whole new identity: a mixture of the work-rate and mentality of German football with the more expressive, flair-based *Oranje* blueprint.

"Jürgen is someone you can't stop learning from because he surprises you so many times," Lijnders said. "He can create a feeling of belief and determination for a whole group of players in two sentences.

Speaking about Peter Krawietz, whose main job is to analyse the opposition, Lijnders told Pearce: "Peter is one of the world's best analysts because he finds solutions to the problems that we are going to face, but he finds them before the problems arise, which is very smart."

Krawietz then joins Klopp and Lijnders in trying to plot ways to win the game, with Andreas Kornmayer analysing the workload from the day's training, to monitor every last ounce of energy expended; while Lijnders himself will watch the sessions on video. "Andreas will provide us with the data of the session, how many sprints, how much high-speed running."

Everything is planned in terms of how many days it is until the next match; Lijnders speaks of no reference to days of the week, but "matchday -1 or -3".

In the second part of his interview with James Pearce, Lijnders discussed the tactical balance required at Liverpool; and how the style of play has had to evolve, in response to teams sitting back against the Reds. "Balance is everything. It's about how we've developed but don't forget it's always about the opponent as well. Teams mainly set up to counter-attack against us. You play always two games. The first one you see on the scoreboard. The second one is 'our way' and 'our style'.

"The first one you can lose sometimes but the second one, never. And this is where our focus lies. It comes back to the same thing – our process."

It seems only a matter of time before Lijnders is presented with another chance in management, but with any luck (from a Liverpool perspective) he will use the NEC experience as proof that the grass isn't always greener on the other side, and that job stability, at a massive club, is nothing to sniff at. Another three years at Liverpool would still see him in his 30s if he wants to try that route again. Indeed, he could even be a natural successor to Klopp, should the German choose to move on.

Dutch Cycle

Football goes in cycles. For a while, Dutch players, managers and coaches were the gold standard; from the 1960s onwards they essentially reinvented the game, not least with 'total football'. But in recent years the Dutch national side hit some difficult lows – the kind of which prompted a root and branch rethink of German football a decade earlier, as a generation of coaches, including Jürgen Klopp, reinvigorated the national game. Almost unthinkably, the Netherlands failed to qualify for both Euro 2016 and the 2018 World Cup, having been at every major tournament since 2002.

Brazil has also had its problems in recent years. Brazilian players – the kings of the game until the '70s – have also taken a bit of a fall from grace, even if they are still *amongst* the best around – just not necessarily *the* best (and certainly underperform as the national team, ever since 2002, when the elite nationalities became European, mainly Spain, but briefly Italy and Germany).

Growing up in the 1970s and '80s, if you could have had three Dutchmen and three Brazilians (one voted the best in Europe) in the squad you'd have thought you were in dreamland. (Of course, you could only have three overseas players back then, so it would also have been breaking the rules.) Perhaps in 2019, that has returned to being a wonderful thing, even if the trio of Dutchmen and the three Brazilians aren't exactly typical to the stereotypes of players from those countries.

What's strange is that Liverpool, with the transfer policy since 2015, haven't *gone German*. One of the obvious benefits of Liverpool appointing the best German coach would have been attracting the best German players. In the 1990s Arsène Wenger went French: Patrick Vieira, Emanuel Petit, Nicolas Anelka, Thierry Henry, et al; Rafa Benítez went Spanish: Xabi Alonso, Luis Garcia, Fernando Torres, Pepe Reina, et al; and Jose Mourinho went Portuguese, with Ricardo Carvalho, Paulo Ferreira, Tiago, José Bosingwa, et al. But rather than go German – albeit after a couple of low-cost punts in 2016 – Liverpool have *gone Dutch*. That said, there has been a big Bundesliga signing since Klopp was appointed, but it just happened to be a Guinean.

Which isn't to say that Klopp didn't have big German targets; German journalist, author and Klopp biographer Raphael Honigstein said that Liverpool, before the manager was persuaded to take Mo Salah, were going for Julian Brandt – a player still being linked with a move to the Reds. No matter how good Brandt is, it's hard to imagine anyone else making the kind of impact that Salah immediately did.

Indeed, Naby Keïta's playing time after his arrival from RB Leipzig was in part inhibited by the further improvement of Gini Wijnaldum. Midway through the 2018/19 season, the ex-Feyenoord, PSV Eindhoven and Newcastle utility man belatedly got some praise in the mainstream media, although he remains largely understated; not always highly visible in games, but the importance of his play, from a tactical point of view, is discussed in a later chapter of this book.

And how long before there's a third Dutch player regularly in the Liverpool team?

"'Unbelievable,' was the usually understated Neil Critchley's response to Ki-Jana Hoever's U23 debut", according to the *Liverpool Echo*, after a win at leaders Everton. "Sixteen years old? Just... wow, really! I thought his calmness and assurance, his decision-making, his intelligence without the ball, it was terrific. Playing against a good player, I was very impressed with him indeed."

According to reports in Holland, the teenager was pursued by Chelsea, Manchester United and Manchester City, but perhaps Liverpool's increasing Dutch connection helped sway his decision.

Hoever arrived from Ajax in the summer of 2018 but it took a while to get international clearance. Under-18s' manager Barry Lewtas only had Hoever briefly; he shone so much he was promoted to the U23s in almost no time. Lewtas is quoted in the *Echo* as saying: "Ki's just been away with the national team and played right-back, but he's [also] played centre-back. He's got a load of real positive attributes.

"Blimey," Lewtas added, "Moving out at 16 to another country. Credit to him, he speaks fantastic English so that'll help him settle. I think his English is better than mine! It's big for kids to move to university at 18 – and that's down the motorway. So for a boy to move country, I wouldn't underestimate the time it takes to adapt."

But in no time at all, Hoever was in the U23 squad, then almost as quickly, training with the first team on a regular basis. Within another month he was making his first-team debut, coming on after just five minutes for the injured Dejan Lovren in the cup tie away at Wolves; and *still* only 16.

Plenty of other promising players have made their debuts at 16 or 17 and then largely vanished; because, after all, it's one thing to be given a taste, and another entirely to be ready for *regular* first-team football at that age. A player like Hoever would be doing incredibly well to be a serious candidate for the Reds' first team by the age of 19 or 20, let alone having only turned 17 a short while after his debut in January 2019. Eventually thought to be a centre-back – the position he played at Wolves – he has gone through the usual blooding at right-back, both in Holland and with Liverpool's youth and U23 sides. A tall player with pace, and real talent on the ball, the natural progression would eventually be back towards the centre; and in time, depending on Joe Gomez's fitness, he could end up partnering a certain compatriot who, people say, *can play a bit*. In the 2019 U17 European Championship, playing at right-back, Hoever scored a remarkable goal – skill to bamboozle the defender and finish – and, in the final, also hit the inside of the post with a free-kick that ran to a team-mate to score, as the Dutch won the trophy. It was even more abundant why Ajax were so sad to lose him.

Still, there's a long way for Hoever to go to be the equal of someone like van Dijk, the best player in England in 2018/19.

Virgil van Dijk, Dutch Demigod

As the game neared its conclusion, with Jürgen Klopp having switched to a 4-2-4 system in desperation to grab a winning goal, Spurs, having pulled it back to 1-1, broke towards the Anfield Road end of the famous stadium; two fast players against just one Liverpool defender.

But Virgil Van Dijk, as a one-man colossus, stared down Moussa Sissoko whilst simultaneously blocking the pass to the more talented Son Heung-min, as the Dutchman backtracked – one eye on the man with the ball, without ever losing the sense of the speedster ready to run in behind him. He forced the goal-shy Sissoko to shoot, and to shoot with his weaker foot. Like Riyad Mahrez's penalty earlier in the season, it soared like a fighter plane on takeoff.

Joshua Robinson, writing in the *Wall Street Journal* days later, in April 2019, talked of the coup Liverpool had pulled off almost 18 months earlier: "The transfer made van Dijk the single most expensive defender in the history of the game. And yet he might have been undervalued. Since he arrived at Liverpool, no Premier League team has conceded fewer goals."

Of course, Robinson – while clearly right about van Dijk being a bargain – was not using inflation. With inflation, van Dijk ranks as only the 99th costliest player in the Premier League era, and the 12th-most expensive defender. Remember, also, that he cost £75m at a time when the world-record fee was £200m; whereas in July 2001, Zinedine Zidane broke the world transfer fee record at £46m, and a year later Rio Ferdinand broke the British transfer record at £30m (although it could have actually ended up being £33m after clauses). So not only was Ferdinand a British record fee *overall*, at £30m he cost 65% of the overall world record, whereas van Dijk cost only 37.5% of the world record. The notion of suddenly singling out a defender as the most expensive in the world *in his position* was perhaps an example of how undervalued they had become.

The following players all cost more than van Dijk once inflation is applied:

1 Ferdinand (to Man United) £197,930,506
2 Ricardo Carvalho (to Chelsea) £146,105,116
3 Rio Ferdinand (to Leeds United) £125,837,529
4 Eliaquim Mangala (to Man City) £106,443,648
5 Ashley Cole (to Chelsea) £103,937,149
6 Jaap Stam (to Man United) £98,931,509
7 Paulo Ferreira (to Chelsea) £97,158,062
8 Joleon Lescott (to Man City) £92,556,408
9 Luke Shaw (to Man United) £79,832,736
10 José Bosingwa (to Chelsea) £75,843,204
11 Glen Johnson (to Liverpool) £75,727,970

As such, I've been saying for years that centre-backs now seem to be undervalued and, most bafflingly of all, goalkeepers rarely seem to move for big fees; which is all the more odd when you consider it's such a specialist position that they occupy. That said, Gianluigi Buffon cost Juventus an estimated £220m in current-day money; with the estimation due to our inflation model, TPI, tracking only *Premier League* spending (with the fee in 2001 of €52m equating to £33m, and £33m being £220m, but inflation in *Serie A* will have run at a different rate). As such, as with the relative cost of the van Dijk fee, Alisson Becker still only cost Liverpool roughly a third of the world's best goalkeeper of the 2000s. For all the talk of a world-record fee for a goalkeeper and a world-record fee for a centre-back, the pair, combined, still only cost two-thirds of the overall world-record fee. As such, is it any wonder they now look like bargains?

The *Wall Street Journal* article on van Dijk continued: "Not only is he built like a Spartan warrior, but he has the skill, intelligence, and vertical leap to neutralise entire offences. The last time anyone dribbled past him was more than 50 games ago, according to Opta Sports. Most people brave enough to try it are still picking grass out of their nose.

In December, the fastest player in the Premier League – Adama Traoré, the ex-Barcelona and Middlesbrough, and current Wolves winger – tried to 'do' van Dijk for pace. A couple of months earlier, the *Birmingham Mail* had written about Traoré's record-breaking speed: "Wolves star Adama Traoré may be the fastest footballer in the world. The Molineux ace is certainly the quickest player currently plying his trade in the Premier League. Remarkably, the star was once clocked at 37 kilometres per hour. This is the equivalent of 22.99 mph ... Usain Bolt was running at an average speed of 23mph when he won the 100m sprint in the 2009 World Championships."

Trying to out-sprint van Dijk on the inside-right channel, Traoré – a man who can't really do *close* control – knocked the ball and ran. But van Dijk got there first. Others had tried a similar tactic, and failed; many soon stopped even trying.

(It was later revealed that van Dijk clocked the fastest sprint of any player in the Champions League, in the away leg at Barcelona.)

"I could write a book about his skills, his strength, how much I like him," Klopp said after the win in Munich, the centre-back rising to thump home a towering header, having been impeccable all night in defence, and also having hit a 50-yard pass to Sadio Mané that moved through the air with whip and spin, and landed – also with some skill on Mané's part – on the attacker's bootlaces. "Without writing a whole book," Joshua Robinson wrote in the *WSJ*, "describing van Dijk boils down to this: he is the most complete defender in the world today."

In the article, Robinson examines some of van Dijk's physical prowess. "Perhaps more than any defender on the planet, van Dijk, 27, looks the part. He is 6-foot-4, 203 pounds, and has probably never even looked at a doughnut.

"He is only two inches taller than the average Premier League centre-back. But his weight, and how he carries it, make him one of the most immovable objects in English soccer. He is a full 21 pounds heavier than the average central defender and 29 pounds heavier than the average striker. In boxing terms, that translates to two whole weight classes.

"If you thought that heavyweight carriage might be hard to shift in sprints or aerial duels, van Dijk will happily prove you wrong. He was clocked earlier this season at 21.5 miles per hour by Opta. Only six other defenders have gone faster this season and all of them were smaller."

While 21.5mph isn't as fast as some wingers' top speeds, van Dijk has that extra intelligence and anticipation to given himself the edge; after all, if someone like Traoré is going to beat van Dijk with a dribble or burst of pace, he first has to be *in front* of the defender, from the Dutchman's perspective; you can't dribble past someone if you're already past them with a run off the ball. It's usually tough for a bigger man to be quick off the mark, but van Dijk is *quick enough* from a standing start; and then effortlessly moves through the gears. But most of the time you don't even see his pace get called upon, as he's no Micah Richards or Kyle Walker – fast defenders who couldn't/cannot read the game sufficiently well. Even at top speed, van Dijk rarely looks like he's breaking sweat.

The superb Barney Ronay, writing in *The Guardian,* summed up his qualities: "Mainly he just stood there being Virgil, appearing at times like the only grown-up on the set. Van Dijk is a fascinating leader. He doesn't yodel and bang his chest. It is more a question of presence, a way of standing. Even watching from the seats you feel somehow that you're going to find that train home, that the half-time queues will be short, that whatever it is that's happening in parliament will work out."

After any teammate scores, van Dijk makes a point to have a moment alone after the other players have made a fuss, to personally congratulate him. And when Arsenal defender Sead Kolašinac began to hassle Mo Salah as the players walked off at half-time, having been incensed that Salah had the gall to fall over after he'd twice been kicked in the area by the clumsy defender (I know, *how dare he?*), van Dijk swooped in, like a father seeing his young son being bullied by some thug; Kolašinac was less keen on taking the fight to the giant Dutchman.

Rob Bagchi wrote in *The Telegraph* in March that "Liverpool's Virgil van Dijk deserves to overcome the institutional blindspot of awards towards centre-backs and be crowned player of the year

"… The Lagonda smoothness of Van Dijk's running, his reading of the game, sound judgment and the sharp nose for danger evident in his thwarting of Everton's long throws and hounding of Theo Walcott into panicky offloads in Sunday's derby showcase his range of qualities. There are contrasts, too, he can nip in and tackle stealthily or challenge lawfully with the full weight of his body to rattle an opponent's bones and resolve."

In October 2018 Troy Deeney – the Watford street-fighting striker who terrorised Martin Škrtel – stated, once again, how much he cannot stand facing van Dijk. "I've said it many times … I hate going up against him. He's too big, too strong, too quick, too good on the ball, loves fighting, a good head of hair. One of those guys that sprays on his top as well, so it smells lovely!"

Deeney played against van Dijk twice in 2018/19 after making that comment, and as well as not getting a kick, he didn't get a *head*, either. He wasn't the first, and he wouldn't be the last.

Van Dijk ended the season as the PFA Footballer of the Year and Premier League Player of the Season – having marshalled the best defence in the top flight (most clean sheets, fewest goals conceded), and scored six goals in the final five months of the season, five of which were from the end of February onwards; including key goals against Bayern Munich, Porto and Newcastle. He also ended it with a Champions League winners' medal, and the Man of the Match award. And, as widely noted, it had been 64 games since someone dribbled past him.

With several assists as well, including the sumptuous long pass to Sadio Mané in Munich, he really was the most complete player in England in 2019.

Pressing, Passing, Possession and Tactics – the DNA of Liverpool in 2019

Against Spurs at the end of March – the Reds' 32nd league game of the season – the midfield was yet again outlined as a weakness in this Liverpool side, when in truth, *it gets results*.

The Reds' trio of Jordan Henderson, Gini Wijnaldum and James Milner attracts a lot of criticism as a unit (and Henderson as an individual), but much of it seems unfair. They often play as a trio against the best opposition, so they will shine less often and have lower win-percentages when deployed together, but against Spurs the whole team seemed nervous for much of the game, as was to be expected. And despite Fabinho coming on to make an impressive late cameo, which helped to win the game, Spurs could have scored from three or four breaks, one of which was a two-against-one, which Virgil van Dijk, standing alone and exposed, dealt with like a master.

A week later, it needed Henderson and Milner to come off the bench at Southampton, to help turn a 1-1 draw into a 3-1 win; Henderson assisting the Mo Salah breakaway goal with an incredible header – the ball flying at him at great speed from a Sadio Mané block-tackle, but somehow the captain managed to deliberately angle his head to add direction to the pace that was already on the ball, and send it beautifully into Salah's path inside his own half, so that the Egyptian could sprint away and finish into the bottom corner (as if he wasn't on a nine-game scoring drought). Six minutes later Henderson, playing in a more advanced role, stole in to score in the six-yard box, befitting of the player who used to bring 5-7 goals from midfield. (It was the 10th season in a row in which Henderson had scored a Premier League goal, a feat that only three other current Premier League players could match; one being Daniel Sturridge.) The game at Southampton also highlighted Naby Keïta's attacking prowess, with a goal and a clear penalty denied by yet more baffling refereeing; but the Guinean also struggled for large parts of the match in midfield, as did Fabinho.

Statistically – in terms of who creates the team's chances – it would seem that Liverpool are now essentially an amorphous side when attacking, with, rather than a single focal forward, three ultra-mobile goalscoring wingers (or in Roberto Firmino's case, a converted attacking midfielder) who can switch positions at will; but where, for all the interchanging, there's a certain preset narrowness to the *de facto* attack –

the width provided by the full-backs who essentially play as wingers, with the wingers playing as inside-forwards.

In February 2019, Benjamin Magnusson – a teenage tactical prodigy who has already worked with a top-flight Danish club – wrote an article for *The Tomkins Times* about Jürgen Klopp's two preferred formations across the campaign (4-3-3 and then 4-2-3-1), and how he'd switched between the two. The use of Liverpool's full-backs was at the heart of the analysis.

Benjamin noted that Liverpool's use of full-backs was fairly traditional, in that it's been a long-established notion that they should attack, with overlaps and crosses; although I would argue that the fact that *both* full-backs often stay upfield at the same time is a relatively new phenomenon in the game, with the old wisdom being that if one goes, the other 'stays'. (Indeed, Alan Shearer, in an early *Match of the Day* from the 2018/19 season, stated – with a large dose of 'in my day' – it was *wrong* that both of Arsenal's full-backs were so high up the pitch at the same time, and were frequently caught upfield; where, the truth was, it was the failings of Arsenal's system – presumably the midfielders – to cover for that tactic on the day, given that the full-backs were clearly under instruction to do that job. The tactic itself is increasingly common in better teams.)

Benjamin noted the more radical development by Pep Guardiola at Bayern Munich of the "inverted" full-back. "Since then," Benjamin stated, "[Guardiola] has carried this idea to Manchester City. The main idea is simple enough: when in possession, the full-backs move infield in order to occupy the half-space [the half-space being the channel between the wing and the centre of the pitch, seen vertically] rather than the wide-space, which they normally do. This, in turn, means that City's wingers are now tasked with operating in the wide-spaces in order to provide width. At the same time, this gives greater freedom for players like David Silva, Kevin de Bruyne and Bernardo Silva to attack through the half-spaces, and considering the technical ability of someone like David Silva, it makes sense to give him greater responsibility in the attacking phase."

With the graphic Benjamin shared, it was possible to see that, actually, both Liverpool and City often had five players in the final third, but with alternating accentuations; for City it was the wingers who stayed wide, and Sergio Agüero who stayed high and central; whereas Sadio Mané and Mo Salah would be as high up the pitch as City's three attackers, but more narrow, in the half-spaces, or channels; and Roberto Firmino, the third Liverpool forward, would be as central as Agüero just a bit deeper (but where he'd often arrive a bit later in the box to score goals). City's two Silvas would be in the same half-spaces as Mané and Salah, just deeper, whereas Robertson and Alexander-Arnold would be in the same wide spaces as Leroy Sané and Raheem Sterling, but like the Silvas compared to Mané and Salah, just a bit deeper. The end result was five players very high up the pitch for both teams. The difference was that two of the Liverpool players were nominally full-backs, but when you look at their chance creation stats, you can see why, as arguably two of the best crossers of the ball in world football right now. (One rare weakness of Andy Robertson's game is that he can't really dribble infield, nor go outside his man with skill, but most of the time he doesn't have to; using the old David Beckham trick of *letting the cross do all the work*. Trent Alexander-Arnold has more pace, and can go past a man, but also has that Beckhamesque ability to just whip in the cross first-time.) Liverpool's full-backs became the most creative pairing for the position in Premier League history, both getting into double figures for assists.

While Benjamin noted that Man City's full-backs will overlap on the occasions when their wingers head inside, another tactic of Guardiola's "inverted" full-back was to head infield; where they'd advance up the field, but to nowhere near the kinds of degrees that Liverpool's full-backs regularly did. Equally, these deeper half-spaces are the kind of areas Liverpool's midfielders would cover – where you'd expect to find Fabinho, or Jordan Henderson, before the latter was moved further forward.

In Klopp's system – where the full-backs are quasi-wingers – the midfield's job is mostly to recycle the ball, rather than be the all-creative, swashbuckling model of midfields of bygone eras. While some teams still play with all-conquering midfield generals (and while football fans, on the whole, still seems to crave them), Liverpool's system is set up to service the front three and the full-backs; its job, in one way or another, is to get the ball to the "front five" whilst protecting the centre of the pitch.

Data shows that Liverpool's centre-backs frequently play the ball out wide, and from those wide positions, the full-backs will advance and play the ball inside further up the field; so the midfield becomes like the eye of a hurricane, as everything else swirls around in an almost circular motion, from back to front and, if the passing lanes are blocked, from front to back. Indeed, as teams crowd towards one flank, Robertson and Alexander-Arnold, if they don't play back and can't play forward, will look for quick switches to the other flank, sometimes finding each other, other times finding Salah or Mané. Even an overhit cross that curls backwards a little will usually end up as a pass to the other full-back, with the inside-forward from that flank having darted infield, into the six-yard box, dragging the opposing full-backs with him. Then, depending on which flank the ball arrives at, either Robertson or Alexander-Arnold has the chance to cross again.

To have midfielders constantly getting ahead of the play when both full-backs are often as high up the field as *any* attacking Liverpool player would be to leave dangerous gaps. Apart from special occasions when someone like Gini Wijnaldum was given clear licence to drive beyond the opposition defence time and again, as he did when scoring against Bournemouth (with his third or fourth off-the-ball run of the game; therefore it was no accident), the midfield was there to maintain a solid base, around which the rest of the team can quickly rotate. And when Joël Matip broke the lines from the defence by running 40 yards with the ball, the midfield needed to be alert, to cover the space; just as they needed to cover the full-backs. In the easier games, a more attacking player filled one of the three midfield roles – either Xherdan Shaqiri, Adam Lallana or Naby Keïta – but in the tougher games Klopp tended to favour his most experienced midfield trio. (Regarding experience, only Lallana is older than Henderson and Wijnaldum, but after years spent in the lower leagues, he has fewer international caps and top-flight games than any of Henderson, Milner and Wijnaldum. Lallana has also been at the club longer than Milner and Wijnaldum, but missed so much football that this particular midfield trio became the heart of the side that made it to the Champions League final in Kiev, and as such, they had the best "fit" in the terms discussed earlier in the book.) Fabinho gradually edged his way into the side, to break up the trio on several occasions, and Naby Keïta finally started to look like a regular until a groin injury curtailed his season.

Those looking for the eye-catching, swashbuckling brilliance of someone like peak-years Steven Gerrard need to understand that the team is geared towards getting the best out of the players already in the team; and while you could rebalance things by adding a Gerrard (if such a player could be found again), then it would mean losing something from the front three, as *not all of them* – as well as a new Gerrard – could dominate the ball. For most of the time in which Gerrard shone at Liverpool there was little quality on either flank; the team was more spine-centric. Under Gérard Houllier the full-backs were initially 6ft centre-backs (the "four oaks" as they were dubbed), and then under Rafa Benítez the full-backs were more ambitious, but he struggled to find wingers of sufficient quality and consistency to play just in front of them (Harry Kewell, Antonio Nunez, Albert Riera, Jermaine Pennant, Ryan Babel, Yossi Benayoun all hit and miss, or just mioo), with Dirk Kuyt ultra-reliable at getting into the box from the right flank, but where he wasn't going to beat players with skill or pace out wide. Back then the strength was almost entirely in the spine – Javier Mascherano and Xabi Alonso winning or recycling the ball further forward to Gerrard, who would feed – or work off – Fernando Torres.

Henderson, in particular, suffers for not being Steven Gerrard. But quietly effective players get chosen by managers for a reason; and to date, Kenny Dalglish, Brendan Rodgers and Jürgen Klopp have all relied on him, as have successive England managers. That said, his position as an automatic starter for Liverpool has been weakened by the arrival of Fabinho, in particular, but he did find a late spark as a more attacking midfielder.

The one midfielder who can "do it all" (bar dominate aerially), Naby Keïta, has been hampered by adjustments to life in England and the pace of the game, as well as niggling injuries. But perhaps he also hasn't been the creative fulcrum that he was at RB Leipzig because a lot of his play – by design, and/or by a sense of inhibition – has been to give the ball to the front three, or play it out wide to the overlapping full-backs. If Liverpool's game is purposefully geared against the pot-luck of long-range shooting, then that's one less area for him to "wow" as he did in Germany; with frequent long-range efforts in open play essentially part of a club's pecking order, just like who gets to take free-kicks. (The established top players are the ones who are "allowed" to take the long-range punts.)

Instead, Keïta often tried to either run a quick ten yards with the ball (which worked so well for Alex Oxlade-Chamberlain in 2017/18, and indeed, worked so well for Keïta in his earlier games), or to try and jink past three or four players in the box. Also, in the easier home games in the middle of the season, Xherdan Shaqiri often started as the advanced midfielder, or the little Swiss would move to the flank, Salah to the centre, and Firmino would drop into the no.10 role; where he would replicate some elements of Gerrard's barnstorming play, without ever being quite so deep or box-to-box.

If you look at Man City, they have an abundance of skilful lock-pickers, but their full-backs aren't as progressive, even for a team as apparently attack-minded. Even Benjamin Mendy, when fit, doesn't have the space to move into like Liverpool leave for their full-backs, as City have their wingers positioned wider. So you could compare the midfields and say that "Liverpool need to be like City", but City have a much bigger collection of expensive attacking midfielders, and get less from their full-backs.

As Andrew Beasley wrote for *TTT* in late March 2019, "Andy Robertson and Trent Alexander-Arnold ... [don't] just [have] impressive figures by Liverpool standards either; both players are currently in the Premier League's top 14 players for expected assists, and the top 17 for xA per 90 minutes (for players with a minimum of 1,700 minutes played)."

And this was before the Spurs game, when Robertson racked up an actual assist, to take him to nine – behind only two players (both attackers) – in the Premier League rankings, and Alexander-Arnold "assisted" Mo Salah's header that Hugo Lloris fumbled before it deflected off Toby Alderweireld for the winning goal. Both players continued to add assists as Liverpool won the final nine league games.

"Strip out set-pieces to compare them with other top-flight defenders," Andrew Beasley noted, "and their impact is even more stark. Robertson has amassed 4.88 expected assists in open play, the most in the division. Lucas Digne is next on 4.57, followed by Alexander-Arnold on 4.09.

"Patrick van Aanholt [of Crystal Palace], with 3.34, is the only other player to register more than three expected assists in open play from defence this season. Liverpool's full-backs are simply streets ahead of almost all of their peers when it comes to creating goalscoring opportunities. The Reds lead the way in the field of open play chances from their right- and left-backs."

So it's clear that you cannot have three creative forwards and two creative full-backs, and still expect the midfield to be *just as creative*. You can't have six players making the same killer pass in the same move. Perhaps you could have them in the same team, *capable* of making such a pass; but their individual figures will be diluted by sharing the responsibility.

Liverpool's midfield is mostly there to shuffle, harry, press and make simple but effective passes. It is there to help form a solid square in front of the goalkeeper, with two midfielders sat just ahead of two defenders; to protect the key part of the pitch. And it's there because Salah and Mané are not asked to track back, unless the Reds are under the cosh. It's a constant game of brinksmanship, with Salah and Mané forcing the full-backs – if the opposition plays a back four – to drop deep and go narrower, which then opens it up for the Reds' quasi-wingers to do their thing. And until teams find a way to consistently blunt Robertson and Alexander-Arnold, why would Liverpool want "more" from the midfield, if it risks unbalancing the side?

Equally, someone like Alex Oxlade-Chamberlain – an elite presser – had the skillset to be an important player in 2018/19; but alas, not the knee ligaments.

DNA

I spent the second half of the season working with Andrew Beasley to find the statistical vital signs of this Liverpool side, for both the website and also this book.

Towards the end of the season he wrote: "Long-time subscribers may recall I wrote about ball recoveries in the final third (a.k.a. final third regains/FTRs) back in 2011/12 during Damien Comolli's tenure. According to 'The Secret Footballer', the first director of football appointed by FSG had a selection of statistics which he fetishised in players, with one in particular being winning the ball in the opposition's defensive third."

This, of course, is a big trait of a Jürgen Klopp side, with Klopp famously saying that the pressing to make a final third regain is better than the most creative no.10 in the world.

As Andrew noted, "In April 2012, Liverpool had averaged 3.31 FTRs per league match, the most in the division. The players most frequently responsible for them, who had played at least 1,000 minutes, were Luis Suárez (with one every 100 minutes), Steven Gerrard (134 minutes) and Craig Bellamy (155 minutes).

"Players and managers have come and gone in the intervening half decade or so, but winning the ball high up the pitch has always been a theme for Klopp teams. Sure enough, in 2017/18 his charges collectively made 4.47 final third regains per game, an increase of 35% on a team supposedly assembled with this specific attribute in mind.

In 2017/18, five Liverpool players bettered the above figure posted by Gerrard during 2011/12. "Firmino won the ball in the final third every 96 minutes in 2017/18, to better the efforts of the Tasmanian Devil-like Suárez."

But as Andrew notes, *he wasn't the leading man.*

"Top spot belonged to Alex Oxlade-Chamberlain. In his debut Liverpool campaign, the former Gunner recovered the ball in opposition defensive thirds every 83 minutes. While I haven't monitored this stat over the years, I wouldn't have expected anyone to better Suárez's efforts, never mind by roughly a sixth.

"Yet, believe it or not, this season someone has moved up again. Firstly, we have to give credit to Mohamed Salah. The Egyptian king is the only man to appear in every match day squad so far this season, but despite this lack of a break – current international fortnight aside – he has improved his FTR rate from every 108 minutes last term to every 83 this, matching the efforts of Oxlade-Chamberlain. Has this apparent increased work rate dulled his senses in front of goal? Something to ponder."

And remember, for all Salah's diminishing goal return in the second half of 2018/19, he ranked 2nd *in the whole Premier League* for sprints.

But there was one really big surprise from Andrew's data. "Something else to contemplate is the work of Xherdan Shaqiri. Despite relatively limited time on the pitch, he has made more final third recoveries than everyone bar Salah and Firmino, at an incredible rate of one every 78 minutes. And Charlie Adam, a veteran of the 2011/12 side lest we forget, thought Shaqiri didn't work hard enough."

(Judging by Charlie Adam's subsequent career, he seems to have pork pies where his brains should be.)

"Shaqiri's form in this field, combined with increased rates from the likes of Milner, Alexander-Arnold and Robertson (alongside Salah) means the Reds have made 5.13 FTRs per league match in 2018/19. Small sample results such as this can easily distort percentages, but that's a 55 percent increase on Comolli's team."

So it seems clear that the creative forces of the Liverpool team were the full-backs, the front three, and *the whole team pressing*.

Pressing From the Middle

Earlier in the season – back on November 19th 2018 – long-time TTT subscriber Will Gurpinar-Morgan, shortly before taking up a job with analytics giants Opta, wrote an article for the site about the changes in the Reds' pressing.

"In order to investigate this, I'm going to use the pass completion model that I employed previously to analyse the midfield options available to Jürgen Klopp this season, in a similar manner to an analysis I did last season [for *Statsbomb*] on Liverpool's pressing. While passing data doesn't provide a direct measure of the pressing strategies deployed by a team, they can provide an indication of them, while also benefiting from the large number of passing events in a single match that aids identification of clear statistical fingerprints.

"The pass completion model is based on the start and end location of the pass plus whether it was with the foot or not, which provides a probability value for how likely a pass is to be completed or not. So for example, relatively short backward passes by a centre-back to their goalkeeper are completed close to 100% of the time, whereas medium-range forward passes into the centre of the penalty area have pass completion rates of around 20%.

"… In Klopp's debut season, the team really blunted the passing game of their opponents high up the pitch and led the league when combining the midfield and opposition defensive zones. This was largely the case in the following season, with the team coming second in the rankings behind Tottenham. Both Liverpool seasons rank in the top five across the past four seasons.

"Last season [2017/18] saw a slight shift, with the team dropping to third in the rankings but unlike prior seasons, they were well behind Tottenham and Manchester City. The current season sees Liverpool in seventh place in 2018/19 and twentieth across the past four seasons; this season has seen a substantial change for both Manchester City (slightly ahead of Liverpool) and Tottenham (below Liverpool), which is an intriguing shift especially with a number of other teams now adopting a high-pressing approach. The radical change for Liverpool has been high up the pitch, with the opposition completing passes at a close to average rate in their defensive midfield and defensive zones."

All of this seems to suggest Liverpool were pressing less intensely from the front. But with all the criticism of the midfield, it's important to note the following *vital* passage from Gurpinar-Morgan's analysis (with the emphasis in italics mine).

"The midfield zone is as strong as ever in terms of pass disruption *and leads the league this year by a wide margin*, ahead of Tottenham in second … Furthermore, this season ranks 4th across the past four seasons if we only include Klopp's matches in 2015/16, which would rank second behind Manchester City last year.

"… Analysis by the *Anfield Index Under Pressure* podcast, the *Played Off The Park* blog and *StatsBomb* all indicate that Liverpool's ability to generate attacks via pressing has increased this season and the defensive performance has been excellent, so it is hard to fault the approach thus far."

Gurpinar-Morgan concluded back in November that Liverpool still pressed from the front, which is backed up by Andrew Beasley's final third regains data. But the Reds no longer frequently swarm forward in *packs* that can be easily bypassed as opponents wise up to the tactic; and, if not bypassed, there's the constant high-risk, high-reward style of it leading to a goal, or leading to a massive opportunity to be countered against; the more harum-scarum style seen previously under the German.

With Liverpool leading the way for midfield pressing, this seems an easily overlooked benefit that the maligned trio of Milner, Henderson and Wijnaldum provide (although all the other midfielders are fine pressers, too, as seen when Naby Keïta pressed so remarkably in the first 10 seconds against Huddersfield that, mere seconds later, he had scored). Assists and goals were simply not the way to judge *this* midfield, and with the Reds racking up the third-best ever points total in English football, it seemed churlish to focus on the very few points Liverpool dropped when, in truth, they were winning points at an almost unprecedented rate.

Midfield Possesses

Another area where the midfield improved was in keeping possession. If the central trio didn't create loads of chances or score a lot of goals, they at least helped the Reds to keep the ball better; enabling Jürgen Klopp's team to take the sting out of games, and also, in away fixtures, wear the opposition down with constant recycling of the ball, often in order to do more damage in the second half.

Liverpool changed from a team that either blew the opposition away or blew themselves out – by the 70-minute mark – to a team that led the league in late goals (scored in the last 15 minutes), with 25 – one shy of the club's Premier League era record, which was set in 2008/09. In previous seasons Klopp's hard-pressing front six often looked dead on their feet by that stage of a game.

Part of the problem is one of perceptions, with the game at the elite level moving faster than the average fan's expectations of what a player is *supposed* to look like. The idea of a "false 9" was largely ridiculed, particularly when Roberto Firmino first started adopting the role in red, but a few years on the average observer has caught up with the concept that the striker doesn't just have to play on the shoulder of the last defender, or be a giant totem pole, and bang in goals; although plenty still feel this way.

As noted earlier in this chapter, the *instinct* is still to want the midfielder to resemble Steven Gerrard, with an all-action style, combative tackles and 30-yard Exocets from the laces of his boots; to yearn for the days of Roy Keane and Patrick Vieira kicking the living daylights out of each other. But while there will always be room in the game for such talents, the job of the midfielder has evolved; although again, much depends on the other players in the team, and their own strengths and weaknesses, as to how everything balances out. The aim of the midfielder, just like the aim of the striker, is *to help the team win as many matches as possible*. It's now appreciated by those who study the higher form of the art that the thumping tackle is often less important than the timely interception – even if, in English football, a crowd will react to the former as if a goal has been scored. As the game grows more and more scientific – with players' movements trackable to the nth degree – the emphasis shifts to positioning, and closing off passing lanes, rather than thundering into a 50-50.

Indeed, I felt as far back as 1997 that for all the added aggression Paul Ince gave Liverpool, he'd give the ball away a lot more than John Barnes was doing up to that point, and if Ince won it back half the time, that was still a downgrade; and while Barnes' shelf life was running out due to age and fitness, Liverpool lost something that couldn't be regained by Ince, no matter how many crunching challenges he put in. The thing that pretty much every Liverpool fan at the time felt the Reds' needed – steel – came at a cost. Though he's rarely credited as such, Barnes was actually a prototype for the modern midfielder: just don't give the ball away very much. And while most of us fans could appreciate that aspect to his game, it felt somewhat disposable, and totally unexciting. It would take another seven years for Xabi Alonso to arrive and give back that calm assuredness in the midfield, with Gerrard – the hitherto box-to-box sensation – gradually moved further up the pitch by Rafa Benítez, to allow room for Alonso to control the game, and to take away the need to add greater tactical discipline (which may not even have been possible) from the more free-spirited, street-style player.

With the tackling laws much stricter, the blood-and-thunder of such midfielders has been largely neutered. Gerrard played his best football under the Spaniard, but having been sent off four times prior to Benítez arriving (some of which was down to naivety), Gerrard was only dismissed once during the Spaniard's six seasons; and then, in the five years after, sent off twice more; meaning that six of his seven red cards came either side of what was the best period for the Reds in the Premier League era prior to Klopp arriving. While Gerrard's own managerial career got off to an impressive start at Rangers, particularly as they operate on around just one-third of Celtic's budget, that his team had picked up an astonishing *twelve* red cards suggests his old personal habits have followed him north of the border. It's hard to see what is gained by players missing so many games due to suspension, and the balance between intensity and *legality* is one that successful teams can muster. Playing no fewer than three games with nine men cannot be good for legs.

Writing in March 2019 for the influential analytics website *Statsbomb*, Nico Morales noted the change in style of the modern midfielder, and amongst several players highlighted across Europe, one of Liverpool's is worthy of several paragraphs.

"What strings these elusive transfer targets [the most coveted young midfielders in Europe] to players like Georginio Wijnaldum or Miralem Pjanić, however, is how they distribute the ball. The common, almost necessary attribute underpinning any well-known midfielder of this ilk is their intelligence on the ball.

"… These players are not only ensuring the passage of possession to the final third, but they're distributing it in a way that protects the team from a counterattack. It's what coaches like Pep Guardiola and Mauricio Pochettino are talking about when they refer to players who 'see the space.' It's not about directly assisting an attacking player or literally playing a forward into an open area; it's about ensuring the entire team is at equilibrium. Possession nowadays is more about knowing how to possess the ball than it is merely maintaining the players and structures to do so."

Morales discusses some of the elite midfielders in Europe, then returns to Liverpool's largely unsung midfield maestro. "It's a similar case with Georginio Wijnaldum. Though his performance in many of the categories pales in comparison to his midfield compatriots, Wijnaldum finds himself an increasingly important cog in Klopp's current Liverpool. With their greater emphasis this season on beating teams who ask questions of their possession game, Wijnaldum's intelligence in distribution sees him selected over players who are more gifted in other, more directly observable ways. As much as Liverpool fans might cry out for a more ostensibly attack-minded midfield option, because of how he moves the ball, he's as essential to the chances their front three ends up creating as he is snuffing out the moments where Liverpool are vulnerable. It's Liverpool's system that has the most influential part in creating chances, not the individual brilliance of sole players – an ethos carried over to the dynamic of their title rivals, Manchester City."

So, how has Liverpool's possession changed in recent seasons?

The biggest possession reboot was supposed to be under Brendan Rodgers, who arrived from Swansea, where his low-budget team had been able to keep the ball, but often do so in their own half. Could he now do the much more difficult thing, and keep it in the *opposition* half? And with the way football was moving, was that even a good idea any more?

In an early fan briefing, which was attended on behalf of *The Tomkins Times* by Dan Kennett, Rodgers said: "I've always enjoyed and worked with the statistic that if you can dominate the game, with the ball, you have a 79% chance of winning a game of football. If you're better than the other team, with the ball, you've got an eight out of 10 chance of winning the game."

Writing for *TTT* seven years later, Andrew Beasley said "I've no idea what that claim is based upon. In his first season at the helm, Liverpool's possession average increased to 55.1% [from 53.6%], though it only won them nine more points than they amassed the year before. Indeed, in the 16 matches where the Reds had at least 60% possession (which is the benchmark used for high possession in this article), they only earned 1.63 points per game; a shade above their average for the campaign as a whole, but well short of the form required for a top four finish.

"The following season, everything clicked. Liverpool's overall possession average dipped slightly to 54.7%, but in the 60%+ possession matches, of which there were 14, they averaged 2.29 points. Interestingly, this was again only marginally better than their average figure for the campaign as a whole, suggesting the team were just far better than the year before, and the amount of possession they had made very little difference.

"Unfortunately for Rodgers, as quickly as his team's elite form came together, it fell apart. Liverpool essentially maintained their possession average the following season – it fell just 0.4% from 2013/14 – but their record when they truly dominated the ball collapsed. From the start of 2014/15 to the day Rodgers was sacked, the Reds had at least 60% possession in 17 league matches, and they only averaged a Roy Hodgsonesque 1.29 points per game from them."

Liverpool were keeping the ball, and doing almost nothing at all with it. As Andrew put it, "Liverpool had become the poster boys for sterile domination. In Rodgers' last full season, only four sides averaged more possession than Liverpool, but only four averaged a lower expected goal per shot figure (as per *Understat*'s data), and none of those that did finished higher than 15th."

Liverpool had to find a way to either do more with the possession they had, or to find a different way of playing; keeping the ball and having low-value shots from distance was not the way forward. Indeed, if we continue the metaphor from earlier in the book, rather than have a ton of impressive vital signs, Liverpool were *flatlining*.

Somewhat surprisingly, given that he is seen as the *gegenpresser* and Rodgers the *possessor*, Klopp's teams have actually averaged more of the ball than his predecessor's; although for quite a while that wasn't always proving to be of great benefit.

In researching the development – and effectiveness – of Liverpool's possession in recent seasons, Andrew devised a new metric: xG per possession percentage (or 'xG/Pos' for short), which he went on to apply to the Reds' fortunes with the ball.

"The average expected goal tally by a Premier League team over each of the last four full seasons has been 49.04, which isn't far from the possession average which is obviously 50%. So while they're on different scales – xG ran from 26.5 to 91.4, while average possession covered 40.7 to 66.4% – you can still combine the figures to get an idea of which teams made most effective use of their time on the ball.

"It correlates with success, which you would assume, as the better teams create the best and the most chances. The top ten sides for xG/Pos across the last four years finished 2.5th on average, with just one team finishing outside the top four. It won't surprise you to learn that Leicester's title winners are way out in front with a xG/Pos figure of 1.53, followed by Manchester City's 100 point side, on 1.38.

"Brendan Rodgers' Liverpool clocked in at 0.95 in 2014/15, and 0.93 for his first eight games in 2015/16. It was undoubtedly time for a change.

"Enter Jürgen Klopp, who hadn't founded his reputation on coaching possession-heavy sides. His Dortmund side of 2010/11 won the title with an average of 51.4% possession – the joint-fifth most in the 18 team division – before retaining it with a slightly higher 53.3% of the total attempted passes in their matches in the following campaign."

Andrew pointed out that Klopp's one poor season with Dortmund – his 7th and final one – also had an average possession percentage of 53.3, which goes to show that, in modern football at least, possession has become more of a mixed bag than in the 1990s, when it was seen by many to be the most powerful predictor of success available.

Indeed, the good results in Klopp's earlier seasons at Liverpool were not successfully linked to higher possession rates. "The Reds' 2015/16 stats were virtually identical for those from the previous campaign. Possession increased by 0.7% on average, expected goals per shot went down a touch, xG/Pos went up a few decimal places, nothing major.

"The issues in matches with particularly high possession figures didn't change either. Klopp took charge of 15 league games in 2015/16 in which Liverpool attempted at least 60% of the total passes, and won just 20 points from them. Had it not been for a late surge, the picture would've been even uglier; the Reds won just one of Klopp's first nine league matches which met the high possession criteria.

"After starting 2016/17 with a thrilling win at Arsenal, Liverpool hit their possession nadir. They went down 2-0 at Turf Moor despite having 80% of the possession and allowing Burnley just three shots. The issue was that only nine of Liverpool's 26 shots were in the box, and none of them were clear-cut chances. Klopp may not have sent his side out with the intention of attempting four of every five passes in the match but, once they had the ball that much, they were still unable to create any chances of note with it."

Even then it took a while for Klopp and his team to reverse the trend.

"While the form in high-possession games picked up – with Liverpool collecting 1.77 points per game in 2016/17, and 1.78 a year later – there were still issues on the road. Across Klopp's first two full seasons, the Reds earned 1.97 points per game when they had at least 60% of the possession at Anfield, but only 1.33 in away games.

"However, there were definite signs of progress year-on-year. On average, 41% of shots in the Premier League are taken from outside the penalty box. For Liverpool in high possession games in 2015/16 (under Klopp) their figure was 47%. This dropped to 43% the following season, and then 41% in 2017/18. The Reds weren't exactly tearing it up on this front, but if the stats are progressing in the right direction, then the results should follow."

All of which brings us to this past season. Writing two-thirds of the way through the campaign, Andrew noted: "This has been proven in abundance in 2018/19. In the almost three years between Klopp taking over and the end of 2017/18, Liverpool won 10 away games where they had at least 60% of the possession. But this season they won their first five in a row, in large part by only averaging 32% of their attempts at goal from further than 18 yards out.

"Add in the matches at Anfield, and Liverpool won their first 13 league games in a row where they had a high level of possession this season. Not just with the bar of 60% which has been used throughout this article either; they averaged 68.8% possession, 2.5 expected goals and 2.77 actual goals per match.

"The draws with Leicester and West Ham broke the perfect run, but the win over the Cherries gave Liverpool an average of 2.75 points per game in their 16 high possession league matches so far this season. If we look at the statistics mentioned throughout this article across the last five seasons, the progress which has been made is clear to see."

All of the above was true up to February 9th. Liverpool then went on a run of games that included draws at Everton (despite having 58% possession) and Man United (with Liverpool having a whopping 65% of the ball) – both of which were objectively good results, but which some saw as points *dropped*; despite victories at Old Trafford being rare, and wins at Goodison Park, while more common, still not as frequently achieved as in the previous decade. Watford were beaten with 62% of the ball, Burnley with the Reds having 69%; away at Fulham Klopp's team won with 63%, and at Southampton with 67%. The only league game where the Reds did not have more of the ball was at home when beating Spurs with only 49% of the possession, albeit with the lion's share in the first half. Of the five games in that run where the Reds had over 60% of the ball, they won four and drew away at the biggest of Big Six rivals; another very high average return from games with high possession levels.

Perhaps surprisingly, given how Maurizio Sarri was supposedly making Chelsea a high-possession team, the Reds had 62% in the 2-0 victory in April, while the Reds posted a whopping 74% at the possession-averse Cardiff, under long-ball merchant Neil Warnock, in another 2-0 win. The Reds then blew away Huddersfield with 70% of the ball, and 100% of the five goals, and almost matched that, at 69%, in the late 3-2 victory over Newcastle. And even when it felt like Liverpool were struggling to hold onto the ball, they still posted 59% possession stats when beating Wolves 2-0 on the final day of the league season. All five of these games were won, with four "high possession" performances by Andrew's measure (and the one that wasn't missing out by a mere fraction), and two that fall into Jonathan Wilson's definition of 70%, as noted in his *Guardian* article on the way Man City, and other big clubs, dominate the ball:

"There have always been big clubs before, rich clubs, but never clubs whose status at the top of the game is so systemically secure. In 67 Premier League games this season one side had 70% possession or more; 15 years ago there was one. That is one in six games that are not in any meaningful sense a contest."

One more thing Andrew noticed is that, while the Reds' possession figures have increased, the total shot count has decreased. While this may appear to be a bad thing, it harks back to the expected goals theory: on average, fewer shots from excellent positions are better than a greater number of shots from bad positions. While the total shots figure fell, the percentage of shots *inside the box* rose year on year.

All of which suggests that this is systemic, deep-lying progress by Liverpool on all fronts, and not, as seen in 2013/14, a mere flash in the pan.

Of course, the Champions League final ended up being won with some of Liverpool's worst passing and possession stats of the season, but this wasn't the first time Spurs had out-possessed the Reds in the past year and a half, only to fail to beat them. Spurs seem to be one of the teams the Reds often dare not try too much possession against, preferring to stay in a compact shape and just look for longer-pass counter-attacks. While Liverpool are now *capable* of attaining 70% possession in numerous league games, sometimes they simply don't want to. Indeed, it was almost Mourinhoesque, the final – with his mantra being the team who has the ball is in the greatest danger when it comes to making mistakes. (And so, on occasions where nerves may wreck your composure, it makes some sense.) And as a spectacle it was up there with the "shit on a stick" game between Liverpool and Mourinho's Chelsea in the 2007 Champions League semi-final.

Beautiful, exciting football has been a big part of Klopp's Liverpool tenure; but *occasionally*, winning ugly is all that matters. And in Madrid, no one with Liverpool allegiances cared how the match was won – after some great football and too many near-misses in the past few years – as the players ran around the pitch in utter euphoria and the fans went delirious in the stands.

Set-Piece Redemption: Bigger and Better

As of the end of March 2019, Liverpool had taken just 17 shots at goal from direct free-kicks in the season; scoring just one – from Trent Alexander-Arnold, away at Watford. Xherdan Shaqiri's first free-kick for the club, against Southampton, cannoned back off the joint between bar and post, but Mo Salah had already seemed to know of the little Swiss' plans (after a quick tête-à-tête), and was already following in to score. Otherwise, Alexander-Arnold failed to score with his other six attempts, Shaqiri's further four efforts drew blanks, and none of those taken by Salah (three attempts), Milner (one) nor Virgil van Dijk (one) proved successful. Just on his own, at Derby County, Harry Wilson had scored three free-kick goals in the league, albeit from 28 attempts;

which, at 17, was eleven more than Liverpool either won or elected to shoot from at that juncture. (Wilson also scored free-kicks in the cups, most notably his stunning 'knuckleball' swerver that flew into the net at Old Trafford.) It would appear that this is the one area where Liverpool have a below-par set-piece record, but of course, it also seems that the players are taking fewer shots; instead choosing to pass or cross, to work a different angle. These figures – going indirect from a direct free-kick – would be amalgamated within the *overall* set-piece stats, and hard to separate without watching every game again with just this purpose in mind. Just because it's a direct free-kick, the option to take it as if it were *indirect* still stands.

In the four years between 2012 and 2016, Philippe Coutinho didn't score a single direct free-kick goal in the league for the Reds, but then scored three in 2016/17, and two in 2017/18; with one of the tactics the sneaky "under the wall" ruse, as the defensive players jumped. Before him, Steven Gerrard seemed to score more than his fair share of long-range free-kick goals, although not as many as the memory seems to suggest.

To be frank, Liverpool were an utter set-piece shambles when Jürgen Klopp arrived. It's hard to see another way to describe a side that in 2014/15 had the 5th biggest budget in the Premier League yet won *fewer corners than it conceded;* ending with a set-piece goal difference of -8. (Set-piece data from *Whoscored.*)

In Rodgers' final season, Liverpool scored just six set-piece goals, ranking the club 19th, one place ahead of his former club, Swansea. In return, the Reds conceded a whopping *fourteen*, with only West Brom and QPR conceding more. Overall, Liverpool were the worst team in the league for set-pieces, with both West Brom and QPR scoring enough set-piece goals to end up in set-piece goal-difference credit in West Brom's case (+1), and in the case of QPR – relegated in bottom place – their set-piece goal difference was -6, two better than Liverpool's. Even Swansea, who couldn't *score* set-piece goals, conceded exactly half the amount the Reds did.

In October 2018, Jürgen Klopp spoke to the press about the set-piece improvement, which was clear up to that point of the season: Liverpool having conceded just one set-piece goal, against Spurs in the dying minutes at Wembley, whilst scoring six of their own in the first six league games of the season.

"We did a lot on set-pieces," Klopp said, referring to preseason. "Actually, it's quite difficult to talk about set-pieces because you don't want to talk about it! [For] the routines, there are different runs and different things. We did it in preseason – and it was clear at the start of preseason that we want to focus on it because it was not a proper strength of ours. That's what we do week-in and week-out. It doesn't work out all the time, but I would say it is a different approach that we choose. We have different runs, never the same routine, so it's always something different. We put more focus on it.

"[Sometimes] you really cut off really important training time for set-pieces – and for set-piece training in England, it is quite difficult because it's not very lively. I haven't spoken for a while about the weather because it was so good, but it's rather cold [here] and in Germany it is similar.

"In Spain you could work five hours a week on set-pieces, that's not a problem – but because of the weather in England and Germany it is quite difficult because when it is cold you cannot stand around. It's never very lively, 'you go there, you go there, you run there, you block here…' and at the end everybody is so cold!"

It's interesting that the Reds' set-piece threat initially tailed off as the season unfolded – the further away it got from those summer set-piece drills – with none scored in the Champions League group stages, before, after a gap of several games, seven more were scored in the league heading into winter. In the first 30 games of the season, in all competitions, the Reds conceded just four times from set-pieces; while in the next 22 games eight were conceded – double the amount, in eight fewer games. Overall – and excluding penalties – it means 14 were conceded, and 28 scored, although the definition of set-piece goals varies depending on the source. In this case, analysing the goals ourselves, this includes the second phase of a set-piece, if it was not sufficiently cleared. But by all sources, Liverpool scored the most set-piece goals and had the best set-piece goal difference.

In terms of *efficiency*, a team like Burnley – full of strapping giants – was more effective at scoring from set-pieces (per corner/free-kick), but obviously won far fewer than an elite attacking team in Liverpool. With so many short attacking players, including the full-backs, and only one really tall midfielder, Liverpool had to rely on pin-point delivery and the threat of just two, three or four players.

After the home game against Newcastle on Boxing Day, the regularity of set-piece goals for became more sporadic, and there was a run of conceding a few, too; three in three games in early 2019, after the abortive training camp in Dubai. In the 10 games up to and including the 4-0 win over Newcastle, Liverpool had scored a phenomenal eight goals; having opened the season with six set-piece goals from seven games. Then came just two set-piece goals in the ten games from the 5-1 win over Arsenal to the 5-0 victory over Watford –

which included the costly period of four draws in six games, even if ending the season with one defeat and just seven draws is still far fewer dropped points than you'd expect to see any champions accrue. Had the set-pieces worked a little better in that time, the Reds might have ended up as champions; but there will always be what-ifs. The regular season ended with five set-piece goals scored in the final seven games (before the Champions League final), to almost mirror the opening of the campaign. (One of these goals just happened to be the remarkable vital corner routine which dumped Barcelona out on their backsides.)

And of course, the Champions League final was won by a penalty and a half-cleared corner that Spurs failed to send outside their own box, before the ball, via Matip's touch, fell to Origi, and the game was over.

High

Part of the distinctive setup the Reds deployed was the very high defensive line when defending free-kicks. It looked possible to breach it with a perfect ball, a late run or a quick reworking of the angles, but time and again it either sailed through to Alisson in goal, or more frequently, resulted in an offside flag. While no defensive system can ever be perfect, even the teams that had worked out the weaknesses in the arrangement could not execute the necessary skills to break through, and the tightness of the offside line was almost a work of art in itself. It helped result in a +14 set-piece goal difference, having been at -8 when Klopp arrived.

In the past five seasons, a -8 goal difference on set-pieces has been matched or "bettered" by Watford, Brighton, Crystal Palace, Sunderland, Southampton, Stoke, Aston Villa and Swansea – the kinds of clubs that concede between 200 and 250 corners in a season, and win perhaps only 150. In 2014/15, the Reds won 198 corners and conceded 199; seriously mid-table figures, that were then either scored or punished at relegation rates. Now, corners obviously aren't the only way to score set-piece goals; but it's harder to quantify indirect free-kicks as, unlike corners, they are taken from various positions. So corners make for the best comparison in like-for-like terms.

As of 29 league games played in 2018/19, Liverpool had scored goals from 10 of their 187 corners (5.3%), and conceded just three from the 98 against (3%). Vitally, eight of the 10 goals scored from corners were important within the context of the match: the first goal in a game, or the goals that secured a one- or two-goal victory margin (other goals may have followed after). Only the Sturridge finish to make it 4-0 against West Ham and the Fabinho header to make it 4-0 against Newcastle were essentially nothing more than dressing up the goal difference. None of the three corner-goals the Reds conceded cost any points, although in the case of the ones scored by Burnley (home and away) and Crystal Palace, they did put the Reds under serious pressure, before later goals sealed victories for Klopp's men. The two free-kick goals conceded following the midwinter break to Dubai – against Leicester City and West Ham – were almost ironic, as the trip to the United Arab Emirates was in part designed for set-piece practice, which as Klopp had earlier outlined, is easier in warmer weather, and which had to be aborted due to a food poisoning outbreak. In those two games, Virgil van Dijk was playing having lost several kilos, and, as you might reasonably expect, well below his usual high standards. This is one of those situations where the club were right to make use of the break to go and do some warm-weather training, but where unforeseen circumstances turned the trip into a hindrance rather than a help.

What's most telling about the work Klopp and co. have done – at first, when identifying and buying players who are tall and good in the air (without being technically deficient), and second, drilling them in training – is that the set-piece goal difference has improved every successive season since his arrival, moving from terrible to terrific. It went from the appalling -8 to a fully neutral 0 in 2015/16 (although the German only took charge a quarter of a way into the season); then to +1 in 2016/17 – with 13 scored and a still-alarming 12 conceded; to the +3 of 2017/18, with just 11 scored but only eight conceded; and finally, in 2018/19, 25 scored in the league and 10 conceded, for a +15 goal difference. In all four of the German's seasons the set-piece goals scored column – while fluctuating slightly – has been very healthy, and in each successive season the goals against has dropped by 20-30%.

The best set-piece season for any club over the past five years had been Antonio Conte's Chelsea, who scored 22 on the way to lifting the title in 2017, whilst conceding seven, for a set-piece goal difference of +15. Liverpool matched this in 2018/19. Weirdly, Liverpool scored only three in Europe up to the final – and none in the two domestic cups, which each comprised just one game; but conceded four. Of course, one of these was Lionel Messi's sublime 30-yard free-kick right into the top corner.

By contrast, Manchester City – as you might expect – are a fairly average set-piece team, but obviously have the benefit of scoring more open-play goals than anyone else, and also, conceding, on average, just over two corners per game, due to their high technical skills and domination of possession. They've still managed to concede more set-piece goals than Liverpool, who on average face one extra corner per game than Pep Guardiola's team, but it's tight. However, City are distinctly mid-table for their *own* set-piece goal tallies, despite winning almost eight corners per game, while Liverpool outscore them when winning between 6-7. After 29 games, City had scored just eight set-piece goals, to Liverpool's 17, and their set-piece goal difference was +2, compared with Liverpool's +12. But City are obviously the most intricate, creative side seen in England in many years (and possibly *ever*), and so set-pieces are not so vital to them. However, on a lower budget, set-pieces have to go some way to closing the gap – something Liverpool were failing to do in Rodgers' final 15 months.

And a lot of it comes back to the height issue.

After all, if you buy players like Joe Allen to play the way a Pep Guardiola side might play, you won't get the same output that you would from the real thing – Xavi, Andrés Iniesta or David Silva – and you also won't have the physicality to match the rougher sides. The 'Welsh Xavi' was (and still is) a good player, but if you buy too many diminutive footballers who do not have truly elite-level skills, and are absolutely hopeless at defending set-pieces (and who won't score from any, either), then you are surely putting yourself at a massive disadvantage.

Rodgers' last-ditch solution appeared to hinge around Christian Benteke, and it was possible to see some of the logic behind it; the Belgian being outstanding in the air. However, despite some positives in the theory it failed badly, leaving a disjointed team. The current solution – to have centre-backs and a holding midfielder who are absolutely towering in the air, and to find fast, goalscoring attackers – seems a much more rounded approach, albeit one that relied on finding potentially elite players at affordable fees and helping them to flourish. In addition, it appears that the Reds do a sufficient amount of training ground work on set-pieces, and that wasn't clear prior to Klopp's arrival. You don't have to become a long-ball team, just be able to cope with the opposition's aerial power, and offer something of your own at the other end.

Having written most of this section after game 29 of the 2018/19 season, game 30 obviously had to throw a spanner in the works. Just a few minutes into the home game against Burnley – marked out by yet more utterly bizarre and windy weather befitting of 'global weirding' – the Reds conceded a soft corner (Joel Matip, perhaps spooked by the wind, headed behind) from which Burnley scored *directly*. If the wind had caught the ball and helped it into the far corner, any hope Alisson had of stopping it was denied by Jack Cork backing into him as James Tarkowski jumped over him, using his arms to pin the Liverpool keeper to the ground. It was about as obvious a double-foul as you can see, and the kind most goalkeepers are given.

But that takes us back to the Kop end, and refereeing decisions. Frankly, Liverpool *just don't get them*; one penalty at that end at Anfield since May 2017, whereas Spurs managed two in about 20 minutes in 2017/18. If VAR can undo the Bermuda Triangle of decisions that are the vanishing Kop-end calls that favour Liverpool (but where decisions only disappear in domestic competitions), then the Reds may *finally* win the league.

There have been so many bizarre moments, with referees intent on looking strong in front of the baying Kop. Also in 2017/18, Dominic Solanke's legitimate goal that bounced in off his hand – a rule set to be changed, but which at the time was still legal if unintentional – to grab a late win against West Bromwich Albion, before the officials belatedly disallowed it on the protests of the West Brom players, was another case in point. The corner Burnley scored was another occasion where disallowing an opposition goal at the Kop end would be seen as weakness, even though it was a travesty. The West Brom players got the referee in that aforementioned game to overturn his decision *with their protests*; Alisson's protests simply earned him a yellow card. In the second half a Burnley player blocked a goal-bound shot when turning his back and leaving his arms outstretched to divert the ball, but again, nothing was given; just as a total of no fewer than four really obvious handballs by Stoke and Brighton players at the end of 2017/18 were waved away at the Kop end, one of which was a clearly deliberate forearm smash of the ball.

Liverpool have had almost a dozen legitimate handball claims at the Kop end since James Milner missed a penalty against Southampton in May 2017 (the last time Liverpool won a handball penalty in the league; contrast this wait to that in the Champions League), as well as the über-curious decision to ignore Jamaal Lascelles taking out Mo Salah as the last man in the Reds' 2-0 win.

It is impossible, based on the most basic laws of logic and probability, to deny that Liverpool should have had more penalties in that time. In the time period in question – two full seasons' worth of data – Liverpool had the über-fast and über-busy attacking triumvirate of Mo Salah, Roberto Firmino and Sadio Mané, with additional, more temporary support from Philippe Coutinho, Daniel Sturridge, Xherdan Shaqiri and others.

In a period of two full years – since the penalty awarded to the Reds (against Southampton in 2017) – Liverpool have taken *over 600 shots at Anfield*, and had over 1,200 touches in the opposition area. If we say that, despite the myth (which may still be true to some degree) that the Reds prefer attacking the Kop, those touches and shots are split evenly between the two ends of the pitch, that will be 600 touches in the opposition area and 300 shots. Add in almost well over a hundred corners that will not result in either a shot or a Liverpool touch in the box – because they hit, or are blocked or cleared by, opposition players – and add maybe a total of 500 crosses in that time (Liverpool average 250-300 crosses per season at home, and 130 corners), we are talking *several thousand moments* in the Kop penalty area in a period of almost two years.

Thousands of moments in front of the Kop, *and one single penalty*, and zero sendings off to opponents.

Double those figures to cover *both* ends of Anfield, and zero handball penalties in those two years (double it again to include away games, and still zero handball penalties won). In that time Liverpool scored one accidental handball goal, and that was chalked off; one single incident, not seen clearly by the officials who were going to give the goal, but punished fully. Ergo, Liverpool have been denied as many accidental handball goals in that period in front of the Kop as they have been awarded penalties.

So are we supposed to believe that in two years, in the face of hundreds and hundreds of shots, there hasn't been a single shot or cross blocked – maybe 1,000 instances where a potential handball could occur – by the hand of an opponent with either intent or an "unnatural silhouette" (i.e. arms outstretched, to make the body bigger, even if not moving hand towards ball)? Almost 700 touches of the ball by Liverpool players in the opposition penalty area at the Kop end, and over 200 shots taken *within the box*, and the only infringement in *all that time* was by an Arsenal player on Dejan Lovren? Meanwhile, the visitors to Anfield average about half as many shots, touches in the area, corners and crosses as Liverpool, yet have won more penalties at Anfield. Again, Spurs – in just eight minutes – won twice as many Kop-end penalties as Liverpool have since 2017. (Of course, Liverpool did get some revenge against Spurs with a European referee.)

This makes absolutely no sense, other than to say that it's a bias on the part of the referees. Liverpool have produced sufficiently outstanding attacking output at Anfield in the league since 2017 to merit maybe a dozen penalties, on the law of averages. I could list at least ten that *should* have been given. Something that should be favouring Liverpool – playing at home (which, in terms of winning penalties, favours all other major clubs) – is being used against them by referees.

Below are the percentages of penalties won by the Big Six at home in the previous five years. Bear in mind that the average for all clubs in the Premier League era is around 66% of their penalties won at home, even though the home side tends to average at "only" c.55% of the key metrics in a match: Chelsea 83.3%; Manchester United 75.0%; Everton 66.7%; Manchester City 65.8%; Tottenham Hotspur 60.7%; Arsenal 50%; and Liverpool … 41.9%. When I discussed this on Twitter in 2018, Daniel Storey of *Football365* made the understandable point that surely Liverpool just therefore win more penalties away from Anfield than they should. My argument, given the low *volume* of Liverpool penalties overall – the club rank 11th on average number of penalties won per season in that five-year period – is that Liverpool get a normal number of penalties in away games and an abnormally low number of penalties in home games.

Things improved slightly in 2018/19, and particularly December, which also happened to be the best month in the entire history of Liverpool Football Club (seven league games won in a calendar month for the first time ever). Mo Salah was awarded a penalty for clearly "going down easily" – but only after being fouled – against Newcastle, at the Anfield Road end of the ground. (Again, look at players who stay on their feet when impeded, for the reason why so many players go to ground when touched.) Then came Michael Oliver, who until December had been the only referee to award Liverpool a penalty in 2018/19 – away at Crystal Palace at the start of the campaign – and who, in the past two seasons, remains the only ref to send off a player in the league against Liverpool (again, at Crystal Palace). Oliver, deemed by many to be the league's best referee, gave the Reds two further penalties – both against Arsenal. The first was for a clear trip on Mo Salah when he got in behind the Arsenal defence, and the second was for a push on Lovren at a corner.

Salah then won a penalty at Brighton, awarded by Kevin Friend, when he was clipped not once, not twice, but *three times* by Pascal Groß; as clear a penalty as you will ever see, but because Salah tumbled to the ground in an unusual manner – not least because he was totally off-balance after the fouls – he was accused by some of diving. This was the apex of the outrage about Salah and Liverpool winning too many penalties; the "Penaltypool" jibes that surfaced a few years ago back in force. Between that outcry and the away game at Fulham over three months later, Liverpool did not win a single penalty. Just two were awarded to the Reds between January and May.

The notion that referees just give what they see is utterly ridiculous; people can see only what they want to see, if they are duly primed. A whole host of biases come in to play before anyone makes a decision. And inattentional blindness means referees can miss the obvious, especially if they are predisposed to a certain way of thinking. As explained on *Wikipedia*: "… inattentive blindness results from a lack of attention that is not associated with vision defects or deficits, as an individual fails to perceive an unexpected stimulus in plain sight."

We think of officials as making decisions with clear eyes and a clear mind, but all kinds of strange things influence those tasked with making judgements.

There's also some research from 2011, which, according to *The Guardian* "examined judicial rulings by Israeli judges who presided over parole hearings in criminal cases, found that judges gave more lenient decisions at the start of the day and immediately after a scheduled break in court proceedings such as lunch. Jonathan Levav, associate professor of business at Columbia University, who co-authored the paper, said: 'You are anywhere between two and six times as likely to be released if you're one of the first three prisoners considered versus the last three prisoners considered.'"

The list of the top penalty winning-clubs in the last five seasons appears to show how some kind of bias is at work. They are, in order: Leicester City, Crystal Palace, Manchester City, Brighton & Hove Albion, Bournemouth, Everton, Tottenham Hotspur, Manchester United, Stoke City, Southampton, and joint 11th, Chelsea, Watford and Liverpool.

There's a logic to only one section of the table: teams in the lower reaches will, on average, win a steadily descending number of penalties from 14th down to 20th in relation to their eventual finishing position; i.e the teams who finish 16th will win a slightly higher number of penalties than the team that finishes 17th, and a slightly lower number than the team that finishes 15th. But how does that explain why teams that finish between 8th and 14th win, on average, a higher number of penalties than the teams that finish 1st-7th?

I addressed this issue on *The Tomkins Times* in February 2019 after *Sky News* ran an opinion piece from a journalist who is a Watford fan (Adam Parsons) – days before Liverpool played Watford at Anfield – that claimed the big clubs like Liverpool get more of the big decisions in their favour. "Deny Watford a goal wrongly, and it's awkward," the journalist wrote. "Deny Liverpool a goal, and you could change the whole course of the Premier League title."

Except, Watford have won as many penalties per season in the last five seasons as Liverpool, and Liverpool have either been competing for the top four or the title (i.e. with something tangible at stake) –

while Watford have largely stayed mid-table, neither threatened by relegation nor in danger of being denied decisions that could put them into the Champions League. Any trawl through the comments during a *BBC* website match commentary will see fans of smaller clubs bemoaning how the bigger clubs "get all the decisions". And someone like Neil Warnock will say it virtually every week.

Well, the team to win the most penalties in a single season since 2014? Leicester City, with 13, on the way to the title. Of the top five penalty-winning teams since the start of 2014/15, four are smaller clubs: Leicester, Crystal Palace, Brighton & Hove Albion and Bournemouth, with only Man City, ranking 3rd, in amongst them.

So my argument here would be the exact opposite of Mr Parsons' – that actually, being mid-table makes it *easier* for referees to give a decision, as less is at stake. *Avoiding* decisions is what the modern referee seems to specialise in, perhaps understandably so, given the outrage to every decision – and of course, something that goes unpunished leaves no mark on the record books, unlike a wrongly allowed goal or incorrect dismissal. The reason VAR is so essential is to take that fear away from the referees and to allow them to punish what they see, although even then the rules are often vague and open to all manner of interpretation and fudging, such as the ludicrous offside situations where an offside striker can go for a ball and not be given offside as he's not interfering *until* he touches the ball, and can be played onside by the touch of a defender who is only touching the ball to stop it getting to said striker. Consistency will still be hard to find, but if it means a greater proportion of the *obvious* decisions are given correctly – such as the foul on Alisson by the two Burnley players that was beyond debate when viewed from pretty much every television angle – then it will be for the greater good of the game. The only worry would be referees simply not referring anything to VAR as they do not want their decisions to be challenged.

This should probably mean the Big Six getting more penalties than they currently do, and while it's hard for fans of other clubs to feel sympathy for anything that makes the gap between the haves and have-nots even wider, an adherence to the rules has to be better than something affected by biases. The evidence clearly shows that Liverpool, based on the past five seasons, are punished more harshly when it comes to winning penalties than other Big Six clubs, which must surely be a remnant of the myth of the Kop "winning" so many penalties – which of course may have been true back in the days when the referee only had 50,000 swaying bodies to appease, whereas now the people in the ground are just a tiny fraction of the overall audience who will be reacting to events. Now, the TV stations, media and social media are who the referees have to most publicly answer to.

Despite my own clear bias, I think the evidence offered is strong. Indeed, my bias *simply drove me to go and research the facts*, in contrast to the aforementioned "opinion piece" on *Sky News*, which used no data at all, and just the author's biased assumption that smaller clubs get more harshly treated than bigger clubs – and argued his case based on one single anecdote where he felt Watford should have had a penalty against Liverpool and that, if it was the other way around, Liverpool would have got the decision. When a team as mediocre as Watford – average position of below mid-table – wins exactly as many penalties per season as Liverpool – average league position of just better than 5th – then you can say that the premise is false, and bigger clubs – with better teams – do not get more favourable decisions, certainly as far as winning penalties is concerned. And in 2018/19, Liverpool had two players sent off, despite having the fewest bookings by any Premier League club in 14 years, but only one opposition player was dismissed.

When Stoke City have won more Premier League penalties per season after 2014 than Liverpool (albeit their top-flight run ended in 2018), or when Leicester, Crystal Palace, Brighton and Bournemouth average far more penalties per season than the Reds, you know something isn't quite right. When Spurs win more league penalties at Anfield in front of the Kop *in one half of a league game* than Liverpool have won in 34 halves attacking that goal, you also know something isn't quite right. What are the odds on these events being logical and just?

While Man City traditionally win a lot of penalties (and did so on the way to 100 points in 2017/18), that wasn't happening in 2018/19 – although they did correctly win, and thankfully miss, one at Anfield in the 0-0 draw in October. After that burst of penalties in December, Liverpool moved three penalty awards clear of City, and with a better (i.e. perfect) conversion rate. But then, in early 2019, after City as a club went to the referees, to claim they have not been getting the calls they merited, they then won two vital spot-kicks, one of which was from zero contact – and zero *attempted* contact – on Bernardo Silva, that saw him hit the deck against West Ham; the resultant penalty winning the match for the home side. Next came the bizarre offside goal Raheem Sterling was allowed to score to break the deadlock after half-time in their home match against Watford.

For Liverpool to win the title against the might and talent of City it needs a bit of luck, without doubt. But once referees stopped cancelling out what appeared to be a slight advantage to the Reds, City were able to turn the screw.

Ex-referee Keith Hackett, writing for the *Daily Telegraph* on March 11th, was in no doubt that refereeing standards were tumbling, after a weekend of fixtures that saw at least half a dozen major errors, three of which could have directly affected Liverpool's title chances: Man City able to break the deadlock with a most obviously offside goal; Alisson fouled for Burnley's goal to open the scoring at Anfield; and even Moussa Sissoko committing "two red-card offences against Southampton, including a butt, and was not sent off" – when Spurs' next league game was a trip to Liverpool. (Sissoko had a late run on goal to win the game for Spurs, before the Reds grabbed a vital goal. Of course, Sissoko also played a key role in handing Liverpool a penalty in the Champions League final, so perhaps it was fitting.)

"Liverpool's title aspirations could easily have been undermined by a poor decision from the referee," wrote Hackett, "when Ashley Westwood's goal was allowed to stand despite a clear foul on the keeper Alisson.

"On a weekend that featured far too many incorrect calls from officials, meanwhile, Manchester City were given a goal despite Raheem Sterling having clearly been in an offside position before scoring the opening goal. These were just two mistakes in a round of Premier League games that should concern the authorities. The standard of refereeing is in decline and measures must be taken to address the problem.

"Take the Alisson incident. Burnley clearly set out to block and impede the keeper, with a player positioned both in front and behind him, allowing Westwood's corner to fly directly into the net. Fortunately for justice's sake, Liverpool recovered from the early setback to win the game, but the decision typified an increasing problem of referees allowing unlawful physical contact in the penalty area to pass without sanction."

Another ex-senior referee, Dermot Gallagher, wrote of the decision on *Sky Sports*: "It's a foul. Not only are there arms on the shoulder, but he completely stops him going for the ball and it is just a foul. He has quite clearly held him down and Alisson cannot get the ball, so it should have been a foul."

Both Gallagher and Hackett couldn't believe the offside goal Man City were allowed to score, which was not down to the linesman failing to spot the offside, but the referee, after a three-minute discussion, incorrectly overruling him.

Gallagher: "Paul Tierney has felt that Janmaat has played the ball and therefore he has taken ownership of that situation. But what he has not realised is that Sterling has actually got the drop on him and therefore when they have pooled their resources, Paul has overridden him and said, 'No, I am going to give the goal,' which was incorrect." Hackett said, "At the Etihad, Paul Tierney's decision to allow Sterling's goal was even more perplexing, given that his assistant flagged for offside."

And this was without covering perhaps the biggest mistake of the season, in terms of its timing in the most crucial of games. Man City were drawing 0-0 at home to Liverpool in the first half of a game that could have seen the Reds go 10 points clear, when the most obvious red card of the season was unfathomably treated as just a caution.

Hackett said in his column following the game: "Vincent Kompany deserved to be shown a red card rather than a yellow for his first-half challenge on Mohamed Salah. No doubt about that. The Manchester City captain has used excessive force off the ground as he goes in to challenge the Liverpool forward and is out of control by the time that he makes contact.

"Referee Anthony Taylor could not be faulted generally for his fitness and movement, but on this crucial decision I wonder if his positioning for the challenge allowed him to have the best view. This was yet another clear example of where the video assistant referee would have proved invaluable."

Hackett doesn't even reference the cynical nature of it, with Kompany knowing that he had to take Salah out to stop him running in on goal from the halfway line. Even if it's not a red card offence for the last-man rule, it's a red card for the challenge and a further yellow card for its *cynicism*. It would have been a yellow card had he hauled him back with a pull, yet it was only a yellow card to stop him with both feet, studs-up, into the Egyptian's shins.

Kompany virtually admitted it was a desperate attempt. "On the pitch I felt I got the ball, a bit of the man, but it wasn't naughty. I didn't try to injure him, that's for sure. It was that *or let him go through on goal* and the decision was made very quickly in my head." (My emphasis.)

City's players later sung a song about the incident.

Former highly-rated Premier League referee Mark Clattenburg was another who said Vincent Kompany was "lucky" not to be sent off. "On watching the replay, it is easy to make a case for a red card, because it is clear Kompany lunges with a straight leg and his studs showing," he wrote in a tabloid newspaper.

Kompany had made the assault even worse with his crude comments to Salah as the Liverpool player lay on the ground, which, even in a German newspaper headline, tell the story: "Kompany schimpft Salah: *Steh auf, du Pussy!*". Charming. (German newspaper *Bild* also said: "Klopp in Rage wegen *Brutalo*-Foul von Kompany".) All told, Kompany could have had about three yellow cards for the incidents, if not a red. The "likeable" Belgian escaped with other bad tackles in later games, to help City over the line in the incredible final months of the season.

Even Better?

In truth, the Reds' set-piece record should be even better. The Harry Maguire goal Leicester scored to take two points at Anfield should not have happened; not only could he have been sent off after a last-man foul, but given that it came well over a minute beyond added time, *no one* should have been on the pitch. The Burnley goal straight from a corner was farcical, whilst Burnley's goal at Turf Moor – also from a corner – involved an offside Chris Wood swinging at the ball, and missing, *right in front of Alisson* (the same offence for which Liverpool had goals disallowed at Spurs and Arsenal). If trying to kick the ball right in front of the keeper is not "active", then what is? Why was it active when Liverpool had the same situation in those two big away games?

Then, for James (no relation) Tomkins' equaliser from a corner at home to Crystal Palace, striker Jordan Ayew had both hands around Virgil van Dijk's midriff to stop him jumping for the ball, and, a mere yard away, another Crystal Palace player had both arms around Jordan Henderson's waist. From Palace it was more like a tactic you'd expect when *defending* a set-piece; in this case, Roy Hodgson's men used it to stop Liverpool being able to clear the ball.

Also, West Ham's clever free-kick to equalise at the London Stadium involved Naby Keita being blocked by Mark Noble – which was hard to spot initially, and perhaps just one of those things that you have to accept, and which wasn't as blatant as having both hands around someone's midriff to stop them moving; but something VAR would perhaps spot and punish.

So both Burnley set-piece goals against Liverpool *definitely* should have been chalked off, as should Palace's; while Leicester's and West Ham's costly goals against the Reds were both contentious. Some blocking off is to be expected, but clear cases of holding that deny a goalkeeper or defender the chance to challenge for the ball need to be punished.

Thankfully the Reds had a bit more luck in the Champions League when it came to set-pieces – and certainly penalties – and the frustrations in the league can be put to one side.

PART THREE

The Run-In: So Close, No Cigar

So much hinged on Mo Salah's decision to stay alive to the looping cross to the far past – a Liverpool tactic on second-balls from set-pieces, in evidence from as early as the very first-half of football of the season, when, against West Ham, James Milner kept Andy Robertson's high cross alive, to square for Sadio Mané to score.

Over seven months later, Liverpool were drawing at home to Spurs, having dominated the first half, but were losing ground in the second. Jürgen Klopp, in desperation, had switched to a 4-2-4 formation for the closing stages of the match, eager to gain those two extra points by whatever it took. Spurs had three or four chances to break against the ludicrously top-heavy Reds, but then one of the subs, Divock Origi – the man who popped up time and again in the final stage of the season – powered down the line and won a corner. Though initially cleared, when Robertson hung the return ball up to the far post, Spurs' defenders were caught half-asleep, with their full-backs more intent on switching to their natural flanks than following the flight of the cross. The only player alive to the situation was Mo Salah, goalless in nine games, and playing with some clear anxiety in front of goal. His header was the safe option – back across goal, but with total focus on hitting the target; choosing accuracy, rather than power. As such it was an easy catch for Hugo Lloris, and yet the French World Cup-winning goalkeeper somehow fumbled it, into the legs of Toby Alderweireld, and as the pair got in each other's way as they half-jabbed at it (it clearly needed an old-fashioned English centre-half screaming "get fucking rid!"), the ball trickled over the line. Salah was credited with the goal at the game, but given that the ball was travelling *away* from the goal at the time it struck the Spurs' defender it had to be an own goal. But it proved the turning point for the Egyptian, as – somehow – Liverpool's title charge stayed on track.

The games were coming thick and fast, each the proverbial "cup final", with a few Champions League knockout games thrown in for good measure. At this stage of the season, Europe seemed a mere afterthought. Late wins were the order of the day, with some calamitous goalkeeping thrown in, but this could be seen as part of the pressure the Reds were exerting on teams, especially at the Kop end. Late goals are what the best teams conjure, if the game isn't already won. As Pep Guardiola noted, if it happened once or twice, it's luck; but Liverpool kept forcing those errors.

The victory over Spurs came on the last day of March. Two months earlier had been the back-to-back draws in games that were probably winnable, if not necessarily nailed-on, given that they were against mid-table sides with a smattering of excellent players; with Leicester faced in the most bizarre weather conditions.

After those two midwinter post-training camp slip-ups, and with a 0-0 draw against Bayern in the first leg of the last 16 of the Champions League, the Reds were foist into two away trips that would be tough to win under normal circumstances, but both Manchester United and Everton were going to bring all the noise they could muster to poop the Reds' party. (*Poop* being the operative word when it usually comes to Everton.)

The Reds escaped with a point from both matches, played out as 0-0 draws where the home team was intent on merely spoiling the play; with the shock of Man United – even post-Jose Mourinho – happy to have less than 40% of the possession at Old Trafford. In the other game, the wind was howling around the open-sided Goodison Park, to further add to the drama. A lot was made of Liverpool not going for it against United when they lost three players to injury in the first half, but United survived without any further injury scares; and Liverpool had just played Bayern Munich mere days earlier, while United's Champions League game against PSG was the previous week. So, as ever, the *timing* wasn't great for Liverpool. As with people saying Liverpool should have given more to the away game in Napoli days after the slugfest at Stamford Bridge, sometimes it's just not that easy.

At Goodison Park the Reds had all the best chances, despite Everton having an extra rest day after the midweek fixtures, but Klopp's men fluffed their lines, particularly when Fabinho took a touch rather than trying to blast in from close range; while Mo Salah was in the middle of a nine-game scoring drought, and snatching at chances.

Just days earlier I was lucky enough to be at Anfield for the 5-0 demolition of Watford, on one of those nights under the floodlights when the glow of the green grass was accentuated by the vividness and stark contrast of the red and yellow kits, Salah, despite not scoring, continually tore past their left-back, while Virgil van Dijk was utterly imperious at both ends, denying Troy Deeney in the air, before powering in two headers of his own.

When van Dijk signed I asserted that he could be worth 10 goals to the Reds at each end of the pitch; but in the end – at least until the halfway point of the season – he had probably helped take 20 off the goals-against column, without scoring the amount expected. But by the end of the season he was edging up towards double figures, and adding in the assists meant that he *contributed* in double figures.

Watford midfielder Will Hughes was asked on radio to compare Liverpool and Man City, having faced both in quick succession. "Playing against Liverpool, you hear people talk about them suffocating you and that's exactly what it was like. The atmosphere on a Wednesday night, I've never experienced that in a Premier League game. It was deafening. The title race is going to be brilliant this season I think, and hopefully it goes down to the wire.

Asked to clarify just what was suffocating, he said, "It was both, the crowd, the atmosphere, and as well on the pitch. It felt like they had more players. You know as a team you'll be defending, but when we got the ball, they were on us for the whole 90 minutes. It was an experience I'll never forget."

At this stage of the season Mané became the main man. The 3-0 win against Bournemouth on February 9th was the first game where he showed what became a surprising aerial prowess, while embarking on a run of 16 goals after mid-January, with most of them the vital opening goal for the Reds. Until that point his finishes had been from fine strikes – but not tap-ins – taken inside the area; often powerful, lashed finishes, with the one in the 4-1 victory over Cardiff almost ludicrous in how much power he generated with no backlift. Some were dinked over goalkeepers or thrashed under, with others tucked in after rounding the keeper, as at Crystal Palace and to seal the victory over Burnley; and the inch-perfect curler to help turn that game against Burnley from a 1-0 deficit into a 4-2 victory. And there was the ridiculous backheeled goal for his second of the game against Watford, where a slightly loose touch turned into a powerful reverse shot with his back to goal – with additional lift gained by using his heel to stub the ball into the turf and send it over the bamboozled Ben Foster.

But Mané used his head against Bournemouth, Watford, Chelsea, Huddersfield twice (the second an absolute bullet-header) and Wolves, and in Europe, against Bayern Munich – to make for seven in the final third of the season. In the second half of the season headed goals were also scored by Naby Keïta, Virgil van Dijk (five!), Divock Origi, Gini Wijnaldum and a few by Roberto Firmino too – to show that, while *defending* set-pieces often requires height, if the delivery is perfect from an attacking sense, smaller players can get plenty of goals if those bigger defenders are wrong-footed or out of position (while someone like van Dijk can be impossible to defend against *legally*). Indeed, Mané was the joint-top scorer of headed league goals (six) along with giants Aleksandar Mitrović and Chris Wood.

Midfield Mire?

Throughout the season the Liverpool midfield was criticised for not being creative enough, and not scoring enough goals, but as explained in more detail elsewhere in this book, their main job was to support a front three – who Liverpool obviously do not want to have to spend games tracking back (although they will if under the cosh) – and reinforcing the runs and the spaces left behind the assist-machines that play at full-back.

But then in April it was the midfield's turn to become providers and scorers. It began at Southampton with Naby Keïta opening both the Reds' scoring on the night – to equalise after a rare Shane Long goal – and his Liverpool account, with a far-post header. This was the foothold in the game Klopp's men needed, and with ten minutes to go Jordan Henderson – as mentioned earlier in the book, but worth repeating – *somehow* angled his neck to head, with precision, a ball that absolutely sped at him from Sadio Mané's sensational block challenge; the Liverpool captain not only clearing the ball but consciously sending it 30 yards into the path of Mo Salah, who was then able to run 50 yards before, after a deft touch to manoeuvre the ball, curled a sweet shot into the far corner – for his first goal in nine games. Off came the shirt as he wheeled away in delirium. It was yet another late Liverpool goal, built by pressure and resilience. But there was time for one more – Henderson himself popping up in the box after a delightful turn by Roberto Firmino (which itself came from Alisson feeding Joël Matip, who hit a peach of a long-range pass into the channel), and the captain swept the ball home from Firmino's cross before also wheeling off in absolute delirium, to end no little personal frustration; his first goal in well over a year.

Keïta, goalless in almost 30 games before breaking his duck, knew his luck had changed when, five minutes into the quarter-final against Porto, his shot deflected past a helpless Iker Casillas. It was a strangely low-key major European night, with such a momentous occasion totally overshadowed by the Reds' thrilling league title pursuit.

This was the Reds' seventh appearance at that stage of the continent's premier competition since 2002, and yet it was only the club's third title challenge in that same period. Henderson turned provider again, dissecting the Portuguese back-line with surgical skill to skewer both centre-backs and the left-back, as Liverpool's right-back-cum-right-winger Trent Alexander-Arnold collected yet another assist, putting it on a plate for Firmino.

And then, days later against Chelsea, Henderson continued his transformation from safety-conscious holding midfielder to marauding inside-forward by dancing to the byline and standing up the most delicate of crosses onto Sadio Mané's head. Another three days later and Henderson was at it again, curling in a beauty of a cross right onto Firmino's forehead in Porto, on the way to a thumping 4-1 win, 6-1 on aggregate.

The charge of the central midfield brigade was not done; away at Cardiff, on a pitch left bone dry and with the grass left to grow long, it was Gini Wijnaldum's turn to absolutely leather home a shot, to break the deadlock in the second half. The Dutchman doesn't score a lot of goals, but he is a master of *important* ones; and the benefit of having a redefined – and refined – holding midfielder who has scored more goals in his career than a lot of Premier League strikers. With Mo Salah then winning a penalty for having the tenacity to fall over after being held round the waist not once but twice, before the Sean Morrison's forearm was dug into his neck, it fell on James Milner to take a late penalty – as he had just over a month earlier at Fulham – to seal the victory. The vice-captain – only on because substitute Fabinho lasted a minute before suffering a concussion – proved once again that he has ice in his veins. (His favourite drink may be Ribena, but his second-favourite is liquid nitrogen.)

Then, in the game of the season against Barcelona, Wijnaldum popped up with two vital goals. It took the midfield's tally (if Xherdan Shaqiri can be included) to 23.

But it's not like the midfield were suddenly forced to do *all* the creating and *all* the scoring. The front three were busy taking their total since the start of 2017/18 past 150, and the full-backs remained a vital supply line.

Mo Salah haunts his old club

Chelsea had asked for it. Or rather, a small gaggle of knuckle-headed Chelsea fans had asked for it. And those Chelsea fans, gathered in a bar days earlier in Prague, got it, with both barrels. Liverpool's two Muslim strikers rammed the vile stereotypes back down those ale-addled throats. Muslims 2, bigots 0. There were no bombs, to use a word from their song; just a second-half *bombardment.*

Then, the travelling thousands in the away end asked for it: singing about Steven Gerrard's infamous 2014 slip *before* the game, and then several times during the game. As the Kop, clearly riled up, ran the gamut of songs in a noisy, choral first 20 minutes – serenades for Liverpool players, one after another, or of European travels and glories – the mood was clear. (Regarding the visiting fans, you have to wonder if fans of some other clubs ever sing any songs about their *own* club and its players? Wolves' fans would be the same on the final day, as would Man City's.)

One thing you never want to do in football is give your opponent a reason to be angry at you, and for them to feel slighted; the very reason no manager or player wants to give anything away before a game that could be pinned on the opposing dressing-room wall, hence why all pre-match talk is largely dull platitudes about how good the opposition are, how difficult the game will be, and so on. But in Prague on Thursday 11th April, some absolutely sickeningly stupid and nasty Chelsea fans chose to video themselves singing about Mo Salah – a player who left them in 2015 after 18 months at their club, not through his own choice, and who has never been disrespectful to his former employers – in which they basically called him a terrorist. Not only was it vile, but it was self-destructive; to use their parlance, a dumb-bomb, destined to blow up in their own prehistoric faces.

Do you *really* want to make Mo Salah angry days before you are due to face him? In the build-up to the game Chelsea, as a club (and at that, one in need of the points in the race for the top four), were forced onto the defensive, and Salah – who up to that point had looked a bit sheepish against his former clubs (scoring a brilliant goal against Roma at Anfield but, as against Chelsea in 2017/18 when he notched a more simple closer-range strike, not celebrating when scoring; and generally looking a bit inhibited in Rome, and in two return visits to Stamford Bridge). Fuelled by smiles rather than hate, he's not the kind of player to be disrespectful to a previous club; but fans of one of those clubs had just claimed he was a terrorist.

It was clear that the gloves were off; any goal would be celebrated, with Chelsea forced to have the nasty words of a small number of fans rammed down their throats. In this instance it was a football-shaped ramming rod travelling at about 80mph.

The move started with a trademark Virgil van Dijk long pass, out to the wing. Salah's first touch was tidy, and he took the ball inside his ex-Roma colleague, Emerson Palmieri. Before one of the centre-hacks could get close enough, Salah drew his foot back and launched a strike so sweet that, despite travelling almost 30 yards, the ball itself did not make a full rotation between leaving his boot and bulging the net. From where I was sitting I assumed it to be a badly mishit effort destined for the Kop, but it simply soared into the top corner.

The deadlock had just been broken less than two minutes earlier by Liverpool's other Muslim striker, Sadio Mané. Not only did that further extend Mané's lead as the top scoring Premier League player when penalties were excluded – something he went on to cement in the final games – it was yet another header, and yet another vital goal. As Andrew Beasley noted in his column for *The Liverpool Echo* after the game, "The Senegalese star has had a real knack for breaking the deadlock recently. In the last nine matches where the Reds have scored first, Mané has been the man responsible seven times. Liverpool were now in command of the match. It's been two years since they lost a league game at Anfield, which was also the last time they scored first and lost. Having won 42 of the 51 league games when netting first since, Mané's header was a big step towards securing the points."

Chelsea responded with two big chances for Eden Hazard, but Alisson closed him down quickly for the first, which – in order to beat the keeper – had to be aimed below the Brazilian's outstretched leg, and that meant little room for error; and, as such, it bounced back off the foot of the post. The next chance Hazard didn't quite fully connect with, but again Alisson's reflexes were razor sharp – just as they had been at Stamford Bridge earlier in the season.

All the fatuous, ubiquitous talk of 2014 and Gerrard's slip was wiped away by the 2-0 victory, and after the match Jürgen Klopp saluted the Kop with his trademark trio of fist-pumps, each cheered by the whole stand, which was still full and still in fine voice. Nothing had been won, but in order to win things *the game had to be won*. And, of course, there was the issue of winning the day's battle, if not the war; and of silencing bigots.

Victory took Liverpool to the utterly insane rank of 2nd in the all-time "points after 34 games" chart (85, with 12 more still up for grabs), ranking behind only 2017/18's record-breaking Man City side; albeit City had the chance to knock the Reds down to 3rd if they won their 34th game – which they duly did, a little nervously, with a 1-0 win over Spurs. City's 35th game of the season felt like it would be the key: away at Manchester United, who were coming off the back of a stinging week that saw them ship seven goals and score none in away games at Barcelona and Everton. Liverpool needed a big favour from the old enemy; a favour many United fans had been saying they would not want their own team to give.

Liverpool's own 35th game was won 2-0 away at Cardiff. Prior to the game, Klopp had made sure that the grass was grown long at Melwood and left unwatered in anticipation of the awfully dry and stodgy pitch that Cardiff were likely to present; which they duly did. This seems like smart thinking, that not every manager would come up with. Football will always present you with nasty surprises, but the more you prepare for the difficulties you can foresee the less spooked you will be.

After the game, in his role as a *Sky* pundit, it was a joy to see Graeme Souness – a man whose most gleeful expression is still little more than the disgusted stare of someone who has just seen a drunken interloper take a dump on his doorstep – gushing like a five-year-old to Jürgen Klopp about just how "proper" his team is; how it has no clear weaknesses; and how it "*will* win things".

Game 36 was probably the biggest home-banker of the season, with Huddersfield arriving long-since relegated, and with just 14 points on the board (74 behind Liverpool, which must be some kind of record), most of which they had accrued in the first half of the season.

But they *came to play*, as the saying goes, and within 10 seconds they had been robbed by a 20-yard Naby Keïta dash, closing like a demented dervish to win the ball, and with his block the first part of a quick one-two with Mo Salah – which added another few seconds to the game – the Guinean had tucked the ball past the visiting goalkeeper with inch-perfect precision. By the end Liverpool had run in five goals, to take the title down to the wire.

The Reds faced Newcastle away in their penultimate game of the league season – on a Saturday night – and it was another humdinger, with the St James' Park faithful full of sound and fury (and possibly ale) in their last home game of 2018/19. The Geordies, finally safe from relegation, were able to play with a freedom rarely seen in a dogfight of a season, and Rafa Benítez was the ultimate professional against his former club. Newcastle fought tooth and nail, and sometimes with studs showing; Matt Ritchie constantly fouling Mo Salah all match.

Virgil van Dijk opened the scoring with an unmarked header from a corner after Newcastle's man-marking (in contrast to what Benítez used with Liverpool) resulted in both sets of players blocking each other, past which the Dutchman sauntered to head home. But Newcastle equalised from Christian Atsu, after Trent Alexander-Arnold had handled Salomón Rondón's effort on the line. The letter of the law meant that the young full-back would have been sent off had the rebound not been tucked home; and presumably Newcastle were happier to have a five-yard tap-in, with a 99% scoring probability, than the 70-80% eventuality of a penalty. Mo Salah then beautifully tucked home a second for the Reds, to restore the lead, but Rondón, who was a handful all night, powered home a second-half equaliser after the visitors only half-cleared a Newcastle corner; the final goal Liverpool conceded all season. The night would get even worse when Mo Salah became the second Liverpool player struck by a concussion in the run-in, after Fabinho's recent clash of heads. Salah, when running towards the goal, was caught on the side of the head by the Newcastle keeper's hip, and while not out cold, was clearly groggy. It cost him a chance to play in the Champions League semi-final second leg against Barcelona, with Roberto Firmino also missing both the trip to Newcastle and that huge Anfield occasion.

But cometh the hour, cometh the Origi. On to replace the stricken Salah, Liverpool were now reduced to a front three that contained only Sadio Mané from the famous trident. As against Huddersfield, and as against Barcelona days later, the Reds made an on-field decision at a set-piece – van Dijk over-ruling an out swinger by Alexander-Arnold in favour of an in-swinger from Shaqiri (another sub) – that the little Swiss curled in perfectly onto Origi's head. Perhaps the big Belgian only got a mere dreadlock on the ball, but in the challenge with the Newcastle defender it flew into the net. The pressure was back on City for the weekend ahead, but alas, with the score at 1-0 after a super-rare Vincent Kompany long-range goal, Iheanacho stabbed a late chance for Leicester to equalise well wide, and City then just had to win at Brighton on the final day, and anything Liverpool could do against Wolves would be academic. (The less that's said about that Iheanacho miss the better. It may not have been deliberate, but it *was* awful).

I left Anfield on the final day of the league season, after the 2-0 win against Wolves, not in regret or sadness but suffused with a Reds-red – *that specific scarlet* – glow of pride in the glorious Merseyside sunshine: at the team, the manager, the backroom staff and executives, and at the Liverpool fans, who were just majestic throughout the game, as they had been on all my recent trips. It was all slightly surreal, in that there was a party atmosphere before the game, but also, with nothing won, a party atmosphere afterwards, too. The entire stadium stayed behind for 30-45 minutes after the final whistle, to congratulate a team that would have been champions in 125 of the 127 other seasons; a team that took the record-breaking, financially-doped Man City to within 60 minutes of stealing the title. And of course, a team heading for the Champions League final in Madrid.

On the south coast, at Brighton, Pep Guardiola's men overturned a surprising one-goal deficit – conceding after 29 minutes before equalising after 30 – to run out 4-1 winners, but not without some jitters. Liverpool's display against Wolves was fairly nerve-free until news of the Glenn Murray goal for Brighton at the Amex had the whole of Anfield in disbelief, and a surreal atmosphere befell the game. Everyone around me was turning to those a few rows above in the executive boxes, who had televisions showing updates from the south coast; with sign language quickly explaining that it was 1-1 in that game and not, as people seemed to think, 2-0 to Brighton.

The match at Anfield then fell apart somewhat when news of Chris Hughton's men taking the lead spread like wildfire around the ground – the players caught up in the momentary hysteria – before news filtered through, a minute later, that Sergio Agüero had equalised. If anything, Brighton had gone too early, and incurred the wrath of a side who, rather than draw, now had to win. From that point on, the Liverpool crowd – mocked by the visiting Wolves fans in just the latest example of the crass nature of football support these days (focussing on trolling, rather than supporting their own team, who themselves had recently thrown away a 2-0 lead in an FA Cup semi-final) – sang songs of celebration, for a phenomenal effort and a sensational points return.

Liverpool won 14 of their final 15 games in all competitions. But it wasn't enough to land the title, with City winning all of their final 14 Premier League fixtures. You cannot deny that City were worthy champions, in terms of the football they played, but had it gone the other way there could be no arguments either; and Liverpool, by contrast, were not under a cloud of alleged financial impropriety. To make matters worse for City, further dark clouds emerged in the build-up to their FA Cup victory over Watford, as Uefa announced they were going to recommend pressing charges; and then, when City trounced Watford 6-0, huge sections of the media seemed to turn against them, as if they had rigged the system so much in their favour that it was destroying the "sport" of the game. At the time when they wanted their greatest adulation, they received plenty of brickbats. To many, the game no longer seemed fair; in part due to how brilliant Pep Guardiola was, but also due to the financial advantages that may not have been within permitted spending limits. And while City may claim to not care, having sewn up the domestic treble, they seemed horrified by the backlash. One of their fans even broke into the media room after the FA Cup final to ask, after perhaps ten too many pints of beer, if the journalists were going to put Liverpool and Mo Salah on the back pages yet again; in so doing, putting Liverpool and Mo Salah on the back pages yet again.

Liverpool's final 15 games of the season across all competitions were even more incredible than City's – due to the quality of opposition faced, and the dual Champions League/Premier League pressures – with the only match not won in that run coming away at Barcelona (a farcical result based on the balance of play), which was duly overturned at Anfield. As such, the Reds won enough games to become Champions of Europe for a sixth time; as, presumably, City's players and fans watched on TV, and – three weeks after their distasteful song about the Reds – could no longer sing about Liverpool winning "fuck all". City had an amazing season; Liverpool had *an even better one*.

How League Titles Are *Usually* Won

Ever since Jose Mourinho credited Chelsea's League Cup final victory over Liverpool in 2005 as the springboard to their league title successes that year, it seems to have become taken as a truth that winning such competitions leads to greater things; like how smoking pot supposedly leads to taking harder drugs, even though millions of people smoke pot – a quick google suggests 13% of Americans say they "regularly" or "occasionally" use or smoke marijuana – and nowhere near as many people take harder drugs (according to one study, just 0.2% of the US population uses heroin, which is just over 1% of the figure that smoke weed).

The League Cup or FA Cup are "gateways to better things", we are told. But just like gateway drugs, it's not necessarily true. It feels like post-hoc thinking; a gateway *only when looked at in hindsight* – when ignoring all the other evidence; dismissing, or just not considering, when either a cup win actually led to nothing, or league titles were won without winning a cup to build up that "essential winning mentality" first. It's just like how the vast majority of those people never move onto smack from dope, as well as the random crazies who go straight from Lucozade to shooting up crack.

The received wisdom is that winning cups is vital to go onto better things, and yet it's stated whilst ignoring strong evidence that cup runs often actually *harm* your league health (a problem that is partially obviated by having a huge squad). It seems to ignore that, actually, you can become a better team over time *without winning anything*; and also, that winning *domestic* cups often involves just five or six games, and the quality of opposition you may be drawn against varies immensely, and therefore it can be random, and ultimately, *unimpressive*. To reach a Champions League final – even to lose it – is a far greater marker of quality, and far more likely to result in some kind of elite education as a result of the tough tests it involves (and how we only really learn when we are pushed past our comfort zone).

When Liverpool exited the FA Cup away at Wolves – hardly a shameful giant-killing – with Jürgen Klopp fielding some kids, and bringing on a 16-year-old Dutch centre-back for his debut just five minutes into the game (following the injury to Dejan Lovren that kept him out for months), there was an outcry in certain sections of the media about not "respecting" the competition (as if the FA Cup still meant what it did 40 years earlier, with its diminished status hardly Klopp's fault); and also talk of it being a failure to instil a winning mentality at Liverpool, who were top of the league at the time (and therefore, presumably *winning quite a few football matches?*). Around the same time, Man City were beating Burton Albion 9-0 at home – but does thrashing Burton Albion in itself have any great significance?

Returning to Mourinho's assertion, Liverpool played Chelsea after the 27th league game of his debut season 14 years ago. At that point the Blues were a staggering *nine* points clear at the top. Effectively, the league was already as good as won. No one – not even Newcastle – has blown a nine-point lead at that late juncture. Ergo, winning the League Cup was largely irrelevant.

I remember writing on the Liverpool website *Red and White Kop (RAWK)* in January 2005 that Liverpool going out of the FA Cup to Burnley was in no way a disaster. (*BBC Radio 5* had a "Liverpool in Crisis" section that month, after the Reds lost away to both Burnley and Southampton.) I pointed out that the Reds were in the aforementioned League Cup final (which while not massively important was not a *bad* thing), but more vitally, *still in the Champions League.*

How did that all work out? Well, Liverpool lost the League Cup final, *but won the Champions League.* But hey, damn that silly Spaniard Rafa Benítez for playing Djimi Traoré and co. at Burnley. How would he ever hope to win anything with an approach like that?

(Ditto that silly Jürgen Klopp, for not trying harder to beat Wolves in the FA Cup, and ending up with just some crumby trophy called the … Champions League.)

So, what about the English champions during the Premier League era? – an era that has helped increase the importance of the league and Champions League but diminish the relevance of domestic and minor European cups. How many title successes were built on recent or concurrent *domestic* cup successes?

Well, Man United won the FA Cup three years before they finally won the title in 1993. Perhaps this achievement did indeed greatly help, not least as it kept Alex Ferguson in a job (amidst banners calling for his departure), at a time when the FA Cup was yet to be subsumed by the all-consuming *Sky Sports*-driven Premier League, and deemed worthy enough to be job-saving for a team that finished 13th. (In recent times, winning a domestic cup saves very few jobs, which in itself should show their relative unimportance.) United then won the European Cup Winners' Cup in 1991, and the League Cup in 1992. But I'd say that more relevant was finishing 2nd in the league in 1992, rather than winning the League Cup that season. Of course, there is some pattern to the improvement, with a cup every season; and then 1993 was their first title in 26 years. So back then – over 25 years ago – winning domestic cups probably *did* help, as part of Man United's overall recovery.

However, the main improvement was in the league, and they had invested very heavily in players in the late 1980s and early '90s – on expensive stars like Paul Ince, Gary Pallister, Paul Parker, Steve Bruce, Brian McLair, and the re-purchased Mark Hughes, plus the mid-priced – but excellent value – Peter Schmeichel, Denis Irwin and Andrei Kanchelskis (and of course the relative bargain that was Eric Cantona); all of whom, over time, formed that title-winning team.

But what about the three cups United entered *during* 1992/93 – the season everyone remembers for those title-winning-knee-slides by its management team? Shouldn't United have been doing well in *those* cups if they wanted to prove themselves that year, and project an air of invincibility? The FA Cup? – fifth round (which they of course only entered at the third round), dumped out by Sheffield United. The League Cup? – third round (having only entered at the second round), to Aston Villa. The Uefa Cup? – first round, out to … Torpedo Moscow. Eek!

Would Alex Ferguson and Brian Kidd have run and slid onto the turf during a game if they instead won the League Cup? To make matters all the more weird, United failed to win any of their first three league games that season (losing the first two), then won five in a row, then drew five in a row – really bizarre form – before losing two on the bounce in a seven-game slump. They spent just one week in the top three before December. Where was the 'momentum' of those cup wins from previous seasons *then*, with five wins from fifteen games, that left them mid-table? As ever, these things are never as clear-cut as often presented.

Go back another year, to 1992 and Leeds United – also winning the title for the first time in decades, in the old English league's final season before rebranding (although *it's still the same damned competition, Sky, BBC, et al.* Liverpool have still won 18 *league titles*). Cup runs for Leeds that title-winning year? None – as bad as United's a year later. But Leeds did finish 4th the year before they won the title – itself coming a year after being promoted – which looked a good stepping stone to being champions, if not exactly an obvious precursor. Was Howard Wilkinson, the last Englishman to win the title, kicking himself because he didn't win the League Cup instead?

Okay, what about the next "new" champions: Blackburn Rovers, winners in 1994/95, after a wait of 81 years (that almost matched the Boston Red Sox' wait for the World Series)? They went out at the first hurdle of the FA Cup that season, and in the 4th round of the League Cup (to Liverpool). They also went out at the first round of the Uefa Cup to … *Trelleborgs*. That all looks pretty dreadful, if you think you have to do well in the cups in the season you win the league.

Indeed, Alan Shearer said something on *BBC One* after Wolves' 2-0 FA Cup victory over the Reds in early 2019 about how going out of the cups doesn't help you win a title; but *his* only title came when Blackburn went out of all three cups at the first few hurdles, playing just eight extra games across the League Cup, FA Cup and Uefa Cup (which back then included replays and two-legged fixtures).

Indeed, it's very similar to Man United in 1992/93 and Leeds in 1991/92. It's almost as if – *unless you're already established as a multi-title-winning financial behemoth* – it's maybe not so good to be bogged down in cup runs when trying to break with recent tradition and win the league. The year *before* they won the title, Blackburn also went out early from both domestic cups, but – and perhaps more tellingly – finished runners-up in the league. (Blackburn reached the League Cup semi-final in 1992/93. That was as good as the cup runs got before they lifted the title.) Blackburn won no cups under Kenny Dalglish, but did win the title, the year after they finished 2nd.

However, Blackburn had also become the joint-most expensive side in the league in the mid-'90s, buying some excellent Premier

League players who cost a pretty packet under the ownership of Jack Walker – to put them on a financial par with the biggest clubs – and had a manager in Dalglish who, at the time, was still as good as you could get. (To this day, Dalglish remains the most recent manager to win the league title with two different clubs.) Perhaps that combination – top manager, good owners, big budget, and a strong mentality brought about by winning an increasing number of league games in the years beforehand – is more relevant to any team's success than the winning of minor trophies? Blackburn and Leeds won the title with absolutely no cups to "prove themselves winners". But they did get used to winning an increasing number of league games.

Next come Arsenal, who won their first Premier Leaguer-era title in 1997/98; a gap of only seven years since their previous title, which is much less time than all the other examples; *but so much had changed in the interim*, from the name of the league to the entire ethos of that club, with its British booze culture replaced by scientific continental methods. So it's worth including Arsenal too, especially as they'd fallen to mid-table (albeit when playing a lot of cup games) in the mid-'90s.

Perhaps tellingly in Arsène Wenger's first *full* season – the glorious one in question – the Gunners went out of Europe at the very first hurdle to lowly Greek side PAOK. Arsenal *did* reach the League Cup semis, and of course, won the FA Cup. But they won the FA Cup final *after* they'd won the league; while the run itself was not particularly challenging. A deeper look at that success shows that they played Port Vale, two games against Crystal Palace (who finished bottom of the Premier League), Middlesbrough (in the 2nd-tier at the time), West Ham twice (8th in the Premier League), Wolves (from the 2nd-tier), and finally Newcastle (13th in the Premier League) to lift the trophy. In essence there were five extra Premier League games there, including the two replays, but none was against an elite opponent or rival, and the second-best team they played was in the final, after the title was secured; and all after going out of Europe at the first hurdle.

And of course, they won the league title with 'just' 78 points, drawing nine and losing six of their 38 games. You could argue that the season in question was therefore more competitive, and it's true that comparing points tallies across different seasons can be a little misleading due to the varying strength of all the other teams, but it shows that it was *a season of general inconsistency*, with no runaway leader at any point. Arsenal were also experiencing very indifferent league form until the second half of the season; and only once they were out of Europe and the League Cup did they put together a run of wins ahead of the FA Cup final. However, if winning the cup itself was an essential stepping stone – as some have argued – then this step came *after* the greater achievement of sewing up the title. Perhaps winning the games to reach the final provided some confidence, but it was not a case of minor trophies leading directly to the majors.

In the previous season, when Wenger had taken charge in October, Arsenal went out of all the cups at the early stages, but did finish 3rd; albeit joint-2nd on points with 2nd-placed Newcastle. So, like Blackburn and Leeds, they were getting more consistent in the league prior to winning the title, but not winning cups. (While Man United had finished 2nd in the league in 1992, but also won some cups.) Go back another year and Arsenal reached the League Cup semi-finals, and then you get back into the George Graham era, where their league form had dipped but they had won a couple of cup competitions. So, their league success was built on zero *recent* minor cup success. That said, it was built on the defence of yore – but many of the key members of that double-winning side in 1998 arrived *after* Graham's cup successes, and certainly after his league titles of 1989 and 1991: Patrick Vieira, Marc Overmars, Nicolas Anelka, Dennis Bergkamp, Emmanuel Petit, David Platt and Alex Manninger (who deputised in goal at a key stage of the 1997/98 season) all signed between 1995 and 1997.

Arsenal's subsequent seasons are also worth looking into, simply because of their relationship between league and cup success. Indeed, between 1998 and 2002 – when they next landed the title – they won nothing. But they did stay 2nd in the league, season after season, before becoming champions again in 2002. They were a *consistent* side, not a *cup* side. The fact that they weren't winning any trophies was not a reflection of their overall quality.

They then won the FA Cup in 2002, to secure a second double, but again, *after* having won the title. And they crashed out early in the League Cup that season, and found themselves out of the Champions League before Christmas. The Gunners then won the FA Cup again in 2003 and 2005, when not winning the title, but had three big cup runs as part of their incredible 'invincibles' season in 2003/04, bowing out at the semi-final stage in both domestic cups and reaching the quarter-finals of the Champions League. That was clearly an incredibly impressive, well-rounded team. But their next FA Cup successes – indeed, their next *trophies* – were in 2014, 2015 and 2017 – which bore no connection to their league form at the time, which had fallen away from the peak of 2004. A much better marker of Arsenal's quality was reaching the Champions League final in 2006 – their last major hurrah – before their star players started to be sold off and, in financing a new stadium, cutbacks were made.

Belatedly winning those domestic cups did not make Arsenal into champions again, did it? – or even realistic challengers. Had they become "winners"? No. It did nothing to change the perception of a club drifting, as they fell from the Champions League qualification spots, and Wenger was sacked in 2018. Why? Because the FA Cup is now almost a vanity project; nice to win it *if you win it*, but not worth much anymore. If almost all clubs that enter then rest key players, the stadiums are half empty, it raises little money, and no one really bothers to watch the final, does it matter anymore? If it's not worthy of an open-top bus procession, is it worth prioritising? Again, it's a nice day out, but domestic cup wins are not remembered in the way they used to be, when it might be the only live club football match you get to see on TV.

I've already mentioned Chelsea in 2005 – the team who usurped the 'Invincibles' – but let's look at their rise in more depth. You can talk of the League Cup being the catalyst, but they had become, by far, the most expensive team and squad in the country; after which they soon won the title. Coincidence? To this day, with inflation, the Chelsea teams and squads of 2004-2007 remain by far the most expensive ever assembled in modern English football history – and presumably, therefore, in *all* English football history. Of course, they finished 2nd in 2003/04, with 80 points (reaching the Champions League semi-finals), so were already a club on an upward trajectory, after just one season of Roman Abramovich's spending. Those two feats, along with the continued investment of the best part of a billion pounds (in current day money) – along with the shock-and-awe tactics of Mourinho, starting in the summer of 2004 – were arguably far more relevant to back-to-back league successes than winning the League Cup in 2005.

Chelsea had won 21 of their 27 league games and lost only once by that February final. So their League Cup success had virtually *zero* bearing on the destination of the title. Maybe it helped in some infinitesimal way, in that it made them feel good about themselves, and if you're in a final it's probably better for confidence to win it. (Although a lot of teams suffer slumps *after* wining the League Cup, as if being sated before March is not a good idea for keeping standards up; a trophy gained can just as easily be a signal to take the foot off the gas – although this probably applies more to smaller clubs, for whom winning a domestic cup is a bigger deal, and when they may have nothing left to play for.) But as mentioned earlier, Chelsea were nine points clear of Man United.

Interestingly, Mourinho's all-conquering team went out of the FA Cup to Newcastle seven days before beating Liverpool in the League Cup final. Did losing to a mediocre Newcastle side in the cup kill their momentum? No. They won the next four league games, as well as the League Cup final. (Something happened with Chelsea in the Champions League semi-finals later that season, but for the life of me I cannot remember what. That said, I do keep seeing flashes of Luis Garcia's face, and a ball just over a goal-line, and the way time seemed to stop when Eiður Guðjohnsen took wayward aim. Maybe one day I'll remember what it all means....)

In the years after Chelsea's dominance ebbed post-Mourinho (a decline that started early in his fourth season), the title mostly went to Manchester United. But the next wave of incredible investment was under way across that city. Manchester City – the next "new" team to win the title (their first since 1968, before any of the current players were even born) – won the FA Cup the year before they won the title. Again, it was labelled as the reason they became "winners". Again, it was probably no *bad* thing, other than it *may* have stopped them making a title challenge that season – having been 2nd at the halfway point, before embarking on their FA Cup run.

With all the investment they still ended up a fairly impressive third in the league that season, and like Arsenal in 1997, were actually joint-2nd on points. City had also become the 2nd-most expensive side in the country (based on £XI), behind only Chelsea, but now narrowly ahead of eventual champions Man United; with the three clubs in the same financial order a year later when City pipped United to the title, and when Chelsea finished 6th, but were busy winning the Champions League.

However, when City won the title in 2011/12, how many cups did they win in the same campaign, to ensure 'momentum'? None. How many finals did they reach? None. They went out of the FA Cup at the first hurdle, and crashed out of the Champions League at the group stage. Perhaps it was said that they would never win the league with such a lack of momentum. Instead, by clearing their schedule, they were able to focus on the league and, on the final day of the season, make a late, late smash and grab.

Leicester – the outliers of all outliers (who *outlie* so far they almost should be lying somewhere in another universe) – also came from nowhere in terms of cup success to win the league, but in decades to come people will *still* be trying to figure out just how they achieved what they did, albeit aided by none of the top clubs being anywhere near their best (all of the Big Six were either in crisis or transition, at a time when – in 2014 and 2015 – no English team made a European final, compared to several before and several after; and of course, all four European finalists this season were from the Premier League). Unlike all the other teams mentioned in this chapter, Leicester had no previous league form that showed they were edging into the frame – aside from a strong response to a relegation dogfight – and had spent no time as possible contenders. Even their manager, Claudio Ranieri, was known for never having won a league title, although at least he, unlike most of the players, had quite a few top-four finishes, and a couple of occasions as a runner-up.

Hitting the Front Late On

Another factor with the majority of these "new" champions is how late in the season they took the lead; and only once was there a runaway "new" winner, who galloped away from the start (and they were Chelsea, the most lavishly funded).

While Man City spent games 8-27 at the top of the table in 2011/12, they then fell behind their city rivals for the next eight match-weeks, due to a run of one win in five for Roberto Mancini's men. It looked like they'd blown the title, in their first proper race in decades. But by winning each of their final six games they not only matched Man United's points tally but, thanks to two dramatic stoppage-time goals, won the title on goal difference. (Cue Martin Tyler exploding, in stark contrast to how he sounds like he's reading a funereal liturgy when Liverpool score.) At that stage – back in 2012 – Man United were the great champions, the team to be feared. But City usurped them.

Leicester's story in 2015/16 obviously still makes no sense, but after a poor start they hit the top after match 13, and despite a couple of wobbles that saw Arsenal go above them for a reasonable period of time, retook the lead and stayed there from game 23 onwards; seeing off the late challenge of Spurs, who were clearly a far more talented team, and with the gap fluctuating for the most part between three and five points. Unlike City, Blackburn, Man United and Arsenal, Leicester didn't need to leave it particularly late, but equally, they never ran up the kind of lead that Chelsea enjoyed in 2005.

The story of quite a few "new" title wins revolved around late drama; rarely was it a procession with winning margins of ten or more points – a phenomenon which seems largely limited to experienced title winners. If retaining the title is seen as harder than first winning it, that's because *you have to have won it first* to face that second hurdle (and obviously, very few teams get to win it in the first place).

After beating Liverpool at the start of March 1993, to send themselves top, Man United endured a four-game winless streak; before winning their final seven games – the first five of which sealed the title. Having first hit the front in December they dropped to 2nd and 3rd on numerous occasions – sitting as far back as 3rd place as late as *the start of April* – before a very late revival, just in time.

In 1994/95, Blackburn hit the front after 16 games. Ten games later they were five points clear of Manchester United, but after 29 games the gap was down to just two points. "Perennial winners" United – as they were starting to be seen at that point – were closing in; Blackburn were choking, or "bottling it", as the popular phrase now seems to be. (If anyone so much as loses a game of football these days they're "bottle-jobs".) However, by game 36 of a 42-game season, Rovers were eight points clear; home and hosed, surely? Yet by game 40 there'd been another swing, with two defeats in three games for Dalglish's men narrowing their lead to five points, with United also having a game in hand – which they duly won. Going into the final weekend, after 41 games, it was 89 points to Rovers, 87 to United. Both teams failed to win their 42nd and final league games of the season – Rovers famously losing to a late Jamie Redknapp free-kick at Anfield – and with Andy Cole misfiring for United at West Ham, the title went to Blackburn, as its manager won the top prize in English football on the old hallowed soil once more. Dalglish's men led for two-thirds of the season, but their lead vacillated quite markedly, and things got very nervy with three defeats in their final four matches.

Arsenal's initial title in the Premier League era saw them as low as 5th after 24 games, before moving up to second; then hitting the top with just six games to go, wrapping up the title within four further matches. And as already discussed, Chelsea's initial success was a blitz almost from the start. They were 2nd from games two to eleven, then top thereafter; unbeaten from games ten through 38. Also as previously highlighted, they were complete financial outliers; something that, in 2019, Liverpool were not.

While Manchester United, Blackburn and Arsenal all had one of the two most expensive £XIs in the season they won their first Premier League-era titles (Blackburn's only season topping the £XI rankings – narrowly – was the one in which they won the league), Chelsea remain the only "new" winners to have an advantage that was *truly significant* – with the next-most expensive £XI (Man United) in 2005 lagging behind Abramovich's project by a whopping 30%. To contrast that to earlier seasons, Arsenal were 2nd in the £XI rankings in 1997/98, but by a margin less than 1%, at a time when the wealth was fairly evenly clustered between five or six clubs; while Blackburn topped the £XI rankings in 1994/95, but by only 5% from Man United in 2nd. In 1992/93, United won the title with an £XI that was 14% more costly than the one ranked 2nd (Liverpool).

Much more recently came Manchester City, in 2011/12. Despite the quick-fire investment of their United Arab Emirates owners, they actually still only ranked 3rd on £XI that fateful season when they finally landed the crown, but they were only a negligible amount below Manchester United in 2nd and Chelsea in 1st (two clubs who obviously hadn't lost their marbles and given away their expensively-assembled squads in the interim). They were three evenly-matched teams, in financial terms; City's £XI, in 3rd, being just 8% less than Chelsea's. When the gaps are this small, a lot more factors come into play in determining who succeeds.

The financial gulf between Liverpool and Man City in 2018/19 was *far more significant*. The Reds were basically operating at less than two-thirds of the budget of their rivals, who pipped them to the title by just a single point. However, the financial gap between the two clubs had closed from what it was just a couple of years earlier: Liverpool's £XI being just 47% of City's – £348m to £754m in 2017/18 – to 62% a year later. This had been achieved through Liverpool reinvesting the Philippe Coutinho money and the funds raised from the Champions League run, as well as City spending a lot of the season without Kevin de Bruyne, whose transfer fee equated to £120m in 2018 money, their second-most expensive current player after Sergio Agüero, at £159.5m. While you don't always get what you pay for, those two ultra-expensive recruits – kept whilst other costly signings flopped and were offloaded – helped fire City to the title in 2018, with Agüero more influential in 2018/19. Ditto Raheem Sterling, whose fee now equates to £106.8m – which neatly shows that a fee of £50m in 2015 is now equivalent to just over twice that amount. David Silva, at £87m, makes it four players who cost more than Liverpool's most expensive (current) player, Virgil van Dijk, who at £75m, remains more costly than anyone else in the squad after inflation is applied to their fees. (Inflation will be applied for the first time to van Dijk's fee when we switch to using 2019 money in the summer of 2019, after this book has been released; but equally, it will also be applied to those aforementioned City players, who will still remain more costly. The Reds' most expensive signing in the Premier League era remains Andy Carroll, at an eye-watering £121.8m.)

So aside from Leicester in 2015/16, when, as a mere tortoise they remarkably beat a somnambulant bunch of out-of-shape hares, Liverpool were trying to achieve the "new" title in the Premier League won at the greatest financial disadvantage. Man United, Blackburn and Chelsea were richer than anyone else when they won their first Premier League-era title; Arsenal and Man City were a mere fraction away from being the richest clubs. Liverpool, by contrast, were punching at just 62% of City's financial weight this past season. Not only did the Reds rank just 4th in the £XI rankings, there was a chasm between their £XI and those of the two Manchester clubs.

Indeed, rarely has a team as relatively inexpensive as 62% of the highest £XI won the title, whether it be their first or their third or fourth. Leicester blew logic out of the water, at just 8% (8%!), almost thirteen times cheaper than Man United that season, who had the most expensive £XI in 2015/16 under Louis van Gaal. But before and since, in the Premier League era, there are only two other champions at 62% or below: Arsenal (62%), in 2003/04, and Man United, at 55% in 1996/97. (And of course, neither of these teams even got to the Champions League final, let alone *winning* it, as Liverpool just did.)

However, even here there are some key differences with Liverpool in 2018/19. First, Man United had already won three of the four previous titles (and their success in 1997 was built on a sensational crop of gradually-introduced youth players dovetailing with the retained purchases), so they were a well-oiled machine undergoing minor tweaks and upgrades; while Arsenal were winning their third title in six years. And second, the richest clubs in 1997 and 2004 were Newcastle and Chelsea respectively; at the time, both were league title virgins, as it were, in the modern era.

Liverpool were not only going up against the costliest team in the league 2018/19, but that club happened to have won three titles this past decade – before you factor in their record-breaking 2017/18, when they finished with 100 points and scored 106 goals, to complete the best single league season in English football history. Even if those levels were nigh-on impossible to sustain, they were unlikely to drop too far, given that there hadn't been a mass exodus of players. (Indeed, they didn't sell or release anyone of note.) They were not doing a "Leicester" and exploding out of nowhere – like a detonation in a fireworks factory – only to fall silently back to earth. Money talks.

In eleven of the Premier League's 27 seasons the costliest £XI has prevailed (41%). But if you widen it out just a bit, you find that 16 of the 27 champions (59%) had an £XI in the 92nd percentile. Widen it a bit more, and 20 (74%) reside in the 80th percentile. So three-quarters of the titles go to *a very expensive side*. And of course, 26 of the 27 – 96% – have been sides that cost significantly more than the average for the league as a whole.

But of course, the Premier League's financial landscape has changed since 2003, when Roman Abramovich pitched up with a platinum-coated flotilla overflowing with rubies and rubles. This widened the gap between the haves and the have-nots, but even so, the average cost of the champions' £XI, if you exclude Leicester, is 90% of the maximum since 2004 (when Chelsea really kicked into shape), but also 90% over the entire 26 seasons since 1992. Ergo, the average champion is *very rich indeed*.

Liverpool spent a lot of money in the summer of 2018, but it was in no small part due to the loss of Coutinho the season before, and also, funded by the road to Kiev. Liverpool were labelled as the big spenders of 2018, but gross spend is the worst financial argument in football, and even *net* spend is deeply flawed. The correlation between what is spent during the season in question and winning the title is virtually non-existent. Obviously sometimes it can help, but it's far from a clear pattern.

The team that won the league in the 27 seasons of the Premier League had a seasonal net spend that, in chronological order, ranked: 13th, 6th, 5th, 20th (when Man United sold players off due to academy successes), 14th, 2nd, 1st, 3rd, 17th, 7th, 1st, 3rd, 1st, 1st, 11th, 9th, 2nd, 2nd, 11th, 4th, 2nd, 1st, 4th, 9th, 3rd, 1st and 10th. Just six times were the champions also the biggest *net spenders* that season, and just under half of the 27 champions were in the top three net-spenders. The average net-spend rank of the champions is 6th. This is why the £XI is a much better predictor of finishing position, with far more predictive accuracy.

Six champions weren't even in the top ten on the net-spend rankings; and that doesn't include Leicester, who ranked 9th in 2015/16 when lifting the crown.

Why? *Because they'd already spent the money.*

The teams that topped the net spending each season? From 1992/93 onwards, in order: Blackburn, Blackburn (both times in seasons *before* being champions but not the season when they *were* champions), Everton, Newcastle, Spurs, Crystal Palace, Man United, Liverpool, Leeds, Fulham, Man United, Chelsea (upon Roman Abramovich's takeover), Chelsea, Chelsea, Chelsea, Man City (upon Thaksin Shinawatra's takeover), Man City (upon Sheikh Mansour's takeover), Man City, Man City, Liverpool (upon FSG's takeover), Chelsea, Man City, Man United, Man City, Man City, Man City and

Liverpool in 2018/19 (with Fulham, eventually relegated, in 2nd place). As you can see, the first half is a fairly bizarre mix of clubs that largely failed to win the title, whereas the latter years see the same clubs featuring time and again, adding new signings to already expensive squads – but not necessarily winning the title in a season with a high net spend.

What you can see is that *sustained* high net spends often lead to success, whereas sporadic splurges can actually do little to improve the value of the squad and the team. Blackburn, Man City and Chelsea each topped the net spend rankings in the seasons *before* they were eventually champions. (Blackburn spent relatively little in the season they won it, ranking 5th; City also won their initial Premier League title when ranking outside the top three on net spend, but having ranked 1st for the preceding three seasons. They topped the net spend rankings in 2018 but were 10th in 2019.) These clubs were stockpiling, and refining their squads; buying a lot of expensive players, keeping the successes and offloading – at a loss – the duds.

This allowed them to overcome Tomkins' Law.

Both Leeds and Blackburn flew too close to the sun, in terms of getting financially burnt; although Rovers did have a league title to show for their investment, as Icarus momentarily made it to the solar corona before the wax wings melted – whereas Leeds just had a lot of fish tanks (and a run to the Champions League semi-finals). In both 1996/97 and 1997/98, Blackburn ranked bottom of the net-spend ranking, as they sold off their players – many of whom wanted out after Dalglish stepped down – to respective profits of £84m and almost £100m (both in 2018 money), and the dream died. However, luckily for them (he said with great irony) Roy Hodgson was now in charge, and after steering them to a healthy 6th-place in the midst of the sales, they then ranked 2nd on net spend the season after (1998/99), with a figure of £151m – but his new buys, who were largely a series of overpriced British journeymen or journeymen-to-be, only took them into the relegation zone, before his inevitable dismissal; with his successor, Brian Kidd, who improved their points per game but not by a big enough margin, getting the blame when they eventually went down. By contrast, Leeds United overspent wildly across several seasons – which, for a year or two, worked; but foolishly budgeting on finishing in the Champions League positions – in addition to reported purchases of office fish tanks the size of Arizona – led to their demise. In 2002/03, in the process of being relegated, they made a staggering profit of £206m (after inflation) on player sales (as a certain 16-year-old James Milner made his debut). It was a fire-sale, as grand ambition gave way to a clearance. Over a decade and a half later they were still fighting to return to the top flight; missing out once again this summer.

In 2011/12, FSG joined the list of new owners who made an initial big net spend to top the rankings – the Reds' first since 1999/00, when Gérard Houllier totally overhauled the squad, to some considerable success; although under FSG this big net spend didn't really lead to any great improvement (initially, at least; a title challenge came two years later, with several of the players involved).

But in 2011 this was a club coming off the back of season upon season of under-investment by warring duffers George Gillett and Tom Hicks. The "cowboys" as they were so unaffectionately known, had also pulled the initial big investment trick, with the Reds ranking 4th in 2007/08, at a respectable £126m (2018 money) that included the purchases of Fernando Torres, Javier Mascherano and Ryan Babel. But in their final three seasons as custodians, the cowboys' investment dried up, and the Reds ranked 15th, 14th and 18th in the Premier League net-spend stakes, as Rafa Benítez bore the brunt of the media criticism when the club fell away after the 2008/09 title challenge.

And while Liverpool's £XI – which still included the transfer fees of some gold-standard signings, like Torres – meant that they should still have been nowhere near the relegation zone – to where Roy Hodgson then took them – the bumbling Londoner's hands were somewhat tied, too. (That said, part of the problem was in not also *gagging his mouth*, to stop him continually shoe-horning his foot into it. Never has a Liverpool manager been so defeatist and insulting to the intelligence of the fans. But that's another story, and perhaps another book – albeit one far too scary to read to your children at bedtime.)

Large net spends can freshen up a squad – they did for Liverpool in 2018/19 – but equally, it can lead to churn, and a lack of understanding and "fit" (as happened with Fulham making more than a dozen signings, and bringing in a further six on loan). Teams that bring in nine or ten new players can end up a total mess. Teams that bring in almost 20 new players are asking for trouble.

How Klopp Triumphed In Germany

In early 2019 some quotes from Jose Mourinho – dating back to his appointment at Man United in 2016 – were rehashed, where he'd said something along the lines of Klopp's titles at Dortmund "not counting" because Bayern Munich were essentially rubbish at the time.

Okay, perhaps that was true in 2010/11, when Bayern – entering the season as reigning German champions and beaten Champions League finalists – fell apart a bit under Louis van Gaal, finishing 3rd. (So Mourinho's dig was *also* aimed at his predecessor at United; don't let anyone tell you he can't aim his bile in multiple directions at once. Unlike his teams, Mourinho can attack from all angles.) But even so, Dortmund were being run on a shoestring budget, so soon after nearly collapsing as a club. They had zero big-name players. They spent almost no money.

For Klopp's men – as outsiders – to win 14 of the first 16 league matches that season was absolutely incredible, given their resources. They only won nine of the remaining 18, but still won the league. Had Bayern been "on it", that may not have happened, in the way that Bayern came back late this time around; but had Bayern been on it, maybe Klopp's Dortmund would have found an extra gear. Who can say?

But any notion that Klopp was in any way lucky in Germany was absolutely blown out of the water the next season. Bayern, with a squad of world-class players, turned back to Jupp Heynckes, arguably their greatest-ever manager (and that includes Pep Guardiola). Bayern reached the German cup final, the Champions League final and racked up almost as many league points as Dortmund had the season before when they won the title. It wasn't enough for the Bavarians, however, as Klopp's men took things to another level, despite still operating on a tiny budget, with a very young team. They lost three and drew another of their first six league matches when defending their title – a poor start – but then didn't lose again all season. With 81 points (from 34 games) they broke the Bundesliga record. And so, yet again, Mourinho was making stuff up as he went along. Indeed, Klopp did something in a major league that the Portuguese has still never managed: winning the title as a massive underdog, with a tiny budget.

Almost!

One thing I've said for years is that if Liverpool are ever going to challenge for the league title it would need to be without a long European run (and/or lots of domestic cup games), because of the extra strain it puts on a squad that still remains outside of the three most expensive in the land. Even Gary Neville chimed in with the same opinion, earlier in the season – justifiably, because of how hard it is to fight on both of the major fronts; but equally, you could not expect Jürgen Klopp to respond with anything other than positivity.

Neville's assertion was that Liverpool should "bin" the Champions League, which was always a bit silly – you can't just dismiss such a competition, even if it is likely to cause a fixture pileup and sap energy. Neville later admitted he was wrong, and of course, I must do so, too. Klopp continues to distort the boundaries of what is possible.

Prior to Liverpool this season, every single English club (bar one) that reached the Champions League final "lost" league points in the process, when compared against their average points totals of the season before and the season after. (We don't have the *after* data for Liverpool and Spurs yet from 2019, as that can only be calculated with genuine 2020 vision, but Spurs' points tally *was* down on their recent average.) On average – prior to this season – the "damage" done by a Champions League run was seven points; with teams outside of the top-three £XI rankings (usually Liverpool and Arsenal, and which will also include Spurs) losing an average of *eleven* points in the season they reached the Champions League final. Indeed, if you want to compare Spurs' 71 points this season with the average of their previous *two* seasons, it is also down by eleven points.

Manchester City edged it in what neutrals called the best-ever title race (it was certainly the one containing almost ceaseless victories for both teams), but Liverpool ended the season as European Champions *with a higher league points tally than any other English European champion* has ever mustered, either in that same season, or in the preceding season. The average tally for previous English winners is 72 points, and never more than 87; English *finalists* prior to this season averaged 75, with 90 the maximum (United 2008/09).

Liverpool racked up 97.

NINETY-SEVEN.

That surely makes it one of the all-time great achievements in English football; arguably – and here I am obviously biased – more amazing than City winning the title with 98 points and landing the two domestic trophies without playing anyone of note (bar Chelsea in one final). It may even top City's 100-point season, too, as a whole body of work – as in neither of their two recent titles did they face the major pressures of even a Champions League *semi-final* to deal with; almost always gargantuan encounters, when almost all English teams drop points in the surrounding league games. (Liverpool were one of the only teams in the modern era to win both league games following the semis, but the wins against Newcastle and Wolves were leggy and hard-fought.) And, of course, City have much greater financial resources than Liverpool, and although not as good as Pep Guardiola made them, many of the squad had won league titles in 2012 and 2014.

Equally, perhaps without City's excellence, as Guardiola took them to a new level, the Reds wouldn't have risen to such heights – like two great athletes pushing each other all the way, to break personal bests and world records.

Therefore, Liverpool's season has a strong case to at least be considered the best all-round campaign in the history of English football, with the third-highest ever total of 97 points allied to winning the Champions League (when almost exclusively facing only top clubs), *all on the 4th-biggest budget in England.*

All of this is beyond what has ever been achieved before. It was nothing short of a miracle.

Come In, Number Six!

Just 22 seconds: the time it took Moussa Sissoko to almost literally hand Liverpool the Champions League trophy, with an arm so outstretched he could have been signalling in semaphore. Utterly accidental, in that he was pointing at someone behind him to run somewhere, he then moved his arm towards the ball, instinctively, after it bounced off his shoulder, hitting him square on the biceps; but maybe intentional on Sadio Mané's part, in seeing an opportunity to force a handball. According to the new laws – which came into play that very June day, and talks of an 'unnatural silhouette' if it strikes an arm – it was a clear penalty; and even by the old rules it might have been given. Yet it was so quick and surreal that it didn't feel like it was truly happening. With the requisite VAR check, it was a minute or so before Mo Salah, in front of the Spurs fans, could take the decisive penalty – rifled fairly centrally, but at an almost unsaveable pace. It may have been enough in itself to secure the win, had Divock Origi not put the result beyond doubt, and denied Spurs the chance, in the final minutes, to throw everyone forward – including the goalkeeper – in an attempt to make it 1-1 via total chaos.

As a game it never really got going, and Liverpool fans cared not one jot.

Madrid Turns Red
As is customary, Liverpool fans took one giant Scouse party to Madrid, and, joined by Reds from around the world who converged on the

Spanish capital, a joyous time was had by all. Fears of any trouble with a rival English team in the final proved unfounded, as both sets of fans enjoyed the occasion, and showed mutual respect. For every fan who turned up either with a ticket, or in the hopes of getting a ticket once there, were several more there simply to drink it all in.

BOSS Night; *The Anfield Wrap*; John Barnes rapping; *Redmen TV* there to capture it all for YouTube; Colin Murray DJing as the crowd sang along to Bohemian Rhapsody. The football wasn't exactly *secondary*, but the before and after parties added so much more to the occasion.

Allen Baynes was just one of a whole host of *TTT* subscribers who descended on Madrid for the weekend. In reference to the way Liverpool fans have made an art of these events, he said on the site:

"If you haven't seen footage of it, it was truly amazing. I don't know what others think but our fanbase is almost becoming a cult. I was struck in Rome last season meeting two lads, one from Denmark and the other from Greenland, who had come not to go to the match but to join the pre-match craic. They just thought it was the best thing they had ever experienced.

"In the middle of the fan-zone on Saturday searching for my nephews I was talking to some lads from Scandinavia and told them when I went to my first game in 1961 I could never believe that we would see such an outpouring of love for my, now their, team. If you haven't seen the rendition of *You'll Never Walk Alone* taken from a balcony above the square you must try and find it on the net."

Over The Line

It wasn't the best final, that much was clear; albeit one played in very difficult circumstances. But the result was *heavenly*. After being the better team in 2007, but losing to AC Milan, and then certainly having the better first half in 2018, until a demented *Madridista* sought to wreck the Reds' dreams, this was perhaps justified in its own way. And, of course, Liverpool had possibly their hardest ever run to a final, to earn the right to win it; they beat a whole host of teams ranked in Europe's top 20, and several in the top 10. This time the tag of favourites seemed to wear a little heavy on Jürgen Klopp's men, in terms of producing a lack of composure in the passing, but the occasion also got to Spurs, who *kinda* controlled midfield and kept possession in deep areas, but didn't attack with any verve until the closing stages, and who snatched at shots and left gaps at the back.

And game-state definitely affected this encounter. When one team gets a penalty after less than 30 seconds, the game-plan for *both* sides effectively goes out the window. From then on, Liverpool looked more concerned with not leaving spaces for Spurs to exploit, rather than committing men forward; contain, and go into a shell, rather than be expansive and echo the gung-ho side from Klopp's earlier days that could thrill but also throw away all kinds of leads. Even so, Liverpool still came closest to scoring as the game wore on, with James Milner – after some fine interplay – inches away after coming on as a sub, until a rally from Spurs in the final ten minutes, which found Alisson Becker again justifying every penny of his £66m fee.

Searing heat, three weeks without a game (all that time to stew on the consequences), and key strikers not fully match-fit; nerves and pressure everywhere, in red and in white – but Liverpool *got over the line*.

Going 1-0 up early isn't *always* a good thing, especially in a season of amazing comebacks, which, in the build-up, were still fresh in everyone's mind; when having the lead breeds fear of all that can go wrong, before a team has even had the chance to get into its stride. On the *Second Captains'* podcast a rather (deservedly) well-oiled Neil Atkinson of *The Anfield Wrap* spoke with great passion and insight to the equally impressive Ken Early in the early hours of the Sunday morning, and one of Neil's points was about how difficult it can be when a team takes a lead it hasn't done enough to deserve; there was literally no time for Liverpool to even *start* playing well before they were 1-0 up. Not only had there been a lack of rhythm due to no game for three weeks (a ludicrous situation), and the tropical heat, but Liverpool no longer had the incentive to try and *find* any rhythm.

In the Premier League, Man City versus Newcastle and Liverpool versus Leicester on the same midweek at the end of January saw early leads taken by the favourites lost to nerves – or just a sense of "this is too easy" – when it looked like both of the title rivals would run away with easy victories. City were then nervous at 0-0 away at confidence-shaken Brighton on the final day but sprang out of their anxiety once 1-0 down; Liverpool were not at all nervous against Wolves *until* they went 1-0 up (and more so when it became clear that City had gone 1-0 down), then it all went very weird indeed – like an absolute terror beset the players, who didn't know what to do (go for another goal, protect the 1-0 lead, or just *boot the ball anywhere?*) It's human nature, when the stakes are enormous. Sometimes going ahead so early means it's definitely yours to lose, and you have 89 minutes to ponder that fact. In the final, *boot the ball anywhere* was perhaps an overused Liverpool tactic but it meant that by retaining their shape it left Spurs no space in behind. Indeed, the one time Virgil van Dijk stepped into midfield there was an instant break in behind him. Usually the coolest man on the pitch – nay, the coolest man in the *universe* – the Dutchman was clearly feeling some pressure.

When Divock Origi slammed a low left-foot shot past Hugo Lloris, van Dijk collapsed to the floor, supine; going one better than Alisson Becker who merely slumped to his knees. There were still several minutes left on the clock; this was not the final whistle. Before the game van Dijk had said that he doesn't get nervous – and it's fair to say that he is one of the most unflappable players the game has ever seen. But here he *was* nervous. He still managed to jump like a basketball player on a trampoline to head various clearances upfield, and found a phenomenal burst of pace to deny Son Heung-min as, for literally the first time in 64 games, someone *almost* dribbled past him – but his composure on the ball was not up to his usual standards. Indeed, no one in the Liverpool side looked composed, but the same can be said of the Spurs players too. The fact that van Dijk was so emotional could be seen in the floods of tears he shed immediately on the final whistle, which seemed so out of keeping; perhaps, now bestowed as the team's de facto leader – with the winning of so many individual awards, and the hefty weight of the oft-noted transfer fee – he felt he was carrying a huge burden. Whatever it was, this meant the *world* to him. The pressure had been lifted. You expected to see Jordan Henderson in tears because of the trials and tribulations of his career, and the special bond with his dad who overcame cancer. But van Dijk blubbing showed just how much pressure the team was under.

Liverpool were also in a very odd situation as the clear favourites – given a 70-75% probability of winning by bookmakers and odds-checkers – but without having that kind of "get this over the line" nous that reduces pressure. If anything, Liverpool had the mountainous weight of history pressing down on them. Yes, they had the recent experience of finals that Spurs did not, but only *losing* them. And yes, there is the history of winning European Cups at the club, but this actual side had none of that – the rest was in the stands, in legends like Steven Gerrard and Ian Rush, and, back in his home city for the weekend, Rafa Benítez. This was not a Bayern Munich or Real Madrid, used to grinding out trophies. This was a Liverpool team that everyone in England (bar Arsenal and West Ham fans) seemed to want to stay trophy-less; that everyone, in the oh-so-modern way, was dying to mock. (Think of all the missed opportunities for 'banter'.) This was a team that the Manchester City players had only just sang about "winning fuck all", in addition to some really tasteless lines from a vile song. This was a Liverpool team who had agonisingly finished runners-up in the previous year's competition, and in the Premier League just three weeks earlier. This was a Liverpool team with a manager who had lost his last six finals, with critics waiting to crow about a seventh.

The Liverpool players knew all this – and while such negativity can serve to motivate, it can also entrap and inhibit, pour concrete into the boots; the people waiting for you to fail can become a spectre if you think too intently about their glee *should they get their wish*. The more you want something, the harder it sometimes gets to achieve. And so it was in Madrid: every ounce of effort by the men in red, as befitting a team so desperate to win, but a fear of losing that set in from the moment it was 90% theirs to lose. Unless there is a total gulf in class between the two clubs, as seen in this season's FA Cup final between Man City and Watford, it becomes difficult to just go for that second goal, when you know you may just expose your defence in the process. Liverpool passed the ball fairly terribly, but they *managed the game* beautifully.

In *The Guardian*, Jonathan Wilson noted Liverpool's evolving approach under Klopp, although the Reds' pass-completion percentage in the final, which was basically as bad as Cardiff's when being relegated (64%), was – to my mind – probably not driven by design but more a mixture of a fear of losing the freakishly early lead, and some anxiety in the heat, with just part of it some tactical plan to ward off the threat of Spurs on the break. Balls hit into the channel to alleviate pressure were clearly *meant* for Sadio Mané or Mo Salah, and not the ballboys to collect from the stands.

"Liverpool worry about pass accuracy far less than many sides," Wilson noted. "Their pass completion rate of 79.9% in the Champions League was the 21st highest of the 32 teams who reached the group stage and beyond this season. They are happy to take risks. They play at high tempo. They are exceptionally good at winning back the ball, which possibly means they protect possession less assiduously than certain sides. They get the ball forward quickly.

"Speed is prized over precision – or, at least, that is how they used to be; that is how the template tells us it should be. This season, though, Liverpool have been notably more controlled. In the league their pass completion was 84.4% as opposed to 83.8% last season. They have not pressed so hard. Regains in the opposition's final third are down almost 9%. Passing sequences of 10 or more resulting in a shot are up 21.5%. They have not gone quite so hell for leather."

When Spurs did break through in Madrid it was without creating a single clear-cut chance, as defined by Opta; the best being a half-chance that fell Lucas Moura's way, after a long-range effort from

Son was saved. They resorted to speculative shooting, some of which was *almost* excellent, some of which was wayward. Nothing they hit was *impossible* to save, but they still hit several well-struck shots, including a curling Christian Eriksen free-kick towards the far corner, and that stinging Son blast from outside the box. But they came up again Alisson Becker, master of the non-flashy two-handed save; not one thought given to doing something "for the cameras" – just keen to get the positioning and footwork absolutely right *in order to beat the bloody thing away*. He also had to get down low to tip a couple of shots away with just one hand, and they were pushed sufficiently clear of danger, with just the right balance between strong and 'soft' wrists (too strong and it goes right back into the centre of the goal, too soft and instead of tipping it round the post it ends up in the far corner of the net).

It was perhaps a cruel reminder of just how poorly Loris Karius had done a year earlier, although his successor never had to deal with the antics of Sergio Ramos. (Although as cool, calm and collected as he is, you sense Alisson might just have headbutted him and been done with it.) And in fairness, Spurs had no Cristiano Ronaldo or Gareth Bale, and the Reds' XI, and bench, was far stronger than a year earlier, too, which meant the goalkeeper was not horribly exposed at any point. Either way, the Brazilian is a clear upgrade on his predecessor, and that's what this latest success was down to: the continual process of finding players that bit better than those the club already had, and then, along with developing some hidden gems, further improving those new players, too.

It was not a memorable game; but it *is* an indelible achievement, with Liverpool's name engraved for a sixth time onto that giant silver trophy. And finals aren't always the most remembered thing; David Fairclough's goal against St Etienne in the quarter-finals in 1977 is arguably more fondly remembered and iconic than the goals in the final that won Liverpool the European Cup for the first time. In 2019, that moment was Trent Alexander-Arnold's quick-thinking corner to Divock Origi, who side-footed the ball into the roof of the net, to leave Lionel Messi and Luis Suárez's Barcelona on the brink of elimination, 4-0 down with ten minutes to play, having won the first leg 3-0.

After five minutes of added time had elapsed, the final whistle sounded. It wasn't quite the dramatic ending that had seen Liverpool beat AC Milan 14 years earlier; indeed, there was no penalty shootout, after the Reds had faced that fate in the finals of various competitions in 2001, 2005, 2006, 2012 and 2016; while several other finals in that time were won or lost by one-goal margins. As such, getting the job done, 2-0, seemed almost anticlimactic; too simple by half.

Players sunk to their knees, or fell onto their backs, as the subs, the squad players and the technical staff, arms aloft, sprinted onto the pitch; not quite sure who to head for first. Klopp, by contrast, was calm and steely-faced, taking time to commiserate with his counterpart in the Spurs dugout, having been in his position 12 months earlier. The German's reaction was in stark contrast to the delirium of the Origi goal against Everton, which – along with Origi's second goal against Barcelona – probably remained the emotional high point of the season, with Origi's goal in the final bringing more of a sense of relief. (All in all, not a bad season for the Belgian striker, whose name – Divock Origi – is worth repeating *ad infinitum*.) In the crowd Steven Gerrard, now manager of Rangers, took high-fives as, down below, Jordan Henderson, the man for so long in his shadow, found his father to share that memorable embrace.

Young Dutch defender Ki-Jana Hoever helped a tearful Virgil van Dijk to his feet, as players in red shirts hugged each other, or hugged the youngsters in grey training tops, and the technical staff in dark tracksuits, and those in suits and red ties; as, around them, Uefa officials ran on with sections of the podium to assemble. Eventually the whole Liverpool contingent ran to the fans, with Mo Salah and Trent Alexander-Arnold allowed to break from their television interview to join the jubilation. In stark contrast to that slightly awkward moment almost four years earlier, after the draw against West Brom, this was pure euphoria.

And then, several minutes later – the presentation. The players filed past the dignitaries, including Spurs' chairman Daniel Levy and Liverpool owner John Henry, to accept their medals. When the last had passed, with gold hanging from their necks, Uefa president Aleksander Čeferin handed the trophy to the Liverpool captain.

As the players waved their hands low down by their feet, Henderson – holding the cup similarly low to the ground – ran on the spot, extending the moment; then the trophy – and all the players' arms – were held aloft as one, and fireworks exploded from behind. On ran the rest of the contingent, to bounce up and down with the trophy, as, a little sheepishly, John Henry ushered Linda Pizzuti Henry – in a Liverpool-red dress – and the rest of the owners into the edge of the frame. Everyone on that plinth had earned the right to be there, and Liverpool were back on their European perch.

After being thrown in the air by his players, a clearly emotional Klopp described the win as "the best night of our professional lives".

"Did you ever see a team like this, fighting with no fuel in the tank?" he said, after a gruelling season that was not unusual in the *number* of games played (53), but certainly in the intensity, and in the slog in the league and the Champions League from August onwards, following on from a World Cup summer; ten months of *must-win* games.

"I am so happy for the boys, all these people and my family. They suffer for me [in the six finals his teams had lost], they deserve it more than anybody. It was an intense season with the most beautiful finish I ever could have imagined."

But he was also *relieved*. For himself, but also for his players. Asked what he liked most about the achievement? "Jordan Henderson is the captain of the Champions League winners 2019, that's satisfying."

He then referred back to the pre-match press conference. "We were talking the other day about my 'unlucky' career. People can hear it like this, but I don't see it. I think my life is much better than I expected it to be. Winning is good, it's really cool. But it's not so much winning – I'm interested more so in development. We are asked all the time about not winning. Well, now we won something."

As Ken Early noted in *The Irish Times*, "His tone on that last line suggested he didn't believe the actual winning made much difference, and the logic is simple. If things had gone differently on Saturday night – if Son Heung-min had chipped a ball against Jordan Henderson's hand to win Spurs a penalty in the first minute; if Lucas Moura had smashed in a late second goal after a set-piece scramble – it would not have changed a single second of the work Klopp, his staff and his players have done at Liverpool over the last four seasons."

Indeed, if Jan Vertonghen had judo-thrown Mo Salah and then elbowed Alisson Becker in the head, it might have all been different again, through no fault of Klopp. After all, the league title essentially hinged on Vincent Kompany doing to Salah a version of what Ramos had, but using karate rather than judo; and like Ramos, he got away with it. A lot had to happen *afterwards*, too, but no one can mitigate against things like that; just as the Spurs' boss could not have planned to concede a handball penalty after 22 seconds.

If Ramos was the key to Liverpool losing 12 months earlier, another centre-back – Virgil van Dijk – was voted the man of the match. Thomas Schaaf, leader of the Uefa Technical Observers in Madrid, said: "Van Dijk showed outstanding leadership and was

Liverpool's best defender. He made crucial interventions when needed and played with a cool head throughout."

Van Dijk, after collecting his award at a post-match press conference, said: "In the second half we were sitting back a bit and they put pressure on us, but overall I think we're deserved Champions League winners.

"[Klopp] is a fantastic manager and a fantastic human being. It's an amazing environment to be in and I'm really proud to play for this beautiful club. We're all ambitious and we all want to have these kinds of nights so let's go for it – work hard and stay humble. I expect a lot from the party today and tomorrow!"

Miguel Delaney, in *The Independent*, noted the progress made under Klopp: "They [Liverpool] were until very recently a club that could barely get into the Champions League at all. They only appeared in it once between the true rise of the super-clubs, in 2010, and 2017, when they got back there for the first time with Klopp."

Two Champions League campaigns for Liverpool under Klopp, two finals. Three European campaigns for Liverpool under Klopp, three finals. He promised heavy metal; but if anyone still doubts the *mettle* of Jürgen Klopp, then they must have several screws loose.

TTT subscriber Nick Mundon offered an account to the site of his experience of the match: "The view was restricted, I had a huge Portakabin in front of me with a chunk of the corner of the pitch completely hidden. Seriously €145 for that, it was a joke.

"I was pissed off on behalf of all the fans who couldn't get tickets, and I was even more pissed off as the game went on and the girl in front of me proceeded to scroll through Instagram and other stuff throughout the whole game. I should have taken a photo to send to Uefa. Seriously is this what they want the game to be about? People that have no actual interest in the game when others would give over their life savings to be there?"

Paddy Smith, another subscriber, wrote: "We get to our seats high in the top tier, it is baking hot, no air and I've got to admit the occasion has got to me – after the heartbreak last year I'm not sure how we'll handle things if we don't win. I feel sick with nerves and say to myself this is the last final I come to, I'm that bad. We end up sitting in front of our mates by coincidence, and that helps as we chat about our trips, but there's no getting away from my nerves.

"The game feels like a slow journey through a very hot kind of torture, I sit biting one nail down to the bone the whole game not wanting to stop biting in case I jinx the boys, I mean, what the fuck is all that about? I'm a grown man and I think if I stop biting my nail Spurs will score!"

TTT's editor, Chris Rowland, made his way to Madrid in a camper-van with friends, but having attended *all thirteen* of Liverpool's previous European finals he was – just like about 50,000 other Reds – unable to find legitimate spare tickets in the city, and therefore forced to watch this one from a bar in the Spanish capital. Half of his group were luckier in the various ballots, and made their way to the Wanda Metropolitano Stadium, and return like conquering heroes.

"As the celebrations continue in our bar and around the square, we await the return of those who'd been to the match. When they show, there's more hugging and more stories to swap. We wander through the night, end up in the Sol district but many bars are closing early, perhaps fearing trouble or perhaps they'd made their money already. They shouldn't have worried about the former – it must be said that before and especially after the game, when the result was known, putting wild celebration in the path of abject misery, the relationships between the fans seemed impeccable. Spurs fans offered congratulations and you deserved it for the season you've had, and Liverpool fans consoled and congratulated rather than gloated, and reminded them we knew how they felt because it was us 12 months ago. The only tiny jarring note came from one drunken Spurs fan who sang "We pay your benefits".

After the game, Benfica B manager Renato Paiva talked to Portuguese newspaper *A Bola* about their involvement with Liverpool's pre-match preparations (which professional performance analyst Tiago Estêvão translated via his Twitter feed).

"Klopp and Lijnders found similarities in Benfica B and Tottenham's style of play, so Liverpool invited them to recreate what would be the final's tactical match-up. Benfica B's manager was asked to analyse and mirror Tottenham's approach in every way possible:

"We recreated two of their offensive and two of their centre-backs and goalkeeper build-up routines, their 4-2-3-1 defensive shape with the striker cutting between opposition centre-backs and the 10 obstructing Liverpool's 6."

Paiva explained that Brazilian striker Vinícius Jaú was asked to mimic the style of Christian Eriksen, midfielder Bernardo Martins replicated the role of Deli Alli, and Portugal U20 star José Gomes was asked to play like Harry Kane.

"We had adapt to that 4-2-3-1 shape, both defensively and in possession, with two midfielders dropping closer to the centre-backs during build-up to try and attract Liverpool's press. Tottenham would ideally want to attract Liverpool players closer to their box, so after a couple of passes between centre-backs and goalkeeper they can then attack the space in behind with their forwards and full-backs."

Klopp complimented the Portuguese side. According to their manager, the German said: "When you dropped your centre-backs to build-up we immediately set up the same press we used against Manchester City, and you still managed to surpass it three or four times!"

Why had Klopp and Lijnders gone with a Portuguese side? According to Paiva: "They couldn't pick an English team due to information leaks. They couldn't pick a Spanish team because Pochettino spent a lot of years in Spain. They couldn't pick a French team because Hugo Lloris is France's goalkeeper. So they had to go with a Portuguese team." And of course, Lijnders spent years working in Portugal, albeit for Benfica's rivals, Porto. It was just one more detail; one more piece of sharp thinking, in an attempt to find all possible marginal gains.

Afterword

This was the season that, at the outset, was *supposed* to be all about the title. All summer it was title talk, title tittle-tattle. And, after Liverpool just about scraped their way out of the Champions League group stage, whilst topping the league in December, it looked justified. It was all about number 19, after 29 years. It was *on*. And, to be fair, by eventually chalking up 97 points, you can't have asked for any more in that department. It bears repeating: the third-highest total in English football history. Liverpool just happened to lose to the team who racked up the second-highest total in English football history, on the back of the highest total in English football history.

Throughout all this, no one really spoke of number six, 14 years. Just number 19, 29 years. Which is better? In a weird way, Man City would probably prefer the thing they've never won, and Liverpool are long overdue a league title; so a swap might have been more satisfactory to both. And yet ... nothing quite beats a European night; the emotion of a final, usually in May, but this time in June, just, it seems, for shits and giggles. (This was Liverpool's first ever competitive game in June. In the future, why not hold it in Dubai, at midday, in July?)

On occasions football can seem like a terribly overrated and overhyped pastime, made grubby by money, prima donnas and shady characters, but sometimes – just sometimes – its power hits home, to the point where you're the odd one getting strange stares because you're *not* crying. For years it can almost numb you, and you wonder why you invest so much time, money and emotional energy into it, just to be left feeling indifferent or dislocated; wondering if you care enough to even get angry anymore, at another 0-0 draw, or at a petrostate or oligarch pumping so much money into a club they've randomly purchased that there's nothing left for anyone else to celebrate. But then – for most sleeping giants, at least – something truly special comes along every few years, or maybe once a decade, or even once in a generation. Sometimes the stars align, and everyone is pulling in the same direction – team, manager, owners, fans. Sometimes it just all falls into place, even if you don't always see all the hard work that sends the pieces toppling towards their perfect positions.

In some ways you need to feel those lows – and Liverpool have had more than their fair share of those since 1990 (and in more general, *tragic* terms, since 1985) – to provide contrast, to give something dark for the light to shine against. And yet, just when you think the magic is gone, and you feel hardened and cynical – and you think "I'm done with all this shit" – a miracle happens in Istanbul, or a Jürgen Klopp comes along.

Sometimes you need a Kiev to truly feel a Madrid. Sometimes you need to have been lambasted your entire career – or to have felt *for* that young man being lambasted his entire career – to feel the true value in lifting Europe's biggest trophy; and, for that player to have almost lost his dad to cancer in order for the pair of them to find themselves locked in a seemingly never-ending embrace on the side of the pitch – father fully recovered, son *the captain of the Champions of Europe*. Sometimes you need a hapless, cantankerous old English manager who makes you question why you even bother, in order to then, years later, fully appreciate the vibrant, intelligent but also slightly *verrückte* German whose booming laughter blows down walls, and whose football blows away the vanity projects and fat-cat clubs who try to spend so much money that failure is unlikely, and success becomes utterly uninteresting.

Sometimes you need a Jürgen Klopp to come along and remind you that Liverpool are a club capable of truly amazing feats, and that football is possibly the most beautiful and meaningful 'meaningless' pursuit in the grand scheme of things, and that, in those moments, you would swap it for absolutely nothing.

Postscript

Divock Origi. Divock Origi.

Divock Origi.

A BIG THANK-YOU TO OUR BENEFACTOR SUBSCRIBERS

A Coles
Abraham Marret
Agnar Lavik
Aiden Halloran
Akshay Sarangdhar
Alan Raleigh
Alec Foerster
Alkesh Dudhaiya
Allan Høy-Simonsen
Allan Morris
Allen Baynes
Andrew Argyle
Andrew Arrojo
Andrew Chow
Andy Orr
Anthony Burke
Anthony Partridge
Anthony Rodenhurst
Anton Black
Arjun Panchapagesan
Arun Butcher
Ashok Kelshiker
Auwais Khan
Axel Harms
Azeem Khan
A Lamb
B D Atherton
B Wright
Benjamin Cottle
Benjamin Freestone
Benjamin Magnusson
Benji Howell
Bernd Schorr
Bijin Benesh
Bjørnar Mikkelsen
Böðvar Brynjarsson
Boerge Bolme
Booya BBQ
Bradley Knight
Brian Dolphin
Ceri Glen
Charles Morrish

Charles Rowe
Chin Yet Ong
Chris Bracebridge
Chris Timewell
Chris Williams
Christine F Andrade
Chris Christodoulakis
Christoph Tung
Christopher Bruno
Christopher Sewards
Claus Ulrich Dahlfelt
Donald Rock
Danielle Warren
Darren Hanevy
David Evans
David Gilleece
David Hayward
David Miller
David O'Reilly
David Perkins
David Ryan
Deena Naidoo
Delta Driver 8132
Dennis Lindsey Laurie
Donny Gow
Dorin Moise
Eamonn Turbitt
Edward Robinson
Emlyn Conlon
Enock Phiri
Evan Kritikakos
Fung Han Lim
Gareth McMahon
Gary Fowler
Gary OSullivan
George Bevan
George Ebbs
Gina Hoagland
Glenn Perris
Gøran Schytte
Greg Vinikoor
Guðjón Teitur

Sigurðarson
Guohao Li
Guy Parr
Haluk Arpacioglu
Hong Kheng Tan
Ian Hopkinson
Ilan Shaw
Ingimar Bjarni
Sverrisson
Ingvar Juliusson
Iyad Zahlan
J F Nolan
J Knudseth
Jakra Srinaganand
James Fleming
James Kelly
James Melvin
James Russell Johnston
Jason Inge
Jason Ng
Jesper Marcussen
Joe Power
John Clarke
John Goldie
John Gordon
John Hogan
John Lankford
JonasIuul
Jonathan Bolton
Jonathan Sowler
Justin Choong
Karapiah Tamilarasan
Karl Mullins
Karl Su
Kay Zat L
Kelley McDowell
Kevin Gibbons
Kinsley Ransom
Kostadin Galabov
Kris Barber
Kristján
Laurent Sampers

Lee Dowey

Lee Hammond

Lee Smith

Leon Aghazarian

Leon Snoei

Lindsey Smith

Lodve Berre

Luke Ingram

M Begon

M Gordon

M R Dancey

Marco Yeung

Marcus Kelly

Mark Cohen

Mark Jeffcoat

Mark Jefferson

Mark Jones

Mark Wise

Markus Topp

Martin Cooke

Martin McLaughlin

Martin Overgaard

Matthew Beardmore

Matthew Willson

Michael Cheyne

Michael Sum

Michael Thomas

Michael Williams

Mike Hajialexandrou

Mohammad Al Sager

Mohsin Meghji

Murtaza Khan

Mutaz Ahmed

Naomi Wilkie

Neil Gold

Neil O'Brien

Niall O'Harte

Nick Hall

Norman Hope

Orjan Karlsson

Ørnulf Schømer

Patricia Adamiecki

Patrick Higgins

Patrick Smith

Paul Gottshall

Paul Jeter

Paul McCormack

Paul Morgan

Paul Winter

Paulus Adhisabda

Peter Barber

Peter Danes

Peter Doyle

Peter J Robinson

Peter Short

Peter Sweeney

Peter Verinder

Peter Vranich

Phil Collins

Philip Lindsay

Philip Tormey

Phillip Blanshard

Quinn Emmett

Richard Blundell

Richard Harrington

Robert Sangster

Rolf Hoel

Ronny Knutsen

Rune Ersdal

Rune Sollie

Ryonadai

Sacha Pettitt

Sadiq Ahmadu-Suka

Sam Henderson

Sam McMaster

Santhanakrishnan
Periathiruvadi

Saugato Banerjee

Sergio Trevino

Shawki Jounes

Shawn Warswick

Simon Barrington

Stephen Anderton

Stephen Capel

Stephen Farr-Jones

Stephen Rigby

Stephen Robertson

Stephen Rowland

Steve McCarthy

Steven Tan

Stratoe Koutsouridis

Stuart Lloyd

Sujit Dasgupta

Suzanne Wiseman

Sze King Chong

T P Stringer

Tan Francis

Thomas McCool

Tim Collins

Todd Schackman

Tom McCarthy

Tomaz Racic

Torbjørn Eriksen

Tristan Wyse

Vidar Kjøpstad

Waleed Alsager

Wally Gowing

Waqas Kaiser

Wesley Allen

Western Ivey

Divock Origi

Divock Origi

Divock Origi

Divock Origi

Divock Origi

Divock Origi

Divock Origi

Divock Origi

Divock Origi

Divock Origi

Divock Origi

Divock Origi

Divock Origi

Divock Origi

Divock Origi

Divock Origi

Divock Origi

Divock Origi

Divock Origi

Divock Origi

Divock Origi

Divock Origi

25613549R00135

Printed in Great Britain
by Amazon